Zero Administration Kit for Windows®

PRENTICE HALL PTR MICROSOFT® TECHNOLOGIES SERIES

NETWORKING

- Microsoft Technology: Networking, Concepts, Tools
  Woodard, Gattuccio, Brain
- NT Network Programming Toolkit
  Murphy
- Building COM Applications with Internet Explorer
  Loveman
- Understanding DCOM
  Rubin, Brain
- Web Database Development for Windows Platforms
  Gutierrez

PROGRAMMING

- Introduction to Windows 98 Programming
  Murray, Pappas
- Developing Professional Applications for Windows 98 and NT Using MFC, Third Edition
  Brain, Lovette
- Win 32 System Services: The Heart of Windows 98 and Windows NT, Third Edition
  Brain
- Multithreaded Programming with Win32
  Pham, Garg
- Visual Basic 6: Design, Specification, and Objects
  Hollis
- ADO Programming in Visual Basic 6
  Holzner
- Visual Basic 6: Error Coding and Layering
  Gill
- Visual C++ Templates
  Murray, Pappas
- Introduction to MFC Programming with Visual C++
  Jones
- MFC Programming in C++ with the Standard Template Libraries
  Murray, Pappas
- COM-CORBA Interoperability
  Geraghty, Joyce, Moriarty, Noone
- Distributed COM Application Development Using Visual Basic 6.0
  Maloney
- Distributed COM Application Development Using Visual C++ 6.0
  Maloney
- Understanding and Programming COM+: A Practical Guide to Windows 2000 DNA
  Oberg
- ASP/MTS/ADSI Web Security
  Harrison
- Microsoft Site Server 3.0 Commerce Edition
  Libertone, Scoppa
- Building Microsoft SQL Server 7 Web Sites
  Byrne

ADMINISTRATION

- Windows 2000 Registry
  Sanna
- Configuring Windows 2000 Server
  Simmons
- Tuning and Sizing NT Server
  Aubley
- Windows NT Cluster Server Guidebook
  Libertone
- Windows NT 4.0 Server Security Guide
  Goncalves
- Windows NT Security
  McInerney
- Supporting Windows NT and 2000 Workstation and Server
  Mohr
- Zero Administration Kit for Windows
  McInerney
- Designing Enterprise Solutions with Microsoft Technologies
  Kemp, Kemp, Goncalves

PRENTICE HALL PTR MICROSOFT® TECHNOLOGIES SERIES

MICHAEL McINERNEY

Zero Administration Kit for Windows®

PH PTR
Prentice Hall PTR
Upper Saddle River, NJ 07458
www.phptr.com

Library of Congress Cataloging-in-Publication Data

McInerney, Michael
Zero administration kit for Windows / Michael McInerney.
p. cm. — (Prentice Hall PTR Microsoft technologies series)
ISBN 0-13-084786-0 (alk. paper)
1. Microsoft Windows (Computer file) 2. Operating systems (Computers) I. Title. II. Series.

QA76.76.O63 M39878 2000 99-052008
005.4'469—dc21

Editorial/production supervision: Jane Bonnell
Cover design director: Jerry Votta
Cover design: Design Source
Copyeditor: Mary Lou Nohr
Composition: Ronnie K. Bucci
Manufacturing manager: Maura Goldstaub
Acquisitions editor: Mary Franz
Editorial assistant: Noreen Regina
Marketing manager: Lisa Konzelmann

Published by Prentice Hall PTR
Prentice-Hall, Inc.
Upper Saddle River, New Jersey 07458

Prentice Hall books are widely used by corporations and government agencies for training, marketing, and resale. The publisher offers discounts on this book when ordered in bulk quantities. For more information, contact Corporate Sales Department, Phone: 800-382-3419; FAX: 201-236-7141;
E-mail: corpsales@prenhall.com
Or write: Prentice Hall PTR, Corporate Sales Dept., One Lake Street, Upper Saddle River, NJ 07458.

Printed in the United States of America

10 9 8 7 6 5 4 3 2 1

ISBN 0-13-084786-0

Prentice-Hall International (UK) Limited, London
Prentice-Hall of Australia Pty. Limited, Sydney
Prentice-Hall Canada Inc., Toronto
Prentice-Hall Hispanoamericana, S.A., Mexico
Prentice-Hall of India Private Limited, New Delhi
Prentice-Hall of Japan, Inc., Tokyo
Pearson Education Asia Pte. Ltd., Singapore
Editora Prentice-Hall do Brasil, Ltda., Rio de Janeiro

DEDICATION

This book is for Linda.
A day doesn't go by without me wondering
why I should be so lucky.

CONTENTS

PREFACE

In the research for this project, one of the first questions that came up was "What is the Zero Administration Kit?" The question is not an easy one to answer.

If you read the Microsoft promotion of the product, then the Zero Administration Kit is a welcome addition to the Microsoft Management Tools family, provided free of charge to help administrators and IS management come to grips with the ever-escalating costs of running a networked computer system.

If you listen to the more skeptical souls in the Information Technology (IT) industry, the product is a late attempt to make up for the fact that features such as user profiles were provided in Windows NT with no real means of management. This tool is really an attempt to reduce rising costs that are being fuelled by the growing complexity of the Microsoft operation systems, and the fact that the tool is free is simply a testament to this idea.

As always, the reality can be found somewhere in the middle of these two extremes. User profiles have always been an excellent tool for controlling the desktop environment, but they are very difficult to implement and manage in a focused manner without a management tool. System policies have been a helpful feature of Windows NT also, and the management tool was delivered at an early stage. Again, the ability to use these as part of a coherent desktop management plan did not really exist. If used, system policies have been used in a standalone manner.

One of the answers to the question is that the Zero Administration Kit brings together in a coherent manner the features that already exist within the operating system. Examples and test users contained in the kit help you to understand what can be achieved with these features. The kit acts as a catalyst, providing the initial ideas and designs from which you can build your desktop control scenarios.

Zero Administration Kits are available for Microsoft Windows NT 4.0, Windows 95, and Windows 98 operating systems. The methodologies behind the implementation and use of the Zero Administration Kit are the same regardless of which of the three supported desktop operating systems you are using. Indeed, you can use ZAK to implement and control a mixed desktop environment using all three supported operating systems.

A large amount of the implementation and configuration of the ZAK is repetitive between the different operating systems. This is one reason why I have chosen to focus on one of the operating systems supported by ZAK. Another reason for this focus is that the ZAK is primarily aimed at the larger organization where many desktop installations take place and real savings can be made if time is shaved off this process. It is in these organizations that costs can be lowered dramatically if the workstation can be installed with a minimum of effort and the desktop can be secured from unwanted user interference. The desktop operating system of choice for these organizations is generally Windows NT because of the need for security as well as a robust platform from which to operate. Windows NT installation through the ZAK is almost unattended, whereas the installation of Windows 9x desktops is still quite involved.

Audience

Zero Administration Kit for Windows targets systems and network administrators, IS management, and anybody with an interest in finally taking back control of the desktop environment.

Total Cost of Ownership is of ever-increasing concern in the business world today. The ability to reduce costs can give a competitive edge. It is rare to find an organization that is not actively pursuing the reduction of costs in "nonprofit" areas such as the IS department.

To fully leverage the discussions and step-through exercises in this book requires a good administrative knowledge of Windows NT systems. Less technically aware readers and Information Systems (IS) managers will be able to use the book to gain a perspective on the control issues involved in a networked computer system environment and on measures to regain an element of control.

Organization

The main focus of this book is on the setup and implementation of the ZAK for Windows NT 4.0. I have chosen to feature this operating system for the reasons outlined above and because the ZAK setup and configuration is more involved here than with the other two operating systems. Where there are differences between the instructions for setting up for Windows NT and those for Windows 95 or Windows 98, they are exposed. The book is divided into three parts.

Part One begins with an introduction to the ZAK and looks at how it can be used to lower the total cost of ownership for your Windows-based systems. The discussion moves on to the installation and configuration of the ZAK in an evaluation environment and the building of test workstation installations. By the end of Part One you should have built an environment in which you can experiment with the various ZAK settings to see how they can benefit your organization and also have a sound understanding of how the ZAK processes work during an unattended workstation installation.

Part Two looks at the central theme of the ZAK, which is controlling user environments by means of the user profile and system policy features provided with Windows-based systems. User profiles are discussed in great detail, and then the Windows default system policies and templates are covered. The discussion moves on from the ordinary user profiles and system policies to those used by the ZAK to put in place the required controls. This part also contains lab exercises at the end of each chapter to reinforce the discussions of each topic.

Part Three takes you through the customization process. The default installations that the ZAK provides are only the starting point from which you should work. The customization procedures in this part use step-by-step instructions that show you how to make changes that will benefit your own environment.

ACKNOWLEDGMENTS

This is only my second computer book, so I could hardly be referred to as a "seasoned author." I could write books for the rest of my life, and I would still consider myself a hands-on man. One reason why I can tackle this type of project and escape with my sanity is that I am writing about topics that I use every day in my own work. That's one reason. The other reason I can do it is that I am surrounded by a support structure that wouldn't allow me to fail, even if I wanted to.

The support structure starts with my wife, Linda. The extra work taken on by me to carry out this project simply shifted the burden of other tasks onto her shoulders. The burden was never too much for her, and the complaints were always too few. Even in the final stages, her help on the editorial side meant that the project finished on time.

My friends at IBM, Thomas Niestroj, Tina Murray, and Vincent Daly, were instrumental in keeping me on the right track. To Scott McCoy, for his technical review, I give many thanks. A sound technical understanding of the topics (coupled with no fear of upsetting me) led to invaluable insight.

And thanks to the whole team at Prentice Hall. This is only my second book with this publisher but it seems like I'm working with old friends. I thank Mary Franz, my editor and the person who keeps it all on the right track. A professional attitude with a friendly face. I thank Jane Bonnell for her work on editorial and production supervision. Your diligence and understanding make it a pleasure to work with you. Mary Lou Nohr, copyeditor and would-be saint. Anybody who has the patience to work through my grammatical inaccuracies deserves recognition. The whole production team at Prentice Hall who smooth the path and make sure that I don't fall.

Finally, for anybody I may have inadvertently left out, I apologize and thank you for your help and support.

ABOUT THE AUTHOR

Writing is not a new endeavor for me. Although this is only my second published book, I estimate that I have written tens of thousands of pages. Technical manuals and some magazine articles make up the bulk of this work.

As founder and director of Insight Business Solutions, I see my main role as still very much hands-on in the realms of computer security, network design, and technical training. The main business aim for my company is to provide high-quality, focused technical consultancy to both European and U.S. companies. Our client list includes many blue-chip multinationals in the banking, treasury, and manufacturing sectors.

On a personal note, I am a Microsoft Certified Systems Engineer (MCSE) and a Master Certified Novell Engineer (MCNE) and have been working with computers and networks for about 12 years now. Over the years I have worked as a freelance trainer and network consultant in both Microsoft and Novell technologies. My training activities have given way over recent years to seminars, and I have become more closely focused on system security and desktop control.

PART ONE

Evaluation Environment

In This Part

The chapters in this part take you through a stage-by-stage creation of a Windows NT test environment for ZAK. The chapters are intended to be read in sequence so that a firm understanding of the test environment setup is reached.

The goals to be achieved during this first part of the book are simple. By following the instructions, you will install the ZAK for Windows NT and build the supporting structure for a simple installation of both TaskStation and AppStation clients. The installation procedure for these client computers is also discussed in depth.

The supporting structure is made up of the network boot disk, which is essential for an unattended network installation of Windows NT, and the answer file, which provides the input for all of the options available during a manual installation of the operating system. The contents of this part are arranged as follows:

Chapter One looks at the Zero Administration Kit and introduces its main features. Included in this chapter are directions on where to get the kit, as well as overviews on how it will reduce the total cost of ownership for your Windows-based systems.

Chapter Two looks at the general installation process for the Zero Administration Kit for Windows NT. A quick setup guide for Windows 95/98 is also included. The chapter then takes you through the necessary steps for building your evaluation environment including network share creation and user account requirements.

Chapter Three builds on the general installation and looks at the add-on processes required to get to the stage where you can actually run an unattended installation of the operating system. The chapter concentrates on the network boot disk and the unattended installation answer file.

Chapter Four looks at the ZAK based unattended client installation for Windows NT. In-depth coverage of what is happening in the background is included so you can appreciate the internal workings of the ZAK process with a view to adapting the internals to fit your own requirements.

ONE

Introduction to the Zero Administration Kit

In This Chapter

- Introduction
- The Zero Administration Initiative for Windows (ZAW)
- Zero Administration Kit (ZAK) Overview
- System Requirements for ZAK
- Introduction to the Task-Based Worker
- Windows NT File System Access
- System Lockdown
- Unattended System Installation
- A ZAK Comparison: Windows NT vs. Windows 95/98
- Summary

The chapter discusses a topic—total cost of ownership (TCO)—that is becoming more and more important in the lives of all IS managers, administrators and everyone involved in the running of an IS environment. TCO can be used as a measurement of the effectiveness of a particular IS model or for individual parts of the model. CEOs and CFOs are looking at the traditional cost centers of their organizations with a view to reducing the burden while increasing the benefits.

Understanding the general concept of TCO and of where your IT budget disappears can help you define and implement strategies that will lower the TCO in a static environment or prevent growth in the TCO of an expanding environment. To that end, this chapter introduces the Microsoft Zero Administration Kit (ZAK), describing its components and examining how they fit with existing Windows NT technology to provide the tools necessary to lower the cost of owning and running a Windows NT network.

Introduction

The total cost of ownership (TCO) is a buzzword (or phrase, to be more accurate) that specifies the effectiveness of IS departments and most other "cost centers" within all organizations, whether they are small, medium, or large.

In the past it has been difficult to measure different IS models, such as client/server vs. centralized mainframes, because of the difficulty of comparing disparate models. Factors making up the cost of the model (hardware, software, maintenance, user input, downtime, administrative overhead, etc.) made the task even harder. Today, the measurement of the TCO is made easier because of the growing awareness of its importance. This growing importance has led to the development of tools and methodologies that enable a more accurate picture of expenditure to be produced.

One fact that everyone can be assured of in these days of tight margins and lower bottom-line figures is that interest is turning towards the more expensive activities in the organization to look for ways to cut costs without cutting the level of service delivered. And which department generally has the largest budget? It is a rare occasion today when the answer to this question is not the IS department.

The TCO for computer systems can be split into many different tangible areas of cost: hardware and software, staff, training, maintenance, and upgrades. Some less tangible costs have been shown in recent years to outweigh these others quite significantly. Two of these cost areas are closely linked:

- **Loss of productivity**. A large part of the cost of ownership of a networked computer system is the lack of availability of system resources because of user and system downtime. In most large organizations, the IS systems support the main business of the company. The systems are recognized as a necessary investment cost to provide the tools required for the business operations to run smoothly and function competitively. IS systems can have a huge impact on the profitability of your organization's business processes. Severe downtime can have major repercussions in a time-sensitive arena. For example, in banking environments, where daily fund transfers of over one billion dollars are not uncommon, downtime in the payments systems can mean the cost of overnight interest on that amount.

  To a lesser degree, user distraction is also a strain on productivity. Why give a user access to three applications that perform the same job? Simplifying the user interface and providing only the tools necessary for the job at hand can help in this situation.

- **User Maintenance**. Closely linked to the loss of productivity is the cost involved in maintaining the computer systems for users. In recent studies it has been noted with interest that up to 70 percent of help desk support calls could have been avoided if the users were given less access to their system configuration utilities. Inexperienced users, or users with a little knowledge, are the main cause of these help desk calls. Combine this with overgenerous system access on the local computer, and you have the potential for catastrophe. The cost involved in running a help desk and providing support personnel generally rises in proportion to the number of users in an organization. This should not necessarily be the case. With the correct management environment and with the correct support structure in place, the costs of user maintenance should scale upward far more slowly than the number of users being accommodated.

Quite often, the TCO measurement for IS systems does not include the less tangible costs of loss of production and revenue. It is difficult to quantify how much business is lost when your key sales staff are down for two hours. Figure 1.1 shows a breakdown of the average expenditure of an IS department, based on a 1996 report by IDC and the Interpose Corporation.

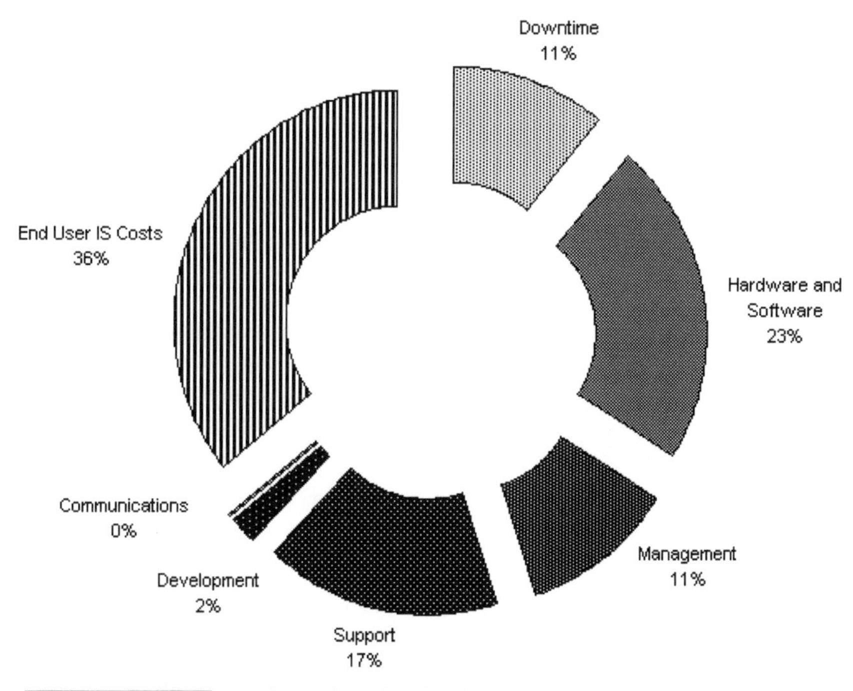

FIGURE 1.1 Budgeted and unbudgeted costs incurred by an IS department

The breakdown in costs shown in Figure 1.1 are drawn from the Microsoft and Interpose model for measuring TCO. The categories listed below include the following items:

- **Hardware and software costs**—Capital expenditure and depreciation costs
- **Management costs**—Administration costs of all hardware, software, network equipment, general labor costs including outsourcing fees, and high-end support structures
- **Development costs**—Development costs including labor for installations, upgrades, and maintenance by development staff or outsourced requirements
- **Support costs**—First-line support, training, general administration, travel, maintenance contracts, and internal costs such as HR cross-charges
- **Communication costs**—Leased line and communications charges
- **End-user costs**—Costs that are unexpected and unbudgeted such as costs arising from self-support efforts by users, including unnecessary and unwanted modifications to the desktop
- **Downtime costs**—loss of productivity and missed business opportunities resulting from any system downtime

The primary budgetary costs being targeted by the ZAK are those of *end-user costs* (36 percent of expenditure) and *downtime costs* (11 percent of expenditure). Further budgetary reductions can be achieved with a properly managed ZAK installation in the areas of *support costs* (17 percent of expenditure) and *management costs* (11 percent of expenditure).

The Zero Administration Initiative for Windows (ZAW)

The overall aim of the Zero Administration Initiative for Windows is to lower the TCO for Microsoft network-based systems. The ZAW is a collection of methodologies that can work independently or together to reduce the administrative overhead of desktop systems within the organization. For the desktop environment, it addresses the arena of productivity loss by limiting downtime to multiples of the desktop environment. (Presumably, server environments are secured from user interference and possible damage.)

The initiative is formed around many tools, one of which is the ZAK and another of which is System Management Server.

The Zero Administration Kit is one tool of many that can be used together to achieve the desired results. It is not dependent on SMS for its functionality and can be downloaded and implemented for a minimal cost. The ZAK provides the capability to configure and distribute system policies, user profiles, and predefined desktop configurations as well as to perform unattended installations of the Windows NT, Windows 95, and Windows 98 operating systems. Using system policies and user profiles, you can allow users access to network installed applications such as Microsoft Office. SMS provides extra and complementary functionality in the areas of network management, software distribution, hardware and software inventories, and remote diagnostic ability.

Zero Administration Kit (ZAK) Overview

The Zero Administration Kit is a tool that, making use of existing Windows desktop technology, allows IS managers and system administrators to implement secure system policies in the desktop environment. It uses existing Windows technology such as system policies and user profiles to store configurations in a central location. You use system policies to override already configured registry entries on the local computer so that you can force a secure and controlled environment. You use user profiles to centrally store preconfigured desktop looks so that only the necessary icons, shortcuts, and programs are available to users. These profiles can be shared so that all users in a particular group can use the same desktop look. You can make changes for all users at the central location, and these will be downloaded the next time the users log on. With these two central themes in the Zero Administration Kit, you can lower the cost of ownership of networked computers by means of the deliverables that the ZAK brings with it. These deliverables are:

- A secure and controlled desktop system that cannot be interfered with by users, thus reducing the number of help desk calls generated by unauthorized system changes.
- The ability to streamline the system rollout procedure. If all systems are configured in the same way, they can be preconfigured in slack periods, ready for new users.
- Central configuration of the desktop so that visits to individual users are not necessary when changes are required.
- The control of application installations, which prevents users from installing unauthorized (and possibly unlicensed) software. This practice will save on user time being spent on unauthorized software and on help desk calls when unauthorized software installation interferes with the system.

The ZAK is based on a set of methodologies defined by Microsoft to lower the cost of management and deployment of desktop systems. These methodologies are based on existing Microsoft technologies available in Windows NT and Windows 95/98, and you are possibly using one or more of these technologies on your corporate network already.

The ZAK brings these methodologies together in two sample installation modes. These can be evaluated in a test situation, and any necessary customizations can be made to fit your own organizational needs. It is highly unlikely that you will be able to (or would want to) roll out the ZAK methodologies using the exact models defined by Microsoft. You must spend time defining your own needs and planning your installation. The default ZAK installations are provided as a starting point from which to begin your adaptation process.

Windows NT, Windows 95, and Windows 98 Support

Zero Administration Kits are available for Windows NT, 95, and 98. The methodologies behind the implementation and the use of the Zero Administration Kit are the same regardless of which of the three supported desktop operating systems you are using. Indeed, you could use the ZAK to implement and control a mixed desktop environment, using the three supported operating systems.

ZAK Availability

You can purchase the Zero Administration Kit for a nominal amount on CD in the United States or you can download it from Microsoft's Web site at `http://www.microsoft.com/windows/zak/getzak.htm`. Instructions for ordering the CD or download the files can be found on this site.

Three different ZAK kits are available today. These kits are for the Windows NT 4.0, Windows 95, and Windows 98 operating systems and are all available on the Web site.

System Requirements for ZAK

The ZAK is a freely downloaded product provided by Microsoft to help lower the TCO for Microsoft Windows NT and Windows 95/98 desktop systems. The minimum requirements for the Zero Administration Kit are set out below.

Network Configuration

- To install the ZAK, you must have a network with at least one Windows NT 4.0 Server running, patched with at least Service Pack 3. This should be configured in a domain structure.
- You must also have at least two client PCs capable of running the desired desktop operating system. See the *Hardware Compatibility* documentation for your operating system for details on your particular hardware.
- TCP/IP must be used on all machines.

Server Configuration

- One primary domain controller
- At least 1 Gbyte of free disk space
- NTFS file system
- Windows NT Server version 4.0 CD
- CD-ROM drive
- At least 32 Mbytes RAM. Adjust this amount to allow for other applications running on the server

Workstation Configuration

The configurations shown below include those for Windows 95/98 as the lower specification.

- The client machine hardware configurations should be as similar as possible in order to limit the number of different configuration files needed for installations.
- The network card installed in the machines must be able to be configured in unattended mode. See *Appendix A* for a list of network cards that can be used in this mode. Check with the NIC manufacturer if you are unsure.
- 486 60 MHz processor (Pentium 90 or higher recommended for Windows NT 4.0).
- 16 Mbytes RAM (32 Mbytes or higher recommended for Windows NT 4.0).
- Floppy disk drive.
- Clean, formatted hard drive with at least 300 Mbytes of free space.
- MS-DOS network boot disk.

Others

- The Zero Administration Kit
- Workstation Resource Kits
  - Windows NT 4.0 Workstation Resource Kit and/or
  - Windows 95 Resource Kit and/or
  - Windows 98 Resource Kit
- Client OS CD (full versions, not upgrades)
  - Windows NT 4.0 Workstation CD and/or
  - Windows 95 CD and/or
  - Windows 98 CD
- Service Packs
  - Windows NT Service Pack 3 or higher and/or
  - Windows 95 Service Pack 1
- Internet Explorer installation files (Windows 95/98 clients)
- Microsoft Office 97 (if using AppStation mode as defined in the ZAK)
- Microsoft Office 97 Resource Kit (if using AppStation mode)

Introduction to the Task-Based Worker

The task-based worker has been defined by Microsoft as a user who has minimal to moderate computer experience. This type of user is responsible for the majority of desktop-related help desk calls, causing loss of productivity and administrative overhead.

The task-based worker has been categorized by Microsoft into two subcategories based on the desktop environment required.

- **TaskStation Mode**. Users who fall into this category use their workstations only to perform very specific tasks. These tasks could be limited to one application within which users perform all their necessary functions. An example of this would be a call center where the call-logger can use one application to log incoming calls, query existing calls, and close off finished calls. The application interface may be a terminal emulation program connected to a large, centralized call-logging system. This user does not require further access to the workstation. The TaskStation user may also have very limited computer skills.
- **AppStation Mode**. Users who fall into this category use a specific subset of applications on their workstation. These applications are well defined, and access beyond these applications to the workstation is not required. An example of the AppStation mode user is secretarial staff

who may use the Microsoft Office suite of programs as well as an e-mail program and an office timesheet program. This type of user normally has at least a basic knowledge of the workstation environment.

The TaskStation and AppStation modes suggested by Microsoft are two starting points from which to build your own customized user modes. The possibilities for customization are almost limitless, as we discuss in *Part Three.*

The TaskStation and AppStation modes are the basis for the ZAK installation as provided by Microsoft. The task-based worker is the most likely culprit when it comes to costs associated with help desk activities and workstation visits by support personnel.

TaskStation Mode

The TaskStation mode provides a minimal interface for the user. The Windows interface is hidden, and the application that is needed for the user to perform work-related tasks is started automatically at logon. The file system is almost entirely hidden, and it is almost impossible for the user to interact with the local system in a way that might cause damage or necessitate a help desk call. Figure 1.2 shows the user interface of a TaskStation worker when the system is set to start Internet Explorer as the one and only available application. This application could be any defined application. Note that there is no taskbar or other icons to distract the user. No context menus are available, and no other features of the desktop environment are exposed. The user is simply provided with the one tool necessary to complete a job role and nothing more. The management of the application, including which application is started and any changes to the startup settings, is controlled centrally from the server.

AppStation Mode

The AppStation mode provides a controlled environment for the user while minimizing the risk of damage to the local system. Only the applications that the user requires for the particular job being performed are available from the Start menu. Access to system files and system programs such as control panel applets or display settings are restricted or denied (changes in these areas are the most common causes of help desk calls.)

AppStation mode minimizes lost productivity due to distractions and local system downtime while still providing access to all of the business tools that the user requires. Again, an important feature here is the centralized administration of the desktop look and feel so that workstation visits are kept to a minimum. Figure 1.3 shows the user desktop set up in AppStation mode. The only available applications are the Microsoft Office suite running from a network share. This set could easily be any combination of applications.

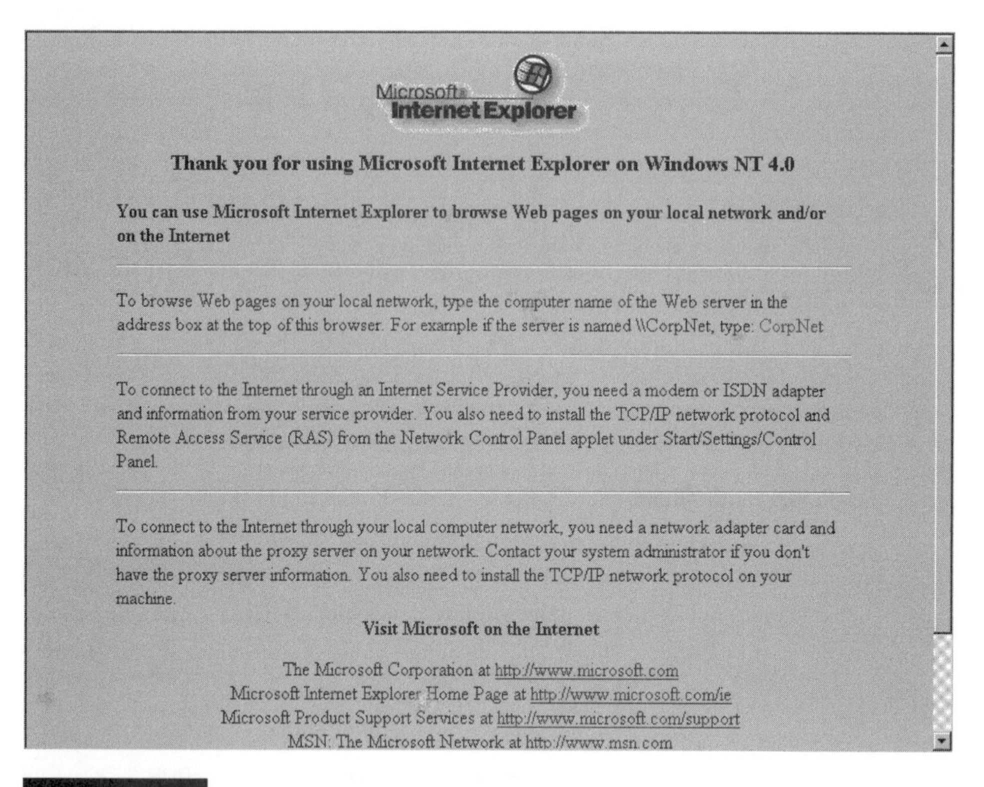

FIGURE 1.2 Single application access for a TaskStation user

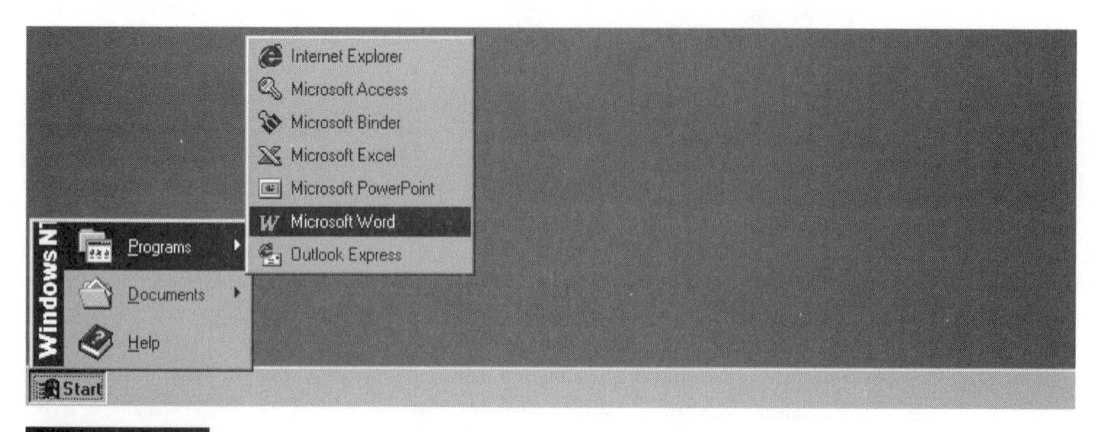

FIGURE 1.3 Only required application access is exposed for AppStation users

Windows NT File System Access

By limiting exposure to the file system so that only the required files are available to the user, you can avoid problems caused by system files being accidentally moved or deleted. The Windows NT ZAK enables you to set Access Control Lists (ACLs) on the local file system at installation time, to meet the needs of the particular user group within your organization. The default installations of TaskStation and AppStation modes will not match your requirements exactly, but you can adjust the installation tools and command files provided to accomplish the setup to implement your individual file system access structure.

System Lockdown

The ZAK uses two main methods of control to lock down systems so that they cannot be adjusted by users, thereby avoiding problems leading to productivity loss and administrative overhead but still providing all the functionality required to perform a job efficiently. These methods are user profiles and system policies.

For the greatest level of security and so that users cannot bypass the lockdown functionality, Windows NT 4.0 Workstation is the required platform. The *Mandatory Logon* process of Windows NT 4.0 prevents users from bypassing the authentication screens upon which the application of user profiles and system policies are based. Using the Windows 95/98 operating systems at the desktop means that you cannot guarantee that users will abide by the imposed rules and system settings.

It is important that you completely understand the abilities and limitations of both user profiles and system policies before you attempt to use the ZAK on your live systems. Fundamental methodologies are used by the ZAK to control and influence the look and feel of the desktop and if used correctly, they complement each other and provide a level of control that can be adjusted to fit almost all requirements. User profiles and system policies are covered in detail in Chapter Five, *User Profiles and Desktop Control*, and Chapter Six, *System Policies*. The following sections give an overview of their benefits and limitations.

Desktop Security

If one of your aims in using the Zero Administration Kit is to help implement desktop security and prevent unauthorized use of, or access to, local system resources, then the only available option is the Windows NT ZAK. The kit for Windows 95/98 does not improve system security on these operating systems. You can implement a common look and feel and you can use the kit for automated installations, but if an even slightly knowledgeable user wishes to, he can bypass the restrictions on the desktop and gain full access to the local machine. As this possibility can lead to downtime and so an increase in desktop costs, you should think carefully about which desktop operating system to implement.

User Profiles

A user profile is a group of settings that together define the look and feel of a user's environment on a Windows NT or Windows 95/98 computer. It is loaded onto the computer when the user logs on. It controls what appears on a desktop or what applications are accessible. User profiles contain settings that can be applied to the desktop environment and can be set up so that users can make changes and save them or so that users cannot save any changes made.

User profiles were designed in part to answer the need for more control over the ever-growing complexity of Microsoft desktop and network systems This growing complexity and functionality has prompted the need for controls over the costs of administration and management at the desktop.

The theory behind user profiles was to give the user a configurable desktop look, similar to the one provided on a Macintosh®. Little thought went into the control of this desktop in an enterprise environment, and no tool was delivered to help administrators manage this feature easily.

On the positive side, with some committed work, administrators can deliver and manage from a central point the look and feel required by the enterprise workforce. Administrators can control user profiles centrally and allow users to take favored settings with them from computer to computer.

User profiles also add an element of security to your NT systems. The control imposed with a user profile can help protect the uniform desktop presentation. The resulting uniform look and feel that are imposed on the client can help in the tracking of security-related incidents.

TYPES OF USER PROFILE

Three types of user profiles are available on Windows NT machines.

- **Local Profiles**. These profiles are local to a given machine and are only available to the user when he logs on to that one machine. These profiles do not move with the user. A local profile is created for every user who logs on interactively to the individual machine. The settings are saved back to the local machine when the user logs off.

- **Roaming Profiles**. Roaming profiles, as the name suggests, are available on any domain machine that a user chooses to log on to. They are delivered from a central source to users at logon and are used by the particular user or groups of users whenever they log on to a machine within the domain. If the roaming profile is not available, users can be logged on with a copy of the profile saved the last time they accessed the machine. When changes are made by the user to the desktop appearance or other object that is stored in the profile, they are saved to the central copy of the profile at logoff time and are then provided to the user the next time he logs on. Roaming profiles can give users a uniform base look on their desktop and then allow them to make changes as necessary.
- **Mandatory Profiles**. Mandatory profiles are similar to roaming profiles except that the user cannot save changes to the profile because it is made read-only. As a further option, the profile can be set up so that the user *must* download the profile in order to log on. In this environment, the mandatory profile must be available to the user or the user cannot log on to the network. It can be available either from the network or from the locally cached copy on the workstation. Furthermore, the mandatory profile cannot be adjusted and stored by the user. Settings are not saved at logoff time, so the same, uniform profile is used the next time the user logs on.

USER PROFILE STRUCTURE

The user profile exists in two separate forms. The first form consists of folders and icons that appear on the user's desktop in various places. These are all stored in a folder structure corresponding to the desktop and Start menu folder structures. The second form consists of a registry hive stored as a file in the folder structure just mentioned.

System Policies

System policies are made up from a set of registry entries that control the computer resources available to a user or group of users. These registry entries can be applied to individual users or groups, or they can be machine specific. System policies control access to many different resources on the local machine. Desktop settings and user access to resources can be controlled easily. Restrictions on the use of control panel or the available options for display settings can be applied by means of system policies.

A system policy editor tool (`POLEDIT.EXE`) is included in Windows NT Server, and you can use it to create policies for your network systems.

For the policies supplied with the ZAK for Windows 95 to work, the policy editor must be capable of loading more than one template at a time. The retail shipped version of Windows 95 policy editor does not allow this loading. Copy the policy editor supplied with Windows NT 4.0 to a Windows 95 system to load more than one template.

System policies are applied either at system startup (for machine settings) or as the user logs on. These settings are copied down from the policy file and permanently change settings in the local registry. The user portion of the system policy is applied to the user after the user profile and overwrites any settings that may have already been applied. In this way an administrator can allow user profiles to be amended by the user and can also apply, by means of the system policy, settings that should not be changed.

When a user profile is applied, registry settings are changed in a registry hive for any portions relevant to the user. User settings are applied to the `HKEY_USERS` hive. The system policy settings relating to the user are made to the same registry hive, and the machine-specific settings are made to the `HKEY_LOCAL_MACHINE` registry hive. Therefore, when you apply a system policy that contains settings that may conflict with profile settings, the policy settings overwrite the profile settings in the registry. This application method gives the ultimate control of the available settings back to the administrator.

System policies can be applied to all users, individual users, groups of users, all computers and individual computers.

The policy editor must be run on the operating system that you wish to configure. Using the NT version of the policy editor on a Windows 95 OS will result in a Windows 95 policy file. Running this same program on a Windows NT machine will result in a Windows NT policy file being created. The policy files are not compatible between different operating systems.

Unattended System Installation

The goal of the Zero Administration Initiative is to lower the cost of owning and running Microsoft Windows clients. One of the time-consuming processes that we all go through is system installation and configuration. If you are faced with rolling out hundreds or even thousands of desktop systems, then you will want to automate the process as much as possible.

Ghosting of complete Windows NT systems has never been supported by Microsoft for many reasons, one of which is the unique nature of the system identifier. Many software vendors claim to have overcome these obstacles, but until their solutions are recognized and supported by Microsoft they may cause problems if used extensively. Another problem with this method of installation is that the hardware must be exactly the same with most of these systems because the systems merely copy files and do not run the setup programs that detect hardware and build the Hardware Abstraction Layer (HAL). The text-based portion of the Windows NT setup process can be safely copied from disk to disk, but the saving is negligible.

Unattended system installations can be achieved with the ZAK and an answer file. This includes the installation of certain applications that lend themselves to the unattended installation process (Office 97 being one of them) and Windows NT service packs. The answer file provides the input that the installer would normally have to furnish. The unattended installation is covered in Chapter Four.

A ZAK Comparison: Windows NT vs. Windows 95/98

You should have a clear picture going forward of what to expect from the different types of ZAK. This understanding can influence your decision on whether to use the ZAK, in the same way that reading the feature list of the operating system will influence your choice of desktop client.

The available ZAKs bring with them many features that support the deliverables listed in *Zero Administration Kit (ZAK) Overview* section. However, not all of the features are available in all of the kits.

Windows NT

The Windows NT ZAK brings with it the capability to run a *near* unattended installation of the operating system. The reason that it is a *near* unattended installation is that a minimal amount of manual intervention is required to remove the floppy boot disk from the drive between the start of the setup and the first soft reboot. The installation runs very quickly, and the end result is a set of computers configured exactly to specification.

System lockdown is made possible by the built-in features of the NT operating system such as system policies and user profiles. Windows NT is regarded as a securable operating system using only its own features. When locked down properly, it can present a uniform look and feel that brings with it the benefits of preventing users from damaging their own system and also from accessing non-job-related features that may cause distraction and loss of productivity.

Windows 95/98

Use of the Windows 95/98 versions of the ZAK has certain drawbacks.

The installations of the operating system require far less manual intervention when using the ZAK than when performing a manual installation.

However, the ZAK-aided installation of Windows 95/98 is still far from unattended. Manual intervention is required at certain stages of the setup, and the value gained in saved time and effort is negligible. Value is added from the setup process because the end result is a machine configured in the same manner as all others, so the benefits of similar desktop configurations on all rolled-out computers is realized.

System lockdown is possible with the same features as described for Windows NT above. System policies and user profiles can present a uniform desktop look and feel, which brings with it all of the associated benefits. However, these operating systems are not considered to be securable by their own features. If you require a secured local system or wish to prevent users from bypassing the desktop lockdown, then the choice really comes down to using Windows NT as the local operating system and using the Windows NT ZAK.

Summary

The need for evaluation of the ZAK in a test environment cannot be stressed enough. The ZAK is not intended to be a product that is simply installed in its default configuration and used in a production environment.

The ZAK aims to implement controls that will limit the amount of damage users can do to their own workstation, thus reducing the cost of managing the desktop environment. These controls must be implemented with your own organizational needs in mind. To implement the default settings without first evaluating them to see if they match your need would be foolish and costly. For some of the same reasons that you may wish to control desktops (to lower costs and reduce productivity loss), you would not want to implement a control structure that does not allow your users to work efficiently. You should use the evaluation to become accustomed to all of the nuances of system policies and user profiles. You should also test network cards which will be used in unattended installations and adjust the answer file to fit your own equipment needs.

Windows NT and Windows 95/98 are operating systems aimed at different target audiences. One of the main benefits of the ZAK is that it brings a predefined level of security to the desktop and prevents unwanted local system access. This is really only true if you are using the Windows NT operating system. The ZAK does not bring with it additional operating system features. Rather, it leverages features shipped with the retail version of the operating system, to implement an environment that can lower the total cost of ownership for IT support and management.

If you require local security to be applied to prevent access to features of the operating system that are not job related, then you should use Windows NT Workstation as the operating system of choice, and use the ZAK for NT to implement the security features that will help bring control to your organization's desktop environment.

T W O

How to Build a Basic Environment

In This Chapter

This chapter takes you through setting up the ZAK for Windows NT 4.0. Step-by-step instructions are included on how to set up the ZAK and configure test users, groups, and installation files. By the end of this chapter, you should have installed the ZAK in a test environment and be ready to move on to the next stage, which is to prepare for the sample client PC installations. As discussed in the previous chapter, the two task-based worker models that are included in the ZAK will not exactly meet the requirements of your organization. These two example modes are supplied as a starting point for you to use and adjust to fit your own needs.

Use the evaluation process shown in this chapter to look closely at all aspects of the ZAK, to help you decide on how you will adjust it to fit your own needs. Experiment with customizing the defined models so that you can look at the effects of changes in a test environment.

Also included in this chapter is an overview of the Windows 95/98 ZAK installation process. This overview briefly describes the creation of users and global groups, to satisfy the requirements of the ZAK installation for these operating systems. As discussed earlier, the deliverables provided by the ZAK for these operating systems are not as extensive as those provide by the ZAK for NT, so the focus of the chapter is on the NT setup. All instructions in the chapter are concerned with Windows NT unless specifically stated otherwise.

Overview

The deployment options covered in this chapter for TaskStation and AppStation computers are used as a starting point, from which you can define your own installation to meet your organization's needs. Remember that these user installations are not intended to be used in a production environment without configuration changes that match your own organizational requirements.

Windows NT

The installation of the ZAK for NT can be loosely split into two different sections, corresponding to the two configuration modes outlined earlier. The setup of TaskStation and AppStation modes are similar, and by the end of this chapter, you should have a distribution point for each type of installation.

You create either the TaskStation or AppStation distribution point in the first part of the setup process. You can run the process twice so that both TaskStation and AppStation distribution points are created. You move the administration files installed in the previous step to their final destination in the next part of the process. After this task is completed, you set up the necessary network shares and apply NTFS permissions to the system folders. You must create test users along with the necessary global groups. After this initial installation, you proceed to the next stage of the evaluation setup: performing test client installations.

Windows 95/98

The ZAK setup process for Windows 95/98 is a very simple one. The instructions contained in this chapter enable you to create a test environment distribution point for task-based worker installations of Windows 95 and Windows 98.

The client setup for both Windows 95 and Windows 98 cannot be considered as being unattended. The amount of input required for the setups can be minimized, but frequent input is required in order to log on to the domain at different stages to continue with the setup.

The installation procedure for each of the Windows 95 and Windows 98 Zero Administration Kits is the same. They can be set up on the same NT 4.0 server distribution point because all of the files that must exist as separate entities are placed under the relevantly named distribution folder (either ZAK95 or ZAK98).

Test Network Requirements

You can adjust the test network requirements set out below to fit your own requirements or equipment that you may have available. The examples and step-through instructions contained in the remainder of this chapter and throughout the book are based on the specifications set out below.

Server

The test environment server requires the following equipment and setup characteristics.

- One primary domain controller (*no* backup domain controllers) with Windows NT Server 4.0 installed
- Service Pack 3 (or greater) installed
- 64 Mbytes RAM (or higher)
- CD-ROM drive
- NetBIOS name **IBSNT04**
- Domain name **NTDOM01**
- ZAK installation software
- At least 1 Gbyte free disk space

Workstation

The test environment requires the following workstation setup.

- Two workstation machines
- Windows NT 4.0 Workstation distribution media (or Windows 95/98)
- NetBIOS names **TaskPC1** and **AppPC1**
- Windows NT 4.0 Resource Kit (or Windows 95/98)
- Office 97 distribution media (for AppStation mode)
- Office 97 Resource Kit
- Floppy disk drive in each machine
- Minimum of 300 Mbytes free disk space on clean hard drive
- Unattendable network interface card in each machine
- MS-DOS boot disk for each different network interface card type

In addition to the preceding requirements, you must have an understanding of the relationship between user profile structures, policy files, and the options encountered in the instructions that follow. For example, you are asked to specify a network connection method for AppStation users to connect to a network application. The entry specified in the test setup is Drive `O:`. If you change this to any drive letter other than the one specified then you must change the user login script. This is because it maps the drive letter `O:` to a share called `Anetapps` that is created. For the test network setup, it is important that the system is defined as described below. When you fully understand the ramifications of changes to these settings and have used the test setup to test any changes, then you can make modifications and build your own design.

NT TaskStation Setup

The TaskStation model is the simplest to install and configure because of the ultimate limitations it places on the desktop environment. This model is useful if users run one application and do not need access to the greater functionality provided with the Windows NT operating system. Users are severely restricted in this mode, but working from a starting point of *extreme limitation* and adding some functionality if required is a good way to secure your desktop environment.

Follow the instructions below to run the TaskStation setup for the distribution point. For this example, the ZAK software is provided in a fully expanded state on CD distribution media. You should be logged on locally to the domain with administrative privileges to perform this installation.

1. Place the ZAK distribution media in the CD drive of the server.
2. Start **NT Explorer** on the server.
3. Navigate to the **\I386** folder on the root of the CD-ROM drive.
4. Double-click the program **ZAKsetup.exe**. Figure 2.1 shows the resulting ZAK setup screen.

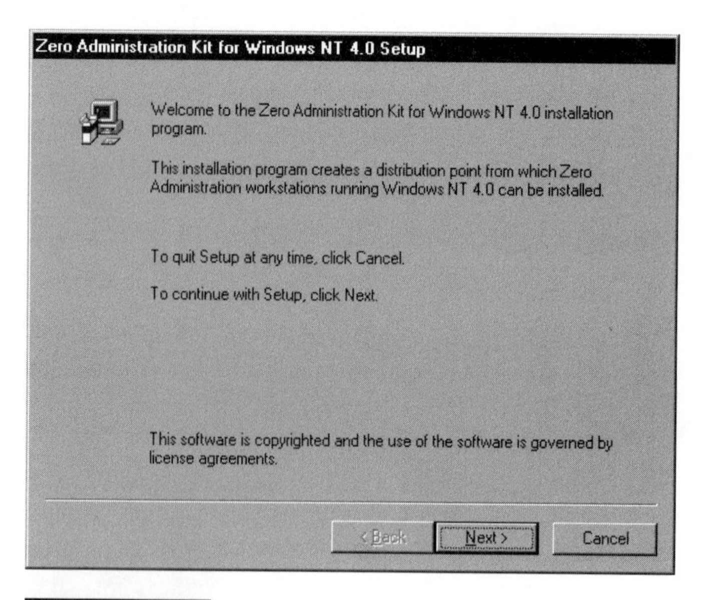

FIGURE 2.1 ZAK setup program initial status screen

5. Select **Next** to display the **End User License Agreement**.
6. Accept the license agreement and select **Next**.
7. Select the **Intel x86 Platform** option. The **NEC** option is for a Japanese version only. Figure 2.2 shows these available options.

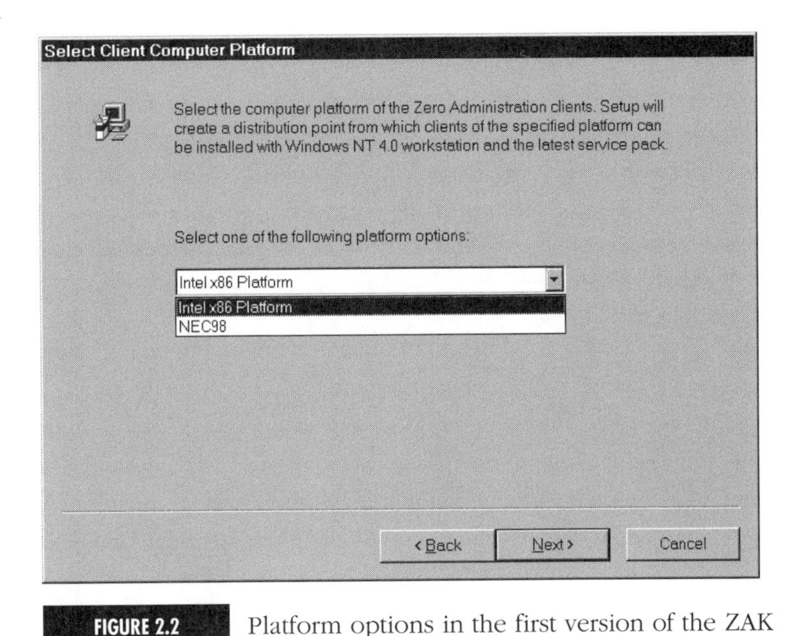
Select Client Computer Platform
Select the computer platform of the Zero Administration clients. Setup will create a distribution point from which clients of the specified platform can be installed with Windows NT 4.0 workstation and the latest service pack.
Select one of the following platform options:
Intel x86 Platform
Intel x86 Platform
NEC98
< Back
Next >
Cancel

FIGURE 2.2 Platform options in the first version of the ZAK

8. Select **Next** to choose which configuration to install.
9. Select **TaskStation**.
10. Select **Next**. You are asked to enter a destination folder for the TaskStation distribution point. Figure 2.3 shows the **Software Location** dialog box. Note the warning about using an NTFS partition so that the distribution point for these files can be protected with NTFS permissions.
11. Enter the destination drive and folder, or accept the default. You can enter a local drive letter, a network drive letter, a UNC path, or browse your connections. Because this designation is used as the distribution point for the TaskStation users, it should be available to these users and should be within the user's domain. This installation presumes the default destination of **C:\ZAKTaskDist**.
12. Select **Next**. You are asked if you wish to create the folder if it doesn't exist.
13. Enter the destination folder for the administration files. This destination should be on an NTFS partition on a domain controller. This installation uses the default of **C:\Zakadmin**.
14. Select **Next**. You are asked if you wish to create the administration files destination folder if it doesn't exist.

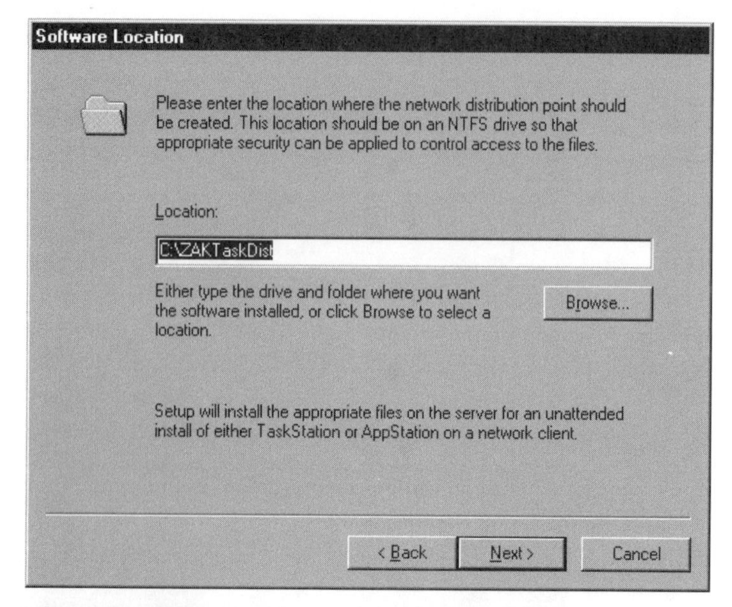

FIGURE 2.3 Configuring the software distribution point for all configurations on an NTFS partition

15. Enter the details of an administrative account in your test domain. These details are recorded in plain text files and so should not be credentials that could lead to your live network being compromised. Figure 2.4 shows the dialog screen completed for the test installation.
16. Select **Next**.
17. Enter a default password and confirmation for the local Administrator user on each configured client PC. This is more secure than leaving the passwords blank on all new configurations.
18. Select **Next**.
19. Enter the default printer information for all TaskStation client configurations. This information should be in the form of a print server name and printer share name. Figure 2.5 shows the information entered for this test system.
20. Select **Next** to begin the distribution file copy to the destination folders designated earlier in this process. The next stage in the process involves copying the Windows NT Workstation installation files to the destination entered in steps 10 and 11 above.
21. When prompted, place the NT 4.0 Workstation media in the CD-ROM drive and enter the source information.
22. Select **OK** to begin the copy operation. This operation takes a few minutes to complete.

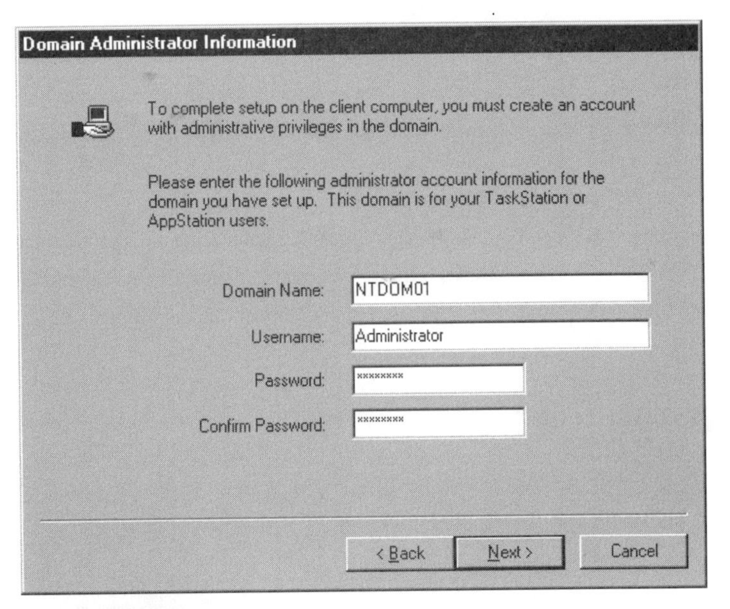

FIGURE 2.4 Administrative account information used to perform the unattended client installation

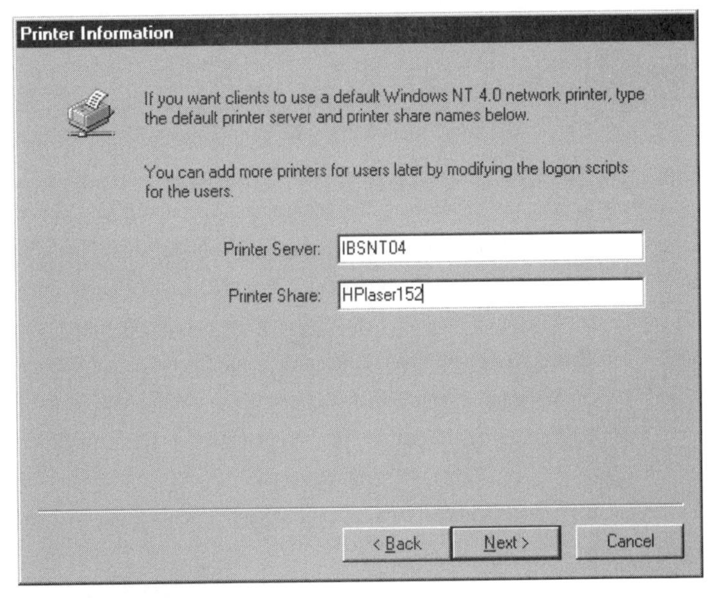

FIGURE 2.5 Printer information defines the default printer for all TaskStation clients

23. You are asked for the source files for Service Pack 3 or greater for the platform you are installing. Place the service pack CD in the drive and enter the drive and folder location.
24. Select **OK**. The service pack files are copied and the installation is complete.
25. Select **Finish** to end the installation. A portion of the ZAK administrators guide is displayed, giving instructions for completing the client setup. Read this file carefully because it may contain up-to-date information for any known bugs.

NT AppStation Setup

The AppStation model uses a more involved installation and configuration procedure because of the extra options available in the desktop environment. This model is useful for users with well-defined application needs who do not need to access the advanced functionality provided by the Windows NT environment. Users are still extremely limited in what they can see and access. Applications are best run from server installations and so should lend themselves to this type of configuration.

Follow the instructions below to run the AppStation setup for the distribution point. For this example, the ZAK software is provided in a fully expanded state on CD distribution media. You should be logged on locally to the domain with administrative privileges to perform this installation. The first part of the installation procedure is the same as that of the TaskStation configuration.

1. Place the ZAK distribution media in the CD drive of the server.
2. Start **Windows Explorer** on the server.
3. Navigate to the **\I386** folder at the root of the CD-ROM drive.
4. Double-click the program **ZAKsetup.exe**.
5. Select **Next**. The resulting screen shows the **End User License Agreement**.
6. Accept the license agreement and select **Next**.
7. Select the **Intel x86 Platform** option.
8. Select **Next** to choose which configuration to install.
9. Select **AppStation**.
10. Select **Next** to specify the destination folder for the AppStation distribution point.

11. Enter the destination drive and folder, or accept the default. You can enter a local drive letter, a network drive letter, a UNC path, or browse your connections. This test setup uses the default of **C:\ZAKAppDist**.
12. Select **Next**. You are asked if you wish to create the folder if it doesn't exist. You are now asked for the distribution point information for network applications. This folder is defined later as a network share from which network applications will be run by the AppStation clients. You must enter the drive and folder information for the network application installation, the server name, and a valid share name to be created on that server. Figure 2.6 shows the dialog box completed with the correct information for this test network.

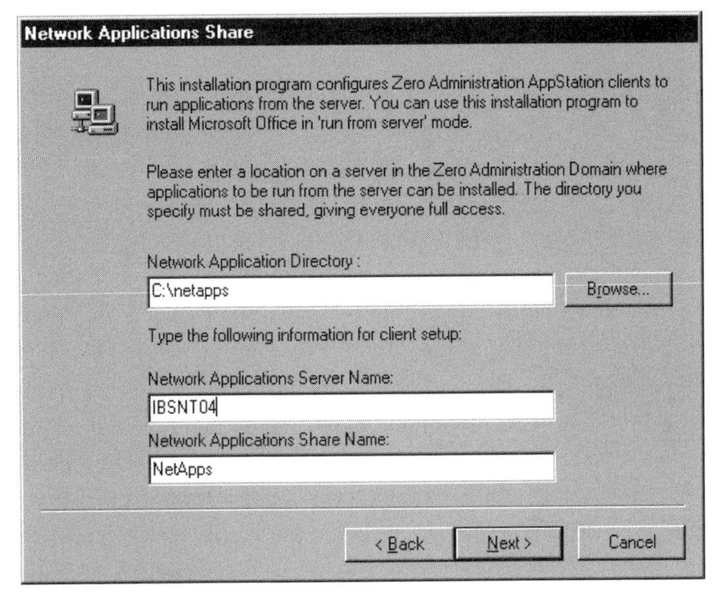

FIGURE 2.6 Share information for network applications, used by all AppStation clients

13. Enter valid information for the **Network Application Share** and select **Next**. You are asked to create the folder if it doesn't exist. This test setup uses the default of **C:\Netapps**. The **Network Application Server Name** should be **IBSNT04**.
14. In the **Network Application Drive** dialog box, you are asked to enter a drive letter that all of the AppStation clients will use to connect to the network applications share. Note that the default offering of drive **O:** is also contained in the user policy file; if you decide to change this, you must also change the entries in the policy file.
15. Accept the default drive letter **O:** and select **Next**.

16. The **Install Microsoft Office** dialog box asks you to confirm that you wish to install MS Office as the network application suite.
17. Ensure that the check box is selected, and choose **Next**.
18. Enter the destination folder for the administration files. This destination should be on an NTFS partition on a domain controller. This can be the same folder as your TaskStation admin files.
19. Select **Next**. You are asked to create the folder if it doesn't exist.
20. Enter the details of an administrative account in your domain.
21. Select **Next**.
22. Enter a default password and confirmation for the local Administrator user on each configured client PC.
23. Select **Next**.
24. Enter the default printer information for all AppStation client configurations. This information should be in the form of a print server name and printer share name. (See Figure 2.5 in the *NT TaskStation Setup* section for an example entry.)
25. Select **Next**.
26. Enter the server name for your Microsoft Exchange installation. This element is optional if you are using Exchange and wish to test Microsoft Outlook client configurations. This test setup does not use MS Exchange.
27. Select **Next**. The distribution files are now copied to the destination folders designated earlier in this process.
28. Place the NT 4.0 Workstation media in the CD-ROM drive when prompted and enter the source folder information.
29. Select **OK** to begin the Windows NT Workstation file copy. This operation takes a few minutes to complete.
30. You are asked for the source files for Service Pack 3 or greater for the platform you are installing. Place the service pack CD in the drive, enter the drive and folder location, and select **OK** to begin the service pack file copy.
31. You are asked to enter the source address for the Microsoft Office 97 files. Enter the source address, and select **OK**. Figure 2.7 shows the resulting information screen. Record the information on this screen for later use.
32. Select **OK** to begin the MS Office 97 installation.
33. Select **Continue** to run the installation.
34. The warning screen shown in Figure 2.8 is displayed. Select **OK** to continue the installation.
35. Enter the company name in the **Organization Information** dialog box.

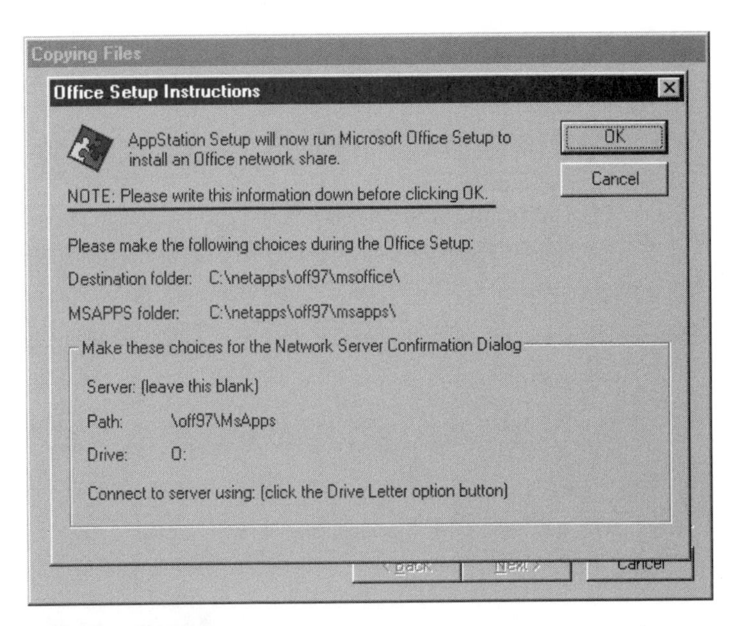

FIGURE 2.7 The MS Office information screen whose content you must record

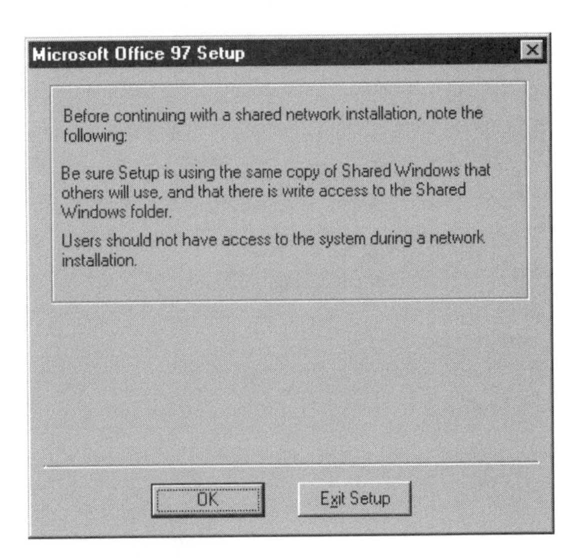

FIGURE 2.8 Warning information from the MS Office 97 shared installation

36. Select **OK**. Select **OK** again to confirm the entry.
37. Enter the **CD key** information.
38. Select **OK**. Select **OK** again to confirm the key information.

39. You must change the destination folder to match the instructions on the information screen shown in Figure 2.7. Select **Change Folder** and enter the correct destination. In this test case, the correct folder is **C:\Netapps\off97\msoffice**.
40. Select **OK**.
41. The shared files for MS Office 97 should be placed in the **C:\Netapps\off97\MSAPPS** folder. This entry should be the default if the previous two steps were followed correctly. If you have chosen your own folder structure then you should amend this entry accordingly.
42. Select **OK**. Figure 2.9 shows the resulting dialog box.

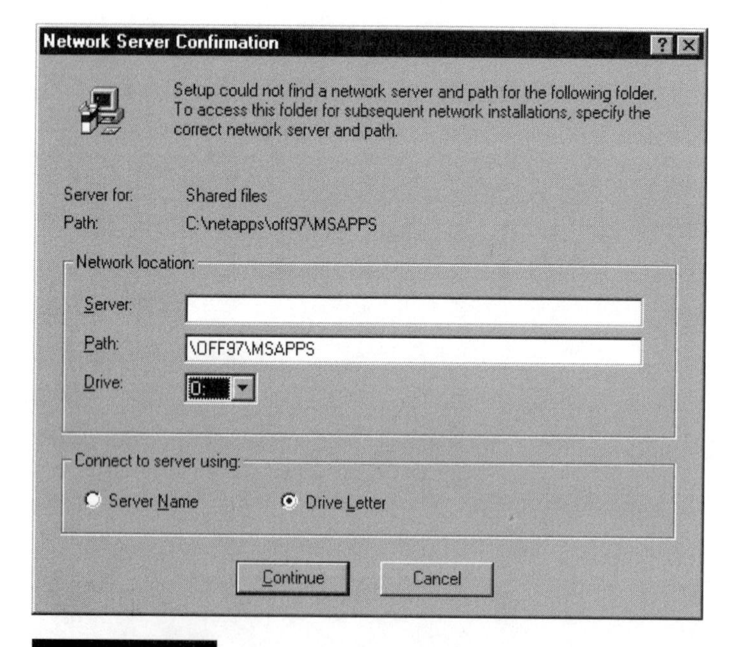

FIGURE 2.9 Carefully fill in the information

43. For this test installation, the **Server** location is left blank. The **Path** is set to **\off97\MSAPPS**. The Drive is **O:**. In the **Connect to server using** section, select the **Drive Letter** radio button. All of this information is given earlier in this section and shown in Figure 2.7.

The settings shown in step 43 are reflected in settings contained in the user profile templates installed for the AppStation user. If you decide to change any of the options contained in step 43 you must make corresponding changes in the user login scripts. The recommendation at this point is to use all of the default settings until you are familiar with the effect that a change in settings has on the user setup.

44. Select **Continue**.
45. Select **Server** as the location for the shared file folder to ensure that all client configurations use the same shared files and that central updates to these files take effect on all clients.
46. Select **OK**.
47. Select the desired **Paper Format** and **Language** option and choose **OK** to continue with the file copy.
48. The MS Office 97 installation completes. Select **OK**. The ZAK setup for AppStation mode continues copying any necessary files.
49. Select **Finish** to acknowledge the end of the installation. A portion of the ZAK administrator's guide is displayed, giving instructions for completing the client setup. Read this file carefully because it may contain up-to-date information on any known bugs.

When installing MS Office 97 in a Zero Admin environment, you must adjust a library file if the Office version is a localized one. You can find the file on the ZAK distribution media in the subdirectory corresponding to the platform you have chosen to install on. For x86 Intel-based systems, the folder is `\I386\fixes\off97` and the file name is `off97_bb.dll`. Take this file and replace the installed file of the same name, which can be found in `C:\Netapps\off97\msoffice`, if you accepted the default settings in the example above.

Windows 95/98 ZAK Quick Setup

The following instructions enable you to create a distribution point for either Windows 95 or Windows 98 client machines.

1. Place the ZAK distribution media in the CD drive of the server.
2. Start **NT Explorer** on the server.
3. Double-click the program **ZAKsetup.exe** at the root of the CD.
4. Agree to the license requirements. Select **Next**.
5. Select **Next** again to display a screen that briefly explains the setup requirements.
6. Select **Next**.
7. Enter the location on the server where you wish to place the network distribution point for the installation files. The default value is **C:\ZAK9x**, where **x** represents either 5 or 8 depending on the operating system involved. Select **Next**.

8. Accept the default offering for the Windows 95/98 distribution point. This is a subfolder of the main distribution point named Setup. The default value is **C:\ZAK9x\Setup**. Select **Next**.
9. Select **Yes** when asked to create a Microsoft Office share point. Select **Next**.
10. Accept the default location, which is a subfolder of the main distribution point called **Netapps**. The default value is **C:\ZAK9x\Netapps**.
11. You are asked whether you wish to create a network boot disk. Select **No**. The instruction for creating this disk are included in Chapter **Three.**
12. Enter your domain name. The test environment used in this book requires the name **NTDOM01**. Select **Next**.
13. Enter a workgroup name, or accept the default name given. Select **Next**.
14. Enter the pass-through validation agent name, or accept the default name **NTDOM01**. Select **Next**.
15. Enter the location for the policy files, templates, and scripts. Place them in the *Netlogon* share by entering the full path name `\%Windir%\System32\Repl\Imports\Scripts`. Select **Next**.
16. Enter printer information if required. Select **Next**.
17. Enter an Exchange server name if required. Select **Next**.
18. Enter the folder name into which the Windows 95/98 will be installed. The default value is **C:\Windows**.
19. Select **Next**. An information screen informs you which file sets will be copied. Select **Next**.
20. The ZAK files are copied to their destination. You are prompted to insert the operating system media into the CD-ROM drive. For a Windows 95 installation, you are prompted for the location of the service pack files, the Internet Explorer files, and the Microsoft Office 97 files.
21. If you chose to install a Microsoft Office share, you are shown a screen with all of the relevant information that you must enter into the Office setup program. Write this information down and enter it exactly as shown when the time comes.
22. The Microsoft Office setup program runs and you are asked for all of the information described in step 21.
23. The ZAK setup finishes, all of the distribution points are created.

You can find more information on this setup procedure in the `\Doc\Zakadmin.doc` file on the Windows 95 or Windows 98 ZAK distribution media.

Network Shares

You must create three network shares to allow access to files that have been installed as part of the ZAK setup process. These shares allow access to the `C:\ZakAppDist\Netsys` folder, the `C:\ZakTaskDist\Netsys` folder, and the `C:\Netapps` folder.

Share Creation

1. Start **NT Explorer**.
2. Navigate to the root of the **C:** drive.
3. Right-click the **Netapps** folder.
4. Select **Sharing**.
5. Select **Share As**.
6. Accept the default share name of **Netapps**.
7. Select **OK** to create the share.
8. Repeat the steps above to create the share **TNetsys** from the folder **C:\ZakTaskDist\Netsys**.
9. Repeat the steps above to create the share **ANetsys** from the folder **C:\ZakAppDist\Netsys**.
10. Set the share permissions for the **TNetsys** share and the **ANetsys** share to be **Domain Admins—Full Control**. Ensure that the **Everyone** group is completely removed from the share permissions **Name** box.
11. Set permissions for the **Netapps** share to be **Domain Admins—Full Control** and **Domain Users—Change**.

WINDOWS 95/98 SHARE

You must create a network share for the Windows 9x installation files. Follow the instructions above for creating a network share. The shared folder should be **C:\Zak9x\Setup** (where **x** represents either 5 or 8), and the share name should be set to **9xSetup**. The share permissions should be set for **Domain Users—Read**.

NTFS Permissions

Apply NTFS permissions to the folders named above to control access. Remember that when NTFS permissions and share permissions conflict, the most restrictive permission is applied.

1. Start **NT Explorer**.
2. Navigate to the root of the **C:** drive.
3. Right-click the **\Netapps** folder.
4. Select **Properties**.
5. Select the **Security** tab.
6. Set the permissions on this folder and all subfolders to be **Domain Admins—Full Control**, **Domain Users—Read**.
7. Select **OK**.
8. Navigate to the **C:\Netapps\off97\msoffice** folder.
9. Right-click the **\Workdir** subfolder.
10. Select **Properties**.
11. Select the **Security** tab.
12. Set the permissions on this folder and all subfolders to be **Domain Admins—Full Control**, **Domain Users—Change**.
13. Select **OK**.
14. Navigate to the **C:\ZakTaskDist** folder.
15. Right-click the **\Netsys** folder.
16. Select **Properties**.
17. Select the **Security** tab.
18. Set the permissions on this folder and all subfolders to be **Domain Admins—Full Control**. Remove the **Everyone** group from the permissions list.
19. Select **OK**.
20. Navigate to the **C:\ZakAppDist** folder.
21. Right-click the **\Netsys** folder.
22. Select **Properties**.
23. Select the **Security** tab.
24. Set the permissions on this folder and all subfolders to be **Domain Admins—Full Control**. Remove the **Everyone** group from the permissions list.
25. Select **OK**.

WINDOWS 95/98 NTFS PERMISSIONS

Set the permissions on the `C:\Zak9x\Setup` folder and all subfolders to be **Domain Admins—Full Control**, **Domain Users—Read**.

ZAK Setup File Structure

If you followed the instructions exactly during the installation phase, then the file structure copied down to the server during the NT ZAK setup contains four directory trees on the root of the `C:` drive.

- `Netapps`
- `Zakadmin`
- `ZakAppdist`
- `ZakTaskdist`

The `\Netapps` folder contains the files copied as part of the MS Office 97 installation. This folder was shared out earlier in the process to provide access to the network applications distribution point. The other three folders are shown in Figure 2.10 below. These folders contain the distribution point files for TaskStation and AppStation clients as well as the administration files (logon scripts, policy files, and templates).

After the installation of both TaskStation and AppStation configuration, two almost identical folder and file structures are created. There are only four differences in the file structure between the `ZakTaskdist` and `ZakAppdist` structures. The files that are different are listed below along with a brief explanation of their function.

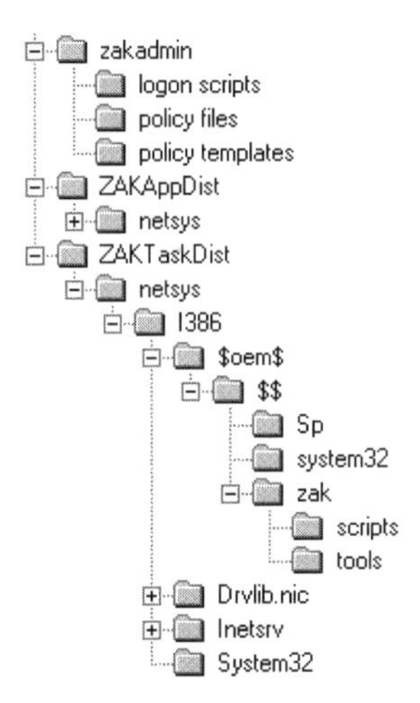

FIGURE 2.10 Folder structures for TaskStation and AppStation are identical

- \netsys\i386\oem\cmdlines.txt. This file calls the configuration-specific command file and exists in both configurations.
- \netsys\i386\$oem$\$$\zak\scripts\acls.cmd. This file sets ACL controls on the ZAK distribution source folders and exists in both configurations.
- \netsys\i386\$oem$\$$\zak\scripts\off97.cmd. This file is AppStation specific when MS office 97 is installed as a network application. The file does not exist in the ZakTaskdist folder structure.
- \netsys\i386\$oem$\$$\zak\scripts\zakb1wrk.cmd. This file runs various command files for the two different configurations. It exists in both configurations.

Move Administration Files

For the task-based worker configurations to function, the administration files that were installed in the *Zakadmin* distribution point must be copied to the relevant folders on the domain controller.

LOGON SCRIPTS

Copy the contents of the \Zakadmin\Logon Scripts folder to the folder on the domain controller shared out as **Netlogon**. This shared is normally \%Windir%\system32\repl\import\scripts, for example, C:\Winnt\System32\Repl\Import\Scripts, as is the case for the single domain controller installation used in this test setup. For a domain with multiple authentication servers, place these files in the replication folders and use the replication service to keep all of the authentication servers in sync.

POLICY FILES

The policy files folder contains two files by default: Zakconfig.pol and Zakconfig.pol.log. These two files contain system policy information for the ZAK configurations. They should be copied to the folder on the domain controller shared out as **Netlogon**. This share is normally \%Windir%\system32\repl\import\scripts, as shown in the previous example above.

POLICY TEMPLATES

The files contained in the policy templates directory are used by the policy editor to present a GUI interface that can be used to apply registry settings to the system in a controlled fashion. Only registry settings defined in the loaded template files are exposed to this manipulation. The template files should remain where they are in the policy template directory. They can be loaded into the policy editor from this directory and will not interfere with the policy template files that are already supplied with the Windows NT Server 4.0 installation on the domain controller.

Default System Policy File Configuration

The system policy editor is supplied as an application with the retail version of Windows NT Server 4.0. System policies are discussed in detail in Chapter Six, *System Policies*. In this example, we load the following template files.

- `Access97.adm`
- `Common.adm`
- `Ieak.adm`
- `Off97NT4.adm`
- `Outlk97.adm`
- `Query97.adm`
- `Winnt.adm`
- `Zakwinnt.adm`

Follow these instructions to start the policy editor, add the template files, and make a change in the AppStation user's policy.

1. Log on to the server as Administrator.
2. Select **Start** > **Programs** > **Administrative Tools** > **System Policy Editor**. The blank system policy editor interface opens.
3. Select the **Options** menu.
4. Select **Policy Template**.
5. Highlight each of the loaded template files in turn, and select **Remove**. The **Current Policy Template(s)** list should be empty.
6. Select **Add**.
7. Browse to the **C:\Zakadmin\Policy Templates** folder.
8. Select the first template file, and choose **Open**.
9. Repeat steps 6 through 8, selecting each template file in turn.
10. When all of the template files are in the list, select **OK** to check the syntax of each of the template files in turn and load them into the policy editor.
11. Select the **File** menu.
12. Select **Open Policy**.
13. Browse to the **Netlogon** share where the policy files were copied to, and select **Zakconfig.pol**.
14. Select **Open**. Figure 2.11 shows the default ZAK policy file.

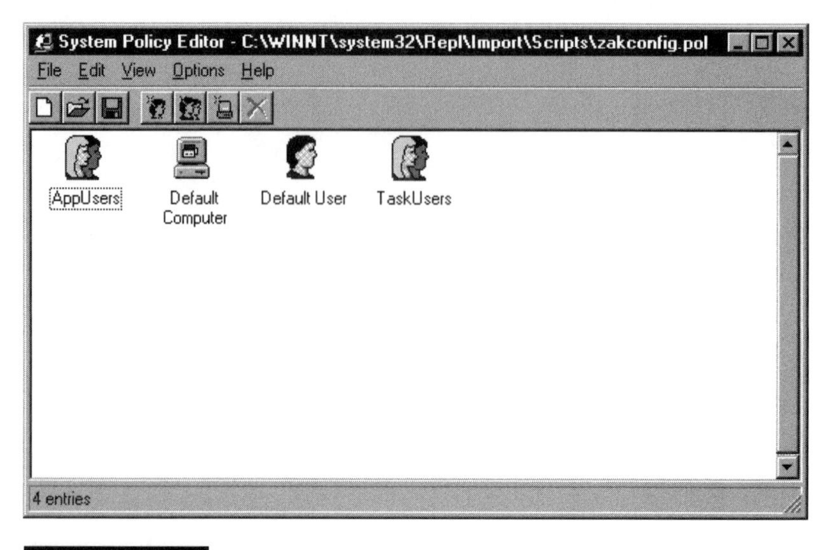

FIGURE 2.11 Default setup for the ZAK system policy

The group entries in the policy denoted by the multiheaded icon are named after the task-based worker configurations. They represent global groups created for the installation later in this chapter. This is an example of why you must make sure that the installation is carried out exactly as shown. If the group names are not spelled correctly when you create them, then these policies will fail to apply to the users when they log on.

You must make one change to the policy file for each of the configuration modes represented by a group icon.

1. Double-click the **AppUsers** icon.
2. Scroll down the list of categories to the **ZAK Policies** entry.
3. Expand the category **ZAK Policies/Windows NT/Drive/Restrictions**.
4. Select the **Show only selected drives** entry. This entry should have a check mark next to it by default. The bottom pane of the dialog box becomes active when you select this entry.
5. From the drop-down list in the bottom pane, select the entry **Only U:**.
6. Select **OK**.
7. Repeat steps 1 through 6 for the **TaskUsers** group icon.
8. Select the **File** menu.
9. Select **Save As**.

10. Enter **NTconfig.pol** as the new file name. This should still be in the **Netlogon** share folder.
11. Select **Save**.
12. Close the policy editor.

The change made in the preceding example allows the users to see only the `U:` drive from their workstations, thus, use the home directory (which we next map to the `U:` drive in the user setup section) and no other network access.

The policy file name `NTconfig.pol` is the default file name looked for when a user logs on to the domain. The next time the policy editor is launched on this machine the template files we just loaded are loaded again automatically.

User Creation

You must define test users on the domain controller so that the evaluation process can take place. This section describes how you set up users and groups. Pay particular attention to the definition of the users and groups so that the installed AppStation and TaskStation models work properly.

Home Directory Share Creation

Create a home directory for the users that will be created in this test setup. Create the home directory share before the user accounts.

1. Start **NT Explorer**.
2. Navigate to the **NTFS** volume on which you wish to place the home directories.
3. Create a new folder called **Users**.
4. Right-click on the new folder and select **Sharing**.
5. Select the **Share As** radio button.
6. Accept the default share name of **Users**.
7. Change the default permissions by removing the **Everyone** entry and replacing it with **Domain Users—Full Control**.
8. Select **OK** to confirm the share creation.

User Account Creation

Now create a test user on the domain controller for each of the two installed configurations.

1. Log on to the server with administrative privilege.
2. Run **User Manager for Domains**.
3. From the **User** menu, select **New User**.
4. For **Username**, enter **Taskuser1**. This user name will be used as a test account for TaskStation mode.
5. Enter a valid password and confirmation password.
6. For ease of use, deselect **User Must Change Password at Next Logon**.
7. Select **Profiles**.
8. For **Logon Script Name**, enter **Tsklogon.cmd**. Be sure to spell it correctly, as shown.
9. Select the **Connect** radio button.
10. Use the drop-down box to select drive **U:**.
11. In the **To** field, enter the correct path to the **Users** share plus the `%Username%` variable. For example, **\\IBSNT04\Users\%Username%**. Figure 2.12 shows the completed dialog box for the user profile.

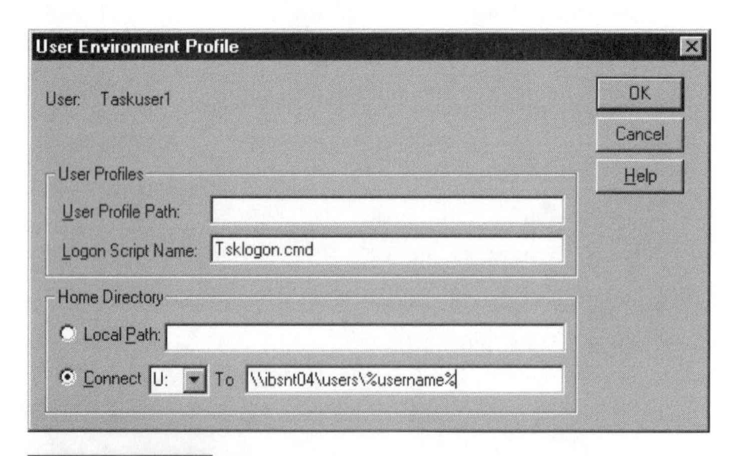

FIGURE 2.12 Entering user profile information

12. Select **OK**.
13. Select **Add** to add the newly defined user.

You should now add a user for the AppStation configuration. To do this, follow steps 4 through 13 above, replacing the TaskStation-specific information with AppStation information, as shown below.

- **Username**. Taskuser1 becomes Appuser1.
- **Logon Script Name**. `Tsklogon.cmd` becomes `Applogon.cmd`.

You can create more users for each test configuration as necessary. In the remainder of the book, we refer to the user names created above when discussing the test environment.

WINDOWS 95/98 USERS

Create users for the Windows 95/98 ZAK environment that can be distinguished from the NT users. The user names that should be created are presented below.

- 9xTaskUser1. No logon script is used for this type of user.
- 9xAppUser1. Enter `Applogon.bat` as the logon script.
- 9xZAKsetup. This user *must* be a member of Domain Admins.

The 9xZAKsetup account will connect to the distribution points and run the setup for Windows 9x.

Global Group Creation

Create a global group on the domain controller for each of the two installed configurations. The users we just created will be added to their relevant global groups.

1. Log on to the server with administrative privilege.
2. Run **User Manager for Domains**.
3. Select the **Taskuser1** account in the top pane.
4. From the **User** menu, select **New Global Group**.
5. In the **Group Name** box, enter **Taskusers**. Be sure to spell it correctly, or the predefined configurations will not work.
6. In the **Description** box, enter **ZAK TaskStation users**.
7. In the **Members** area, the only user should be **Taskuser1**. Remove any other users.
8. Select **OK** to add the new global group; the **Taskuser1** account is a member of the group.
9. Select the **Appuser1** account in the top pane.
10. Repeat steps 4 through 8. Substitute the **Group Name** entered in step 5 with the name **Appusers**. Spell this name exactly as shown. The description for this second group should be **ZAK AppStation users**. The second global group has now been created, and the **Appuser1** account is a member.

WINDOWS 95/98 GLOBAL GROUPS

- TaskUser. Place 9xTaskUser1 as a member of this group.
- AppUser. Place 9xAppUser1 as a member of this group.

You must spell these group names exactly as shown; otherwise, changes will be required in the predefined user setup that come with the kit. Note that the group names are different from those of the Windows NT installation in that they have no letter "s" on the end. This is intentional.

Summary

The installation and configuration processes discussed in this chapter help you install a ZAK test environment so that you can completely evaluate the product. The next stage in the process is to build the network boot disk necessary to connect to the network distribution points and to build the answer file that will help you to perform an unattended client installation.

The ZAK support for Windows 95 and Windows 98 is not as extensive as that for Windows NT 4.0. The setup of the operating system once the ZAK setup phase is complete requires more manual intervention than that of the Windows NT clients. Where desktop security is an issue, Windows NT clients are required so that NTFS permissions can be used to lock down the desktop in a completely secure manner.

THREE

How to Adapt the Basics for Your Requirements

In This Chapter

- Network Boot Disk
- Answer File
- Summary

Once the basic distribution points have been installed for both TaskStation and AppStation clients, you must make adjustments to match the environment that you are trying to build. This chapter looks at the two features that must be created and amended so you can proceed with your first client installation.

The first part of this chapter introduces the network boot disk and its structure. Those of you who have been involved in IT solutions for some years will no doubt be familiar with real-mode drivers and building DOS boot disks that are network enabled. Those people who have not had the pleasure of working with DOS may not be all that familiar with the process. The discussion covers the use of the Windows NT Network Client Administrator as the main method of boot disk creation, and also describes the creation of a disk for an NIC that is not supported by this tool. In the case of the latter, this chapter can be used as an introduction to the structure of the boot disk, providing a starting point from which to work. A network boot disk is a requirement of the ZAK if you wish to perform unattended system installations from network source files.

The second part of the chapter looks at the answer file required to enable an operating system installation to run in unattended mode. This file is looked at in great detail for the Windows NT 4.0 operating system, and changes to the default file provided will almost certainly be necessary before you can proceed with a test installation.

Network Boot Disk

One of the key requirements for an unattended software installation is an access path to the source files. In the case of the test environment that we are creating during this test setup procedure, the source files are stored on a Windows NT Server. The boot disk used for this installation must be able to connect to the server to receive the source files. This means you should use Real-Mode drivers from a DOS/Windows 9x boot disk and either TCP/IP or NetBEUI to connect to the server.

You can use the Network Client Administration tool supplied with Windows NT Server 4.0 to create the network boot disk as long as the NIC that you are using is supported by this tool. If not, you will have to build the boot disk by hand or look to the Network Interface Card manufacturer for help.

NCAdmin

You can use the Network Client Administration tool for Window NT 4.0 to create a network boot disk for one of a subset of supported network interface cards (NICs). This section steps through the creation of one of these boot disks. The NICs supported by the `Ncadmin.exe` tool are listed in *Appendix A*.

1. Run the **Ncadmin.exe** program on a Windows NT 4.0 Server.
2. Place your Windows NT Server CD in the drive.
3. Select **Make Network Installation Startup Disk** and choose **Continue**. The program will usually locate the client files and fill in the required path to the CD-ROM drive. If this is not the case, enter the correct source location.
4. Select **Share Files** and accept the default share name to share out the client files, or select **Copy Files to a New Directory, and then Share** and enter the destination path and name for the new share.
5. Select **OK**. Figure 3.1 shows the completed dialog box.
6. In the **Target Workstation Configuration** screen, select the correct floppy drive specification.
7. Select **Network Client v3.0 for MS-DOS and Windows**.
8. From the **Network Adapter Card** drop-down list select your NIC. (See *Appendix A* for a list of supported NICs for this tool.)

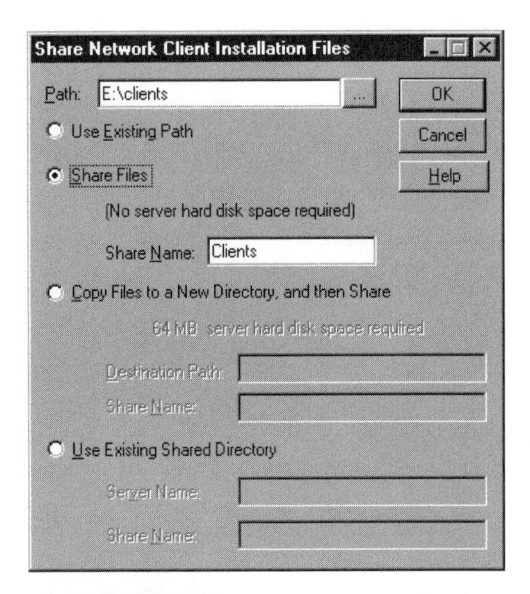

FIGURE 3.1 Share out network client installation files before creating the floppy disk

9. Select **OK**.
10. Enter a unique **Computer Name** for the client PC. This name is only used when connecting to the domain for the first time during the unattended installation.
11. Enter a **Username** and a **Domain** name to connect to. The domain name in this example is **NTDOM01**.
12. Select either TCP/IP or the NetBEUI protocol. This example uses **NetBEUI**. Take care here. The protocol selection drop-down box does not "drop down." It may look as if only TCP/IP is available. Use the scroll bar to move down to NetBEUI.
13. Select **OK**.
14. Insert a formatted **DOS system disk** into the floppy drive; ensure that there are no other files on the disk. If the disk is not bootable, you will receive an error message but can continue regardless. You can place boot files on the disk later.
15. The confirmation screen shown in Figure 3.2 details the information you have entered. Select **OK** when you have checked the information listed.
16. The file copy continues and the process is finished.
17. Exit the **NCAdmin** program.

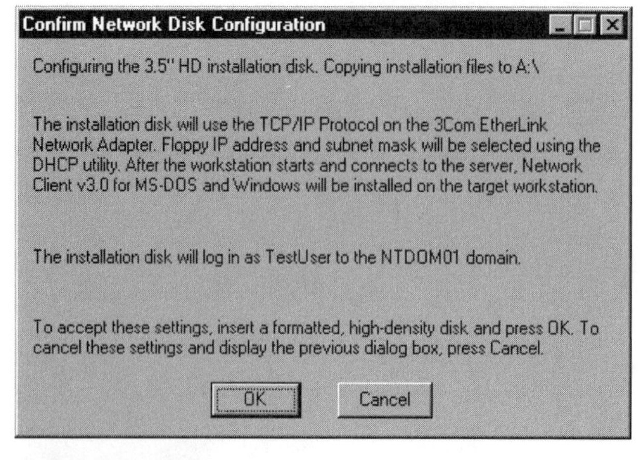

FIGURE 3.2 Check the information carefully before continuing with the floppy disk build

The `Ncadmin.exe` program can only be used to create completed boot floppies for the NICs listed in *Appendix A*. All other boot floppies must be created manually, adjusted from a build made by `Ncadmin.exe`, or provided by the NIC manufacturer.

NCAdmin for Unsupported NICs

You can use `Ncadmin.exe` to build a network boot disk that is close in structure to the one that you require. The resulting boot disk can be used as the base structure for the required disk, and you may only have to substitute driver references to make it work. The process for performing this task is very simple.

In the following example, we use a 3Com® EtherLink III (3C509b-Combo) card to create the initial build, while the target machine contains a 3Com EtherLink XL (3C900-TP) card.

First, you must build a network boot disk using the instructions in the preceding section. Your choice of network card is important. Because this procedure is for unsupported NICs, you will not be able to choose the correct card from the list. Instead, you must choose a card that is very close to the one for which you need to build a disk. You should look for the same manufacturer and the same media type (tokenring or Ethernet). With these two requisites taken care of, you should be able to substitute driver information and make the boot disk function.

Once the boot disk has been built for the 3Com EtherLink III card, place the correct DOS driver in the `\NET` folder on the floppy disk. This driver will be used as a substitute for the original. In this case, the driver named `ELNK3.dos` will be replaced by the `EI90x.dos` driver for the 3Com EtherLink XL card. You must find the correct DOS driver for the network card that you are going to use in the client machines. This particular driver was downloaded from 3Com's site (and also supplied on floppy with the card.)

Within the \NET folder on the newly created boot disk, two files—System.ini and Protocol.ini—contain references to the DOS network driver. You can edit these files with any text editor.

- Protocol.ini. Make a backup of the file before continuing. Then substitute any driver references to ELNK3 with a reference to EI90x. The references are likely to be in the form *DrivernamePrefix*$ (e.g., ELNK3$). When this is done, save the file.
- System.ini. Make a backup of the file before continuing. In the [Network Drivers] section of this file an entry named Netcard should list the driver name ELNK3.dos. Change the entry to Netcard=EI90x.dos. Save the file.

When the changes described above are made, the boot disk is ready to use. Test the disk, and copy any further files into the \NET folder as error messages dictate. This approach may not always work (I have had over 90 percent success rate with this method), but it is much less painful than building a disk from scratch. When the disk boots up and connects to the network, you are ready to move on to the next section.

Manually Configured Boot Floppy

The nature of the NIC industry and the availability of so many different network cards means that this chapter could not possibly include step-by-step instructions for creating every different type of network boot disk.

The previous example used a 3Com Ethernet card to demonstrate the adjustment of a boot disk made with NCAdmin. To ensure that the old-timers don't feel left out, the sample installation in this section uses a client machine with an IBM tokenring network card. I built the network boot disk for this installation from files supplied on the IBM Web site at http://www.networking.ibm.com/support/products.nsf/adapter. Specific downloads for unattended NT 4.0 installations are provided on this site. Other NIC manufacturers provide similar setup downloads.

I had to download the latest NDIS drivers for the NIC that I used in this test setup from IBM's Web site. I copied them to a folder that I created to sit below the Tnetsys share and the Anetsys share created during the ZAK setup. These files could then be copied to the client during the boot operation and used by the client installations as needed.

The folder listing that follows is a complete listing of the boot disk that I used in this installation. The changes that were made from the default download are discussed in the next section. Two separate boot disks were used for the TaskStation and AppStation machine configurations, as there is a slight difference in the Autoexec.bat file which maps the network installation drive to the correct source for each type of installation (i.e., \\Server\AppStationDist or \\Server\TaskStationDist).

```
\autoexec.bat
\bootlog.prv
\bootlog.txt
\choice.com
\command.com
\config.sys
\format.com
\io.sys
\ltc.msg
\msdos.sys
\readme.wnt
\sample1.txt
\sample2.txt
\smartdrv.exe
\unattend.txt
\wp root.sf
\input.txt

\net\administ.pwl
\net\connect.dat
\net\emm386.exe
\net\himem.sys
\net\ibmtrp.dos
\net\ifshlp.sys
\net\la1.msg
\net\ndishlp.sys
\net\net.exe
\net\net.msg
\net\neth.msg
\net\protman.dos
\net\protman.exe
\net\protocol.ini
\net\share000.pwl
\net\shares.pwl
\net\system.ini
\net\wfwsys.cfg
```

In the preceding listing, the contents of the `\Net` folder did not have to be adjusted on this occasion because it holds executables and network support files. The files that feature most in the adjustment process are:

- `Autoexec.bat`
- `Input.txt`
- `Unattend.txt`

These files are discussed below.

AUTOEXEC.BAT

The `autoexec.bat` file for the unattended installation of Windows NT using an IBM PCI tokenring network interface card is listed below. The lines are numbered for later discussion.

1. `echo on`
2. `cls`
3. `format c: < Input.txt`
4. `smartdrv c+`
5. `PATH=A:\;A:\NET`
6. `\net\net start`
7. `lock C: < input.txt`
8. `C:`
9. `md ibmtrp`
10. `net use n: \\IBSNT04\TNetsys`
11. `copy n:\ibmtrp\*.* c:\ibmtrp\*.*`
12. `n:\i386\winnt /U:a:\unattend.txt /S:n:\i386`

Line 3 • The requirements for the unattended installation are for a clean hard disk drive with at least 300 Mbytes of free disk space. This line formats the `C:` partition for this purpose. The file `Input.txt` provides the input to the usual formatting questions so that the process continues without interruption.

Line 6 • This line starts the network client and requires a user name and password for the destination machine, which should be the NT Server used as the source for the installation.

Line 7 • The `Lock` internal command allows direct access to the hard drive.

Line 9 • A folder is created to copy the IBM PCI token ring NIC drivers to the local drive for use during the client setup.

Line 10 • **Important:** This file is from the boot disk of the TaskStation client setup. This line maps the `N:` drive to the `Tnetsys` share created in the Chapter Two. The corresponding line in the `autoexec.bat` file on the AppStation boot disk maps this drive to the `Anetsys` share.

Line 11 • This command copies the NT network driver files for the installed NIC to the local hard disk so that they can be used in the NT setup process.

Line 12 • The `Winnt.exe` executable is run (16-bit NT 4.0 setup program) with the `/U` switch, which specifies the location of the answer file (`Unattend.txt`), and the `/S` switch, which specifies the source folder information for the NT setup files. The setup program for Windows 95/98 could be substituted here for the relevant setup process.

Answer File

The unattended client installation provided with the ZAK allows you to run an installation process for Windows NT 4.0 Workstation, (and MS Office if you use the AppStation configuration), on a PC with a minimum of intervention. You must adjust the supplied answer file to fit your own configuration needs. Armed with this answer file, you will find the installation process quite simple and painless.

You cannot install sound cards when using the unattended installation method. Microsoft has not built that functionality into the ZAK.

The answer file, by default named `Unattend.txt`, can have any valid 8.3 file name. It provides input to the Windows NT setup program to avoid the need for user input during this process. The format of the answer file is key to the smooth running of the unattended installation of Windows NT. The file content must be adjusted to fit the configuration of the machines on which you wish to install Windows NT. This section describes the structure of the answer file and includes a sample file. You can find further samples of the answer file in *Appendix B*. You should use this chapter in conjunction with the samples in *Appendix B* to fully understand how the file is structured.

The answer file generally has three distinct types of content: *section headers*, *keys*, and *values*.

Section Headers

Section headers gather together parameters that are of a similar nature. They can be thought of as group headers. Certain section header names are predefined; others can be user defined. Section headers are contained within square brackets `[ ]`, for example, `[`*`Headername1`*`]`.

Keys and Values

Keys are simply parameters defined within a section header. Certain parameters belong to predefined section headers. Values are assigned to keys. They can be selected from a predefined range (for example, Yes | No), or they can be a string value.

The general format for the key and value pair is shown below. The two are separated by an equal sign, (=), and the value requires double quotes " " around it if it is a string value.

Example: `OemPreinstall = Yes`

In the example above, the key name is `OemPreinstall`, and the value assigned to this key is `Yes`.

File Structure

This section lists all of the predefined and possible user-defined section headers of the answer file, as well as the possible key and value pairs contained in each section.

[UNATTENDED]

A required section header. If this header is not included in the answer file, the file is ignored. It should be placed at the start of the file.

`OemPreinstall`

> **Value: `Yes | No`**
> **Example:** `OemPreinstall = Yes`

This entry determines if the setup is to include OEM information. If the value is `Yes`, then a folder named `\$OEM$` must exist below the `\I386` source directory containing the OEM source files, which are then used during setup. You can use this setting to apply service pack files during the initial installation. When the value is `Yes`, the following section headers and keys are used during the installation. If the value is `No`, these are ignored.

- `[Display]`
  - `InstallDriver`
  - `InfOption`
  - `InfOptionFile`
- `[KeyboardDrivers]`
- `[MassStorageDrivers]`
- `[OEM_Ads]`
- `[OEMBootFiles]`
- `[PointingDeviceDrivers]`

`ComputerType`

> **Value: `<Hal Description> [,RETAIL | OEM]`**
> **Example:** `"IBM PS/2 or other Micro Channel-based PC", "RETAIL"`

Use this setting to indicate the type of machine on which the installation will take place. It defines the HAL to be loaded during the setup process. The key is only valid when the `[Unattended]—OemPreinstall` value is `Yes`. The value `RETAIL` denotes that the HAL to be used is part of the shipped Windows NT 4.0 retail product; a value of `OEM` denotes that it is OEM supplied. In the latter case, the driver must be defined in the `[OEMBootFiles]` section header, and the driver file must be placed in the `\I386\$OEM$\Textmode` subfolder of the installation source. The available retail options for the `[ComputerType]` section are listed in *Appendix C*.

ConfirmHardware

Value: Yes | No

Example: `ConfirmHardware = No`

Use this setting to force the installer to confirm the hardware detected during setup. A value of `Yes` forces the intervention; a value of `No` allows the setup to continue unattended.

ExtendOemPartition

Value: 0 | 1

Example: `ExtendOemPartition = 1`

Use this setting to extend beyond 2 Gbytes the size of the installation partition. It can extend the primary partition size through any contiguous unpartitioned disk space as long as there are no more than 1024 cylinders. More than this number of cylinders will cause the installation to fail. The value `0` indicates that the partition will not be extended, and `1` indicates that it will be extended. When the value is `1`, the `FileSystem` key must be set to `ConvertNTFS` and the installer will be prompted to reboot between text and GUI mode setup.

FileSystem

Value: ConvertNTFS | LeaveAlone

Example: `FileSystem = ConvertNTFS`

Use this setting to force a conversion of the primary FAT partition used on the clean installation disk to the NTFS file system during the setup process. This is a valuable feature for two reasons. First, you can ensure that the final portion of the user setup works properly by providing the means to apply security to the file system. Second, you can run your first test installations with the value `LeaveAlone` so that if the unattended setup requires alterations, you can simply make changes and then reboot from the boot floppy. Because the file system is still FAT, the format command will be able to erase the previous installation attempt.

KeyboardLayout

Value: ***Description***

Example: `KeyboardLatout = "US-International"`

This is a free text field requiring the type of keyboard layout to install. The available options for this key are listed in *Appendix C*.

NoWaitAfterTextMode

Value: **0 | 1**

Example: `NoWaitAfterTextMode = 1`

Use this setting to force an automatic soft reboot after the text portion of the setup process has finished. This reboot is important in an unattended installation. The value of `1` forces the soft reboot; the value of `0` causes the system to prompt for a reboot. This value is ignored if the `OemPreinstall` value is `No`.

NoWaitAfterGuiMode

Value: **0 | 1**

Example: `NoWaitAfterGuiMode = 1`

Use this setting to force an automatic soft reboot after the GUI portion of the setup process has completed. As in the previous case, a value of `1` forces an automatic reboot, and a value of `0` prompts for a reboot.

NtUpgrade

Value: **Yes | No | Manual | Single**

Example: `NtUpgrade = No`

Use this key to perform an upgrade of a previously installed Windows NT version. This key is best ignored because the upgrade version of Windows NT does not work in unattended mode. A value of `Yes` causes the upgrade of the first installation of NT to be found, and a value of `No` causes the installation to halt if a previous version of the OS is found. A value of `Single` allows the setup to continue if only one previous OS installation is found; a value of `Manual` requires user input to define which previous installation should be upgraded.

OEMSkipEULA

Value: **Yes | No**

Example: `OEMSkipEULA = Yes`

Use this setting to skip over the End User License Agreement acceptance screen. Setting this value to `No` will stop the install process until the user accepts the license terms.

OverwriteOemFilesOnUpgrade

Value: **Yes | No**

Example: `OverwriteOemFilesOnUpgrade = No`

Use this setting to overwrite OEM-supplied files with Windows NT native files during setup. The default action is to overwrite OEM-supplied files.

`TargetPath`

Value: ***`Pathname`*** **|** **`Manual`**

Example: `TargetPath = \Winnt`

Use this setting to define the target path for the Windows NT installation. The `Manual` setting prompts for a destination folder. The *Pathname* should not contain drive letters. You specify a drive by changing the WINNT or WINNT32 command line to include the `/T:`*driveletter* switch.

`Win31Upgrade`

Value: **`Yes`** **|** **`No`**

Example: `Win31Upgrade = No`

Use this setting to indicate that a previous version of Windows 3.x should be upgraded (or not).

[DISPLAY]

Specifies graphics adapter settings. The settings specified in this section must be valid for the adapter in question; otherwise, you may be prompted during setup for more information. To find valid settings for this section, you should configure the adapter manually in a working system to the values that you wish to use. Then, you can use the registry editor to look at the active settings, as shown in the following example.

1. Log on locally with administrative privileges.
2. Start **Regedt32.exe**.
3. Change to **Read-Only** mode.
4. Navigate to **HKLM\Hardware\DeviceMap\Video**.
5. Double-click the **\Device\Video0** key to display the registry path to the active video driver. Record the resulting string. In this example, the result is **\REGISTRY\Machine\System\ControlSet001\Services\S3Inc\Device0**.
6. Cancel out of this screen.
7. Navigate to the **HKCC\System\CurrentControlSet\Services\S3Inc\Device0** registry key. You must adjust this key location to fit your own adapter manufacturer's location as listed in the key named in step 5, and you must be logged on and using the same display values that you wish to place in the answer file.
8. Each of the available options for the `[Display]` section header are included here. Double-click each value (which is displayed in hex), and select the **Dec** radio button to convert the value to decimal. See the sample answer files in *Appendix B* for example entries in this section.
9. Close the Registry Editor.

ConfigureAtLogon

Value: `0 | 1`

Example: `ConfigureAtLogon = 1`

Use this key to specify when the graphics adapter should be configured. A value of `1` specifies that the adapter should be configured during the first logon by the user; a value of `0` specifies that the adapter should be configured during setup. Once you are certain that the specified values in the `[Display]` section are valid, this configuration can always be completed during setup to avoid user interference with system settings.

BitsPerPel

Value: ***<Decimal value for bits per pel>***

Example: `BitsPerPel = 32`

This key represents a bits-per-pel value for your graphics adapter. You find a valid value by setting a preconfigured machine to the correct settings and looking in the registry, using the instructions shown above.

Xresolution

Value: ***<Decimal value for X Resolution>***

Example: `Xresolution = 800`

This key represents the horizontal resolution for your graphics adapter. A valid value can be found by setting a pre-configured machine to the correct settings and looking in the registry using the instructions shown above.

Yresolution

Value: <Decimal value for Y Resolution>

Example: `Yresolution = 600`

This key represents the vertical resolution for your graphics adapter. You find a valid value by setting a preconfigured machine to the correct settings and looking in the registry, using the instructions shown above.

Vrefresh

Value: ***<Refresh Rate>***

Example: `Vrefresh = 60`

This key specifies a valid refresh rate for your graphics adapter. You find a valid value by setting a preconfigured machine to the correct settings and looking in the registry, using the instructions shown above.

Flags

Value: ***<Adapter Flags>***

Example: `Flags = 0`

This key specifies any flags which need to be set for the graphics adapter being installed. These will be adapter specific. More often than not the `Flags` setting in the registry will be set to `0` and so this key can be ignored.

`AutoConfirm`

Value: **`0 | 1`**

Example: `AutoConfirm = 0`

This key indicates whether or not the answer file contains all of the settings necessary for your graphics adapter to be loaded. A value of `1` stipulates that all of the necessary settings are contained in the file; a value of `0` stipulates that the user should be prompted for the settings.

[GUIUNATTENDED]

Included only if the `[Unattended]—OemPreinstall` key is set to `Yes`.

`OemSkipWelcome`

Value: **`0 | 1`**

Example: `OemSkipWelcome = 1`

Use this key to skip the Welcome page during setup. A value of `1` skips the welcome page.

`OemBlankAdminPassword`

Value: **`0 | 1`**

Example: `OemBlankAdminPassword = 1`

Use this key to hide the Administrator Password Wizard page from the user. A value of `1` skips wizard page. The default is to show this page (value `0`).

`TimeZone`

Value: <*Text String*>

Example: `Timezone = "(GMT-05:00) Eastern Time (US & Canada)"`

Use this key to set the time zone for the computer. The available values are listed in *Appendix C*.

`AdvServerType`

Value: **`SERVERNT | LANMANNT | LANSECNT`**

Example: `AdvServerType = LANMANNT`

Use this key to indicate the role of an NT 4.0 Server installation. A value of `SERVERNT` specifies a standalone server installation, a value of `LANMANNT` specifies a primary domain controller installation, and a value of `LANSECNT` specifies a backup domain controller installation.

DetachedProgram

Value: ***<Detached Program String>***

Example: `DetachedProgram = c:\runmine.exe`

Use this key to indicate that a detached program should be run concurrently with the setup program. If the detached program requires arguments, they are provided in the `Arguments` key shown below.

Arguments

Value: ***<Arguments String>***

Example: `Arguments = "/T /U"`

Use this key to specify the parameters for the detached program defined above.

[KEYBOARDDRIVERS]

Included only if the `[Unattended]`—`OemPreinstall` key is set to `Yes`. This header defines the keyboard driver that must be loaded during the text-mode setup phase. Without this entry, the setup routine will attempt to detect the keyboard type and load the default Windows NT driver. There is only one key/value pair, which is shown in the example below.

<Keyboard Driver Description>

Value: **RETAIL | OEM**

Example: `"XT, AT, or Enhanced Keyboard (83-104 keys)" = "RETAIL"`

For this key, the value `RETAIL` indicates that the driver is shipped with the retail version of the Windows NT 4.0 product and this driver will be used. The value `OEM` stipulates an OEM driver should be used. Note that this is not the keyboard layout, which is covered in its own section header. The available retail options for this key are included in *Appendix C*.

[LICENSEFILEPRINTDATA]

Only used for Windows NT Server 4.0 installations. The values in this section must be specified; otherwise, the setup process will prompt the user for input.

AutoMode

Value: **PERSEAT | PERSERVER**

Example: `AutoMode = PERSERVER`

Use this key to specify the licensing mode for Windows NT Server. If the value is set to `PERSERVER`, the key `AutoUsers` must be specified. The user will be prompted for input if this value is not specified.

AutoUsers

Value: ***<Decimal Value>***

Example: `AutoUsers = 250`

This key must be specified if the `AutoMode` key is set to `PERSERVER`. The value represents the number of licensed clients that can connect to the server concurrently.

[MASSSTORAGEDRIVERS]

Can be included only if the `[Unattended]—OemPreinstall` key is set to `Yes`. This header contains a list of SCSI devices that must be loaded by the setup routine. This section is useful if the destination drive for the setup routine is on a SCSI device. It corresponds to selecting option `S` during the text portion of the setup process and selecting additional mass storage drivers to be loaded.

<Mass Storage Driver Description>

Value: **RETAIL | OEM**

Example: `"Adaptec AHA-294X/AHA-394X/AIC-78XX SCSI Controller" = "RETAIL"`

Use this entry to define a mass storage driver that must be loaded during the text-mode setup phase. You can list as many drivers as necessary. The value `RETAIL` indicates that the driver is shipped as part of the Windows NT retail product; `OEM` indicates an OEM driver will be used. The OEM driver must be included in the `[OemBootFiles]` header section. The driver should be placed in the `\I386\$OEM$\Textmode` subfolder of the installation source. The available retail options for this section are included in *Appendix C.*

[MODEM]

Specifies that a modem needs to be installed for RAS purposes.

InstallModem

Value: ***<Modem Parameter Section>***

Example: `InstallModem = ModemSection`

This key takes the name of a further section header as the value. The value can be set to any string as long as that string does not conflict with another section header name. In the example above, the value `ModemSection` is used. This value requires that you define a corresponding section header named `[ModemSection]`, containing settings that are listed under the generic section header `<Modem Parameter Section>`.

[<MODEM PARAMETER SECTION>]

Name the `[<Modem Parameters Section>]` after the value given to the `InstallModem` key above. This section defines the settings required for the modem. If you do not supply values in this section, then the setup utility will search all valid COM ports and install any modems that it finds.

`<COM Port Number>`

Value: ***<Modem Description>*** **`[,`*<Manufacturer>*`,`*<Provider>*`]`**

Example: `Com2 = "Sportster 28800-33600 External"`

Use the `<Com Port Number>` key to specify the COM port on which the modem should be installed. The `<Modem Description>` value corresponds to the description of the modem in the `MDMxxx.inf` file for that particular modem. You can find the modem description in Control Panel > Modems on a machine where the modem is already installed. The `<Manufacturer>` and `<Provider>` values are optional and distinguish between two modems where the `<Modem Description>` values are the same.

[NETWORK]

Specifies that networking will be installed as part of the setup process. If this header is missing, no networking will be installed.

`Attended`

Value: **`Yes | No`**

Example: `Attended = Yes`

Use this key to prompt the user for setup information by setting the value to `Yes`. Leave this key out to perform an unattended install.

`JoinWorkgroup`

Value: ***<WorkgroupName>***

Example: `JoinWorkgroup = Workgroup1`

Use this key to indicate the workgroup into which the machine will be installed.

`JoinDomain`

Value: ***<DomainName>***

Example: `JoinDomain = NTDOM01`

Use this key to indicate the domain into which the machine will be installed.

CreateComputerAccount

Value: <*Username, Password*>

Example: `CreateComputerAccount = Administrator, adminpass`

Use this key to create the computer account in the domain and to provide a user name and password combination for the creation process. Remember that the answer file is a plain text file, and so this user name and password combination is available to anybody who can gain access to the file. You should consider creating a new user, with no file system access and only the Add Workstations to Domain advanced user right (assigned in User Manager for Domains). This approach should limit the potential for damage should the user name and password combination be discovered.

InstallDC

Value: <*Domain Name*>

Example: `InstallDC = NTDOM01`

Use this key when installing a primary or backup domain controller. The value is set to the name of the domain.

DetectAdapters

Value: <*Detect Adapters Section*> | ""

Example: `DetectAdapters = AdapterInfo`

This key takes the name of a further section header as the value. The value can be set to any string as long as that string does not conflict with another section header name. In the example above, the value `AdapterInfo` is used. This setting requires that you define a corresponding section header named `[AdapterInfo]`, containing the settings listed below under the generic section header `<Detect Adapters Section>`.
This key can also take a blank value, in which case the first network adapter detected will be installed. You must define this key or the `InstallAdapters` key in order to install a network adapter. The keys defined in the `<Detect Adapters Section>` generic section header will be used to define settings for the adapter that will be installed.

InstallAdapters

Value: <*Install Adapters Section*>

Example: `InstallAdapters = Netcards`

This key takes the name of a further section header as the value. The value can be set to any string as long as that string does not conflict with another section header name. In the example, the section header name `Netcards` is used. This setting requires that you define a corresponding section header named `[Netcards]`, containing the settings defined under the generic section header `<Install Adapters Section>`. The keys in this generic section header define settings for the adapters that must be installed during setup.

InstallProtocols

Value: *<Protocols Section>*

Example: `InstallProtocols = ProtocolList`

This key takes the name of a further section header as the value. The value can be set to any string as long as that string does not conflict with another section header name. In the example, the section header name `ProtocolList` is used. This setting requires that you define a corresponding section header named `[ProtocolList]`, containing the settings defined under the generic section header `<Protocols Section>`. The keys in this generic section header list the protocols to be bound during setup.

InstallServices

Value: *<Services Section>*

Example: `InstallServices = ServiceList`

This key takes the name of a further section header as the value. The value can be set to any string as long as that string does not conflict with another section header name. In the example, the section header name `ServiceList` is used. This setting requires that you define a corresponding section header named `[ServiceList]`, containing the settings defined under the generic section header `<Services Section>`. The keys placed in this section list the network services to be installed during setup.

InstallInternetServer

Value: *<Internet Information Server Section>*

Example: `InstallInternetServer = IISParams`

This key takes the name of a further section header as the value. The value can be set to any string as long as that string does not conflict with another section header name. In the example, the section header name `IISParams` is used. This setting requires that you define a corresponding section header named `[IISParams]`, containing the settings defined under the generic section header `<Internet Information Server Section>`. The keys placed in this section define the setup parameters for IIS during the Windows NT setup.

DoNotInstallInternetServer

Value: `Yes | No`

Example: `DoNotInstallInternetServer = Yes`

Regardless of the value assigned to this key, its very presence means that the installation of IIS does not take place.

[<DETECT ADAPTERS SECTION>]

The name of this generic section header is defined by the value of the [Network]—`DetectAdapters` key previously defined.

`DetectCount`

Value: ***<Decimal Number of Allowed Attempts>***
Example: `DetectCount = 2`

Use this key to define the number of detection attempts the setup process should make for network cards.

`LimitTo`

Value: ***<Netcard Inf Option[, Netcard Inf Option2, ..]>***
Example: `LimitTo = IBMPCITR`

Use this key to limit the scope of the network card detection to the entries listed here. The value must come from the `[Options]` section of the `OEMSETUP.INF` file provided with the network card. If you know that a machine will have one of two networks cards installed, then place the options name of both cards here to limit the detection to these two types of card.

`<Netcard Inf Option>`

Value: ***<Netcard Parameters Section>***
Example: `IBMPCITR = IBMPCITRparams`

Use this key to define a further generic section header that contains the parameters for the network card defined by the `LimitTo` key. The key name is derived from the value contained in the `LimitTo` key above. Multiple entries in the `LimitTo` key above will mean multiple `<Netcard Inf Option>` keys.

[<INSTALL ADAPTERS SECTION>]

The name of the generic section header is defined by the value of the [Network]—`InstallAdapters` key previously defined.

`<Netcard Inf Option>`

Value: ***<Netcard Parameters Section>***
Example: `IBMPCITR = IBMPCITRparams`

This key refers you to the section containing the parameters for a particular network card. The key name is derived from the `[Options]` section of the `OEMSETUP.INF` file provided with the network card. You can include multiple entries here, one for each type of network adapter you wish to install.

[<PROTOCOLS SECTION>]

Contains a list of keys representing supported protocols within Windows NT. The value of each key is a generic section header name where the protocol parameters are listed. Each value must have a corresponding section header defined with the correct parameters. The available protocol entries are listed below.

DLC

Value: ***<DLC Parameters Section>***
Example: `DLC = DLCParams`

Use this key to install the DLC protocol. The corresponding header section must be defined even though the DLC protocol has no parameters to define.

NBF

Value: ***<NBF Parameters Section>***
Example: `NBF = NBFParams`

Use this key to install the NetBEUI protocol. The corresponding header section must be defined even though the NetBEUI protocol has no parameters to define.

NWLINKIPX

Value: ***<NWLINKIPX Parameters Section>***
Example: `NWLINKIPX = NWLINKIPXParams`

Use this key to install the NWLink IPX/SPX Compatible Transport protocol. The corresponding header section must be defined even though the NWLink protocol has no parameters to define.

RASPPTP

Value: ***<RASPPTP Parameters Section>***
Example: `RASPPTP = RASPPTPParams`

Use this key to install the Point To Point Tunneling Protocol. The corresponding header section must be defined even though the PPTP protocol has no parameters to define.

STREAMS

Value: ***<STREAMS Parameters Section>***
Example: `STREAMS = STREAMSParams`

Use this key to install the Streams Environment protocol. The corresponding header section must be defined even though the Streams protocol has no parameters to define.

TC

Value: *<TCP/IP Parameters Section>*
Example: `TC = TCPIPParams`

Use this key to install the TCP/IP protocol. The example shows that the corresponding parameters section for the TCP/IP protocol stack is `TCPIPParams`, represented by the generic section header name `<TCPIP Parameters Section>`. The corresponding header section must be defined containing at least one of the keys listed in the section header `<TCPIP Parameters Section>` for an unattended installation to work.

[<DLC PARAMETERS SECTION>]

Since there are no available parameters to configure for the DLC protocol, this section remains empty but must exist for installation of the protocol.

[<NBF PARAMETERS SECTION>]

Since there are no available parameters to configure for the NetBEUI protocol, this section remains empty but must exist for installation of the protocol.

[<NWLINKIPX PARAMETERS SECTION>]

Since there are no available parameters to configure for the NWLINK IPX/SPX protocol, this section remains empty but must exist for installation of the protocol.

[<RASPPTP PARAMETERS SECTION>]

Since there are no available parameters to configure for the RASPPTP protocol, this section remains empty but must exist for installation of the protocol.

[<STREAMS PARAMETERS SECTION>]

Since there are no available parameters to configure for the Streams protocol, this section remains empty but must exist for installation of the protocol.

[<TCP/IP PARAMETERS SECTION>]

This is the only protocol parameters section that can have any keys defined. You must define at least one key for installation of the TCP/IP protocol.

DHCP

Value: `Yes` | `No`
Example: `DHCP = Yes`

Use this key to specify whether or not a DHCP server should be used to provide the remainder of the TCP/IP parameters.

ScopeID

Value: <***Scope ID***>

Example: `ScopeID = MyScope`

Use this key to define the NetBIOS over TCP/IP scope ID for the computer.

IPAddress

Value: <***IP Address***>

Example: `IPAddress = 10.1.1.240`

This key is required if the `DHCP` key is set to a value of `No`. Use the key to define the IP address for the machine. Multi-homed machines must be configured for DHCP if the setup is to run in unattended mode.

Subnet

Value: <***Subnet Mask***>

Example: `Subnet = 255.252.0.0`

This key is required if the `DHCP` key is set to a value of `No.` The key defines the subnet mask.

Gateway

Value: <***Default Gateway Address***>

Example: `Gateway = 10.1.1.1`

This key is required if the `DHCP` key is set to a value of `No`. Use the key to define the default gateway address.

DNSServer

Value: <***DNS IP Address***>

Example: `DNSServer = 10.1.150.10`

This key is used if the `DHCP` key is set to a value of `No`. Use the key to define the address of the DNS server. You can define three servers in this list.

WINSPrimary

Value: <***Primary WINS Server Address***>

Example: `WINSPrimary = 10.1.1.4`

This key is used if the `DHCP` key is set to a value of `No`. Use the key to define the address of the primary WINS server.

WINSSecondary

Value: <***Secondary WINS Server Address***>

Example: `WINSSecondary = 10.1.1.5`

This key is used if the `DHCP` key is set to a value of `No`. Use the key to define the address of the secondary WINS server.

DNSName

Value: <*DNS Domain Name*>

Example: `DNSName = myone.hometown.com`

This key is used if the `DHCP` key is set to a value of `No`. Use the key to define the name of the DNS domain to which the computer will belong.

[<SERVICES SECTION>]

This section header name is defined in the value given to the `[Network]`—`InstallServices` key. The keys in this section are used to install network services during the setup phase. If you wish to install a service, you must provide the section name where the parameters for that service are defined. In some cases, there are no valid parameters, but you must still include the parameters section name and define the corresponding section name itself, even if it is left empty; otherwise, the installation may fail.

DHCP

Value: <*DHCP Parameters Section*>

Example: `DHCP = DHCPParams`

Use this key to install the Microsoft DHCP Server service on NT 4.0 server. The corresponding section header must be defined even though DHCP has no parameters.

DNS

Value: <*DNS Parameters Section*>

Example: `DNS = DNSParams`

Use this key to install the Microsoft DNS Server service on the NT 4.0 server. You must define the corresponding section header even though DNS has no parameters.

NETmon

Value: <*NETmon Parameters Section*>

Example: `NETmon = NETmonParams`

Use this key to install the Network Monitor Tools and Agent service. You must define the corresponding section header even though Network Monitor has no parameters.

NWWKSTA

Value: <*NetWare Client Parameters Section*>

Example: `NWWKSTA = NWWKSTAParams`

Use this key to install the Client Services for NetWare service. Parameters exist for this service and are defined in the section header `<NetWare Client Parameters Section>`.

RAS

Value: <*RAS Parameters Section*>

Example: `RAS = RASParams`

Use this key to install the Remote Access service. Parameters exist for this service and are defined in the section header `<RAS Parameters Section>`.

SAP

Value: <*SAP Parameters Section*>

Example: `SAP = SAPParams`

Use this key to install the SAP Agent service on NT 4.0 server. You must define the corresponding section header even though the SAP Agent service has no parameters.

SNMP

Value: <*SNMP Parameters Section*>

Example: `SNMP = SNMPParams`

Use this key to install the SNMP service. Parameters exist for this service and are defined in the section header `<SNMP Parameters Section>`.

STCPIP

Value: <*STCPIP Parameters Section*>

Example: `STCPIP = STCPIPParams`

Use this key to install the Simple TCP/IP service. You must define the corresponding section header even though the Simple TCP/IP service has no parameters.

TCPPRINT

Value: <*TCPPRINT Parameters Section*>

Example: `TCPPRINT = TCPPRINTParams`

Use this key to install the Microsoft TCP/IP Printing service. You must define the corresponding section header even though the Microsoft TCP/IP Printing service has no parameters.

WINS

Value: <*WINS Parameters Section*>

Example: `WINS = WINSParams`

Use this key to install the Windows Internet Name service. You must define the corresponding section header even though the Windows Internet Name service has no parameters.

[<DHCP PARAMETERS SECTION>]

Corresponds to the value defined for the `[<Services Section>]`—`DHCP` key. There are no extra parameters to configure, so this section remains empty.

[<DNS PARAMETERS SECTION>]

Corresponds to the value defined for the `[<Services Section>]`—`DNS` key. There are no extra parameters to configure, so this section remains empty.

[<NETMON PARAMETERS SECTION>]

Corresponds to the value defined for the `[<Services Section>]`—`NETmon` key. There are no extra parameters to configure, so this section remains empty.

[<NETWARE CLIENT PARAMETERS SECTION>]

Corresponds to the value defined for the `[<Services Section>]`—`NWWK-STA` key.

[<RAS PARAMETERS>]

Corresponds to the value defined for the `[<Services Section>]`—`RAS` key.

`PortSections`

Value: ***<Port Section Name>*** **`[,`** ***<Port Section Name2>*** **`,..]`**
Example: `PortSections = PortIDs`

This key points to the header section that contains the port names that will be used for RAS. Multiple `PortSections` values can be entered, separated by a comma.

`DialoutProtocols`

Value: **`TCP/IP | IPX | NETBEUI | ALL`**
Example: `DialoutProtocols = TCP/IP`

Use this key to define the protocols to be enabled for outgoing RAS connections.

`DialinProtocols`

Value: **`TCP/IP | IPX | NETBEUI | ALL`**
Example: `DialinProtocols = TCP/IP`

Use this key to define the protocols to be enabled for incoming RAS connections. This key is only valid for NT Server installations.

NetBEUIClientAccess

Value: Network | ThisComputer

Example: `NetBEUIClientAccess = ThisComputer`

Use this key to define the scope of access for incoming NetBEUI connections. The default value is `Network`. This key is only valid for NT Server installations.

TcpipClientAccess

Value: Network | ThisComputer

Example: `TcpipClientAccess = ThisComputer`

Use this key to define the scope of access for incoming TCP/IP connections. The default value is `Network`. This key is only valid for NT Server installations.

UseDHCP

Value: Yes | No

Example: `UseDHCP = Yes`

Use this key to indicate whether or not the RAS service will use DHCP for IP address assignment. The default setting is `Yes`. This key is only valid on Windows NT Server installations.

StaticAddressBegin

Value: *<IP Address>*

Example: `StaticAddressBegin = 10.1.1.100`

Use this key to provide the first IP address in the assignment range. This key is only valid on Windows NT Server installations and requires the `UseDHCP` key to be set to `No`.

StaticAddressEnd

Value: *< IP Address >*

Example: `StaticAddressEnd = 10.1.1.150`

Use this key to provide the last IP address in the assignment range. This key is only valid on Windows NT Server installations and requires the `UseDHCP` key to be set to `No`.

ExcludeAddress

Value: *< IP Address1—IP Address2>*

Example: `ExcludeAddress = 10.1.1.140 – 10.1.1.145`

Use this key to provide an IP address range that is to be excluded from the assignment range. This key is only valid on Windows NT Server installations and requires the `UseDHCP` key to be set to `No`.

ClientCanRequestIPAddress

Value: Yes | No

Example: `ClientCanRequestIPAddress = Yes`

The default value for this key is `No`. This key is only valid on Windows NT Server installations.

IPXClientAccess

Value: Network | ThisComputer

Example: `IPXClientAccess = ThisComputer`

Use this key to define the scope of access for incoming IPX connections. The default value is `Network`. This key is only valid for NT Server installations.

AutomaticNetworkNumbers

Value: Yes | No

Example: `AutomaticNetworkNumbers = No`

This key indicates that IPX network numbers will be assigned automatically. The default value for this key is `Yes`. This key is only valid on Windows NT Server installations.

NetworkNumberFrom

Value: *<IPX Network Number>*

Example: `NetworkNumberFrom = FFFFDDDD`

This key indicates the starting IPX network number address in the hex range 1—FFFFFFFe. This key is only valid on Windows NT Server installations.

AssignSameNetworkNumber

Value: Yes | No

Example: `AssignSameNetworkNumber = Yes`

The default value for this key is `Yes`. This key assigns the same IPX network number to all incoming IPX connections. This key is only valid on Windows NT Server installations.

ClientsCanRequestIpxNodeNumber

Value: Yes | No

Example: `ClientsCanRequestIpxNodeNumber = Yes`

The default value for this key is `Yes`. This key is only valid on Windows NT Server installations.

[<PORTIDS>]

Corresponds to the value defined for the `[<RAS Parameters>]—Port-Sections` key.

PortName

Value: COM1 | COM2 | COM3-COM25

Example: `PortName = COM2`

Use this key to indicate the name of the port to be configured in this port section.

DeviceType

Value: Modem

Example: `DeviceType = Modem`

Use this key to indicate the type of device RAS should install. At the moment, you can only configure the device type of `Modem` through the unattended installation process.

PortUsage

Value: DialOut | DialIn | DialInOut

Example: `PortUsage = DialInOut`

Use this key to define the dialing properties for the ports being configured. The values are self-explanatory.

!DefaultLocation

Value: <*Logon Server*>

Example: `!DefaultLocation = MYNWServer`

Use this key to define the default logon server for the NetWare Client service.

!DefaultScriptOptions

Value: 0 | 1 | 3

Example: `!DefaultScriptOptions = 3`

Use this key to indicate what action should be taken with logon scripts. A value of `0` causes scripts to be ignored, a value of `1` only allows NetWare 3.x scripts to run, and a value of `3` runs either NetWare 3.x or 4.x scripts.

[<SAP PARAMETERS SECTION>]

Corresponds to the value defined for the `[<Services Section>]`—`SAP` key. There are no extra parameters to configure, so this section remains empty.

[<SNMP PARAMETERS SECTION>]

Corresponds to the value defined for the `[<Services Section>]`—`SNMP` key.

Accept_CommunityName

Value: <*Community Name String*>

Example: `Accept_CommunityName = TrapLoc1, TrapLoc2`

Use this key to list the community names from which SNMP traps are accepted.

Send_Authentication

Value: Yes | No

Example: `Send_Authentication = Yes`

Use this key to specify that when an unauthorized information request is received, an authentication trap should be sent.

Any_Host

Value: Yes | No

Example: `Any_Host = No`

Use this key to define whether or not the machine running the SNMP service should accept packets from any host.

Limit_Host

Value: <*Host Names*>

Example: `Limit_Host = Host1, Host2`

Use this key to provide the host names (up to three) from which packets will be accepted. This key is used in conjunction with the `Any_Host` key being set to a value of `No`.

Community_Name

Value: <*Community Name String*>

Example: `Community_Name = Name1`

Use this key to define the community name to which the computer will belong.

Traps

Value: <*Destination IP/IPX Address*>

Example: `Traps = 10.1.1.45,10.1.1.47`

Use this key to list up to three destination addresses for traps.

Contact_Name

Value: <*Name*>

Example: `Contact_Name = "Mike McInerney"`

Use this key to provide the contact name information for the computer.

Location

Value: ***<Location of Computer>***

Example: `Location = "Building 3, first floor"`

Use this key to provide location information about the computer.

Service

Value: Physical, Application, Datalink, Internet, End-to-End

Example: `Services = Internet,Application`

Use this key to list any combination of the five possible SNMP services to be installed. Separate the entries by a comma.

[<STCPIP PARAMETERS SECTION>]

Corresponds to the value defined for the `[<Services Section>]`—`STCPIP` key. There are no extra parameters to configure, so this section remains empty.

[<TCPPRINT PARAMETERS SECTION>]

Corresponds to the value defined for the `[<Services Section>]`—`TCP-PRINT` key. There are no extra parameters to configure, so this section remains empty.

[<WINS PARAMETERS SECTION>]

Corresponds to the value defined for the `[<Services Section>]`—`WINS` key. There are no extra parameters to configure, so this section remains empty.

[<NETCARD PARAMETERS SECTION>]

The section header contains parameters for the network card specified by the `<Netcard Parameters Section>` value in either the `[<Detect Adapters Section>]` or the `[<Install Adapters Section>]`.

<Variable Parameters>

Value: ***Variable***

Example: `MaxTxFramsize = 4096`

The parameters available for setting in this section vary according to the type of network card being defined. The best way to look at valid parameters is to use the registry editor.

1. Start **Regedt32.exe**.
2. Change to **Read-Only** mode.

3. Navigate to the **HKLM\Software\Microsoft\Windows NT\Current-Version\NetworkCards\1**. This entry gives you a value for the key *ServiceName*.
4. Navigate to **HKLM\System\CurrentControlSet\Services*Service-Name*\Parameters**. The parameters listed in the right-hand pane are valid for this network card. The key is the value name (e.g., **Full-Duplex**), and the value in this case is **Yes** or **No**.
5. Close the registry editor.

The example value shown in step 4 would be entered as `FullDuplex = Yes`.

[<INTERNET INFORMATION SERVER SECTION>]

Sets parameters for the Internet Information Server installation during the setup process.

`InstallINETSTP`

> **Value: `0 | 1`**
> **Example:** `InstallINETSTP = 0`

Use this key to specify whether or not the Internet Services will be installed. The default value of `1` specifies that the component will be installed.

`InstallDIR`

> **Value: <*Internet Services Root Folder*>**
> **Example:** `InstallDIR = C:\Inetpub`

Use this key to define the installation folder for the Internet Services components. This key is only valid if the `InstallINETSTP` key value is set to `1`.

`InstallADMIN`

> **Value: `0 | 1`**
> **Example:** `InstallADMIN = 0`

Use this key to specify whether or not the Internet Service Manager will be installed. A value of `1` specifies that the component will be installed.

`InstallFTP`

> **Value: `0 | 1`**
> **Example:** `InstallFTP = 0`

Use this key to specify whether or not the FTP Service will be installed. A value of `1` specifies that the component will be installed.

`FTPRoot`

> **Value: <*FTP Root Folder*>**
> **Example:** `FTPRoot = C:\Inetpub\FTProot`

Use this key to define the virtual root folder for the FTP service. This key is only valid if the `InstallFTP` key value is set to `1`.

`InstallWWW`

Value: `0 | 1`
Example: `InstallWWW = 0`

Use this key to specify whether or not the WWW Service will be installed. A value of `1` specifies that the component will be installed.

`WWWRoot`

Value: <*WWW Root Folder*>
Example: `WWWRoot = C:\Inetpub\WWWroot`

Use this key to define the virtual root folder for the WWW service. This key is only valid if the `InstallWWW` key value is set to `1`.

`InstallGOPHER`

Value: `0 | 1`
Example: `InstallGOPHER = 0`

Use this key to specify whether or not the GOPHER Service will be installed. A value of `1` specifies that the component will be installed.

`GOPHERRoot`

Value: <*GOPHER Root Folder*>
Example: `GOPHERRoot = C:\Inetpub\GOPHroot`

Use this key to define the virtual root folder for the GOPHER service. This key is only valid if the `InstallGOPHER` key value is set to `1`.

`InstallW3SAMP`

Value: `0 | 1`
Example: `InstallW3SAMP = 0`

Use this key to specify whether or not the WWW sample files will be installed. A value of `1` specifies that the component will be installed.

`InstallHTMLA`

Value: `0 | 1`
Example: `InstallHTMLA = 0`

Use this key to specify whether or not the HTML form of the Internet Service Manager will be installed. A value of `1` specifies that the component will be installed.

GuestAccountName

Value: <*User name for Guest Account*>

Example: `GuestAccountName = IUSR_IBSNT04`

Use this key to define the username for the Internet guest access for WWW, FTP, and GOPHER services. In a normal installation of IIS the value is comparable to the created account IUSR_*Nodename*.

GuestAccountPassword

Value: <*Password String*>

Example: `GuestAccountPassword = zxc7Msd8kas`

Use this key to define the password for the created guest account. The key can be omitted, forcing a random password assignment from the IIS installation routine.

[**OEM_ADS**]

Generally only used by OEMs to customize the installation process.

Banner

Value: <*Text String*>

Example: `Banner = "OEM Corp—Windows NT 4.0 Installation"`

The value for this key is a text string which should be placed in double quotes `" "`. This value will only be used if the words "Windows NT" are included as part of the overall text string.

Logo

Value: <*File Name*> [, *Resource id*]

Example: `Logo = CompLogo.bmp`

Use this key to display a bitmap file in the upper right-hand corner of the screen during setup. If you only supply a filename, then the file must be a valid bitmap file and placed in the `\I386\$OEM$` subfolder of the installation source. The `Resource id` value is a base 10 number referring to the resource ID of a bitmap within a `.dll` file. If this value is supplied, the filename should be that of the `.dll` file. This file must be placed in the `\I386\$OEM$` subfolder of the installation source.

Background

Value: <*File Name*> [, *Resource id*]

Example: `Background = Fisbmp.dll,9`

Use this key to display a bitmap file as a background during setup. If you only supply a filename, the file must be a valid bitmap file and placed in the

\I386\$OEM$ subfolder of the installation source. The Resource .ID value is a base 10 number referring to the resource ID of a bitmap within a .dll file. If this value is supplied, the filename should be that of the .dll file. This file must be placed in the \I386\$OEM$ subfolder of the installation source.

[OEMBOOTFILES]

Can be included if the [Unattended]—OemPreinstall key is set to Yes. The section specifies boot files that are OEM supplied. These boot files must be placed in the \I386\OEM\Textmode folder of the installation distribution point. The files can be used by entries made in the [MassStrorageDrivers] section and by the [Unattended]—Computer-Type key.

TXTSETUP.OEM

This file must exist if the [OEMBootFiles] section is defined. It contains the instructions on how to install the OEM drivers.

<HALfilename>

This file describes the HAL that will be loaded for the computer. This key is used when you define the [Unattended]—ComputerType key. This key is rarely used.

<SCSIdriverFilename>

This file is used to install the mass storage device defined by the [MassStorageDrivers] section entry.

[POINTINGDEVICEDRIVERS]

Can be included if the [Unattended]—OemPreinstall key is set to Yes.

<Mouse Driver Description>

Value: **RETAIL | OEM**

Example: "Microsoft Serial Mouse" = "RETAIL"

For this key, the value RETAIL indicates that the driver is shipped with the retail version of the Windows NT 4.0 product and this driver will be used. The value OEM indicates that an OEM driver should be used.

[USERDATA]

Provides some of the user-defined data input during setup. If any of the keys in this section header are missing or invalid, the setup process stops and asks for user input.

FullName

Value: <*String*>

Example: `FullName = "Mike McInerney"`

Use this key to supply the user name for the User and Organization pair during setup.

OrgName

Value: <*String*>

Example: `OrgName = "Insight Business Solutions"`

Use this key to supply the organization name for the User and Organization pair during setup.

ComputerName

Value: <*String*>

Example: `ComputerName = "IBSNT08"`

Use this key to specify the NetBIOS computer name for the installation. The normal NetBIOS naming conventions apply here (e.g., spaces allowed, a maximum of 15 characters).

ProductID

Value: <*String*>

Example: `ProductID = "111-1111111"`

This value represents the CD key, which can be found on the jewel case of the NT 4.0 CD.

Network Card Configuration

One of the most critical processes when you are building the answer file is to define the network card configuration portion. Once the text-based portion of the setup process is finished and the machine reboots for the first time, the DOS-based network drivers are no longer of any use. The network card(s) for your machine should be installed during the GUI portion of the setup.

UNATTEND-AWARE NICS

For the unattended setup procedure to work, the installed NICs must be *unattend aware*. That is, the drivers supplied for these NICs must have a corresponding code entry in the `OEMNAxxx.inf` (or `OEMSETUP.inf` for third-party drivers) file that can detect whether or not the setup process is running in unattended mode. The variable used to check this setting is `STF_GUI_UNATTENDED`. The listing in Example 3.1 shows an entry taken from the `OEMNADTK.INF` file, which is the setup file for the `IBM Token Ring (ISA/PCMCIA)` adapter.

EXAMPLE 3.1 STF_GUI_UNATTENDED tests for unattended installations

```
ifstr(i) $(!STF_GUI_UNATTENDED) == "YES"
   ifstr(i) $(!AutoNetInterfaceType) != ""
     set BusInterfaceType = $(!AutoNetInterfaceType)
   else
     set BusInterfaceType = 1
   endif
   ifstr(i) $(!AutoNetBusNumber) != ""
     set BusNumber = $(!AutoNetBusNumber)
   else
     set BusNumber = 0
   endif
   goto adapterverify
 endif
```

Appendix A contains a list of NICs and associated `.INF` files supplied with the retail version of Windows NT 4.0. The NICs that are unattend aware are noted. You can search any corresponding `.inf` files from third-party driver kits for the string shown above to see if the code exists to check for unattended setup mode. This string must exist as a minimum before unattended network card installation is possible. Extra code may exist to avoid user interaction by avoiding messages such as "Current Netcard Parameters Are Not Verifiably Correct." This message can be produced even if the network card is working with the current settings. This code is produced by the NIC manufacturer.

AUTOMATIC VS. MANUAL DETECTION

The configuration of network cards during the unattended setup process is achieved by two different methods. The method used during setup and the corresponding answer file entries depend on the type of NIC installed in the machine. The two basic types of NIC are; autodetected network cards and manual configuration network cards.

AUTODETECTED NICS

If your NIC is automatically detected during a normal Windows NT 4.0 manual installation, the same will be true during the unattended setup. You should use the `[DetectAdapters]` section in the answer file to configure the NIC. The extract from an unattended installation answer file in Example 3.2 shows a possible configuration option for autodetected NICs.

EXAMPLE 3.2 Network entries in the answer file for autodetected NICs

```
[Network]
DetectAdapters = AdaptersSection
InstallProtocols = ProtocolsSection
JoinDomain = "NTDOM01"

[AdaptersSection]
LimitTo = NE2000

[ProtocolsSection]
TC = TCParameters
NBF = NETBEUIParams

[TCParameters]
DHCP = yes

[NETBEUIParams]
```

The `DetectAdapters` key in Example 3.2 specifies that the network adapter is autodetected during setup (which should be checked during a manual installation). The detection is limited to the NE2000 Compatible NIC by the `LimitTo` key. This key could be left out and the detection would find any autodetectable NIC. Both TCP/IP and NetBEUI protocols are installed, and the TCP/IP protocol is set to use DHCP. This simple example assumes that the autodetected parameters do not need to be changed. If they do, the file would need an extra parameters section containing the settings that are required to be changed and an extra key entered into the `[AdaptersSection]` indicating the link to the new section. A sample of this new information is highlighted in bold in Example 3.3.

EXAMPLE 3.3 Network entries in the answer file used to change default NIC settings

```
[Network]
DetectAdapters = AdaptersSection
InstallProtocols = ProtocolsSection
JoinDomain = "NTDOM01"

[AdaptersSection]
LimitTo = NE2000
NE2000 = NICParams

[ProtocolsSection]
TC = TCParameters
NBF = NETBEUIParams
```

```
[TCParameters]
DHCP = yes

[NICParams]
InterruptNumber = 5
IOBaseAddress = 1
BusType = 1

[NETBEUIParams]
```

MANUALLY CONFIGURED NICS

If your NIC is *not* automatically detected during a normal Windows NT 4.0 manual installation, then you must supply the required information for the NIC installation during the unattended setup. You should use the `[InstallAdapters]` section in the answer file to configure the NIC. The extract from an unattended installation answer file shown in Example 3.4 shows a possible configuration option.

EXAMPLE 3.4 Network entries in the answer file for *non*-autodetected NICs

```
[Network]
InstallAdapters = AdaptersSection
InstallProtocols = ProtocolsSection

[AdaptersSection]
TRP = TRParamSection

[ProtocolsSection]
TC = TCParameters

[TCParameters]
DHCP = yes

[TRParamSection]
```

The `TRP` key highlighted in the `[AdaptersSection]` section of Example 3.4 and the `NE2000` key highlighted in the `[AdaptersSection]` section of Example 3.3 are the names that denote the type of card that you wish to install. This key must be included if the card is not automatically detectable. You can find the value for this key, known as the *Options Name*, by looking in the `[Options]` section of the `OEMNAxxx.inf` file corresponding to the NIC that you wish to install. *Appendix A* contains a list of NICs along with their corresponding Options Name.

The format of the sections for this type of NIC installation does not differ much from that of the automatically detected cards. The important thing to remember is that section headers often contain keys that point to further section headers. The correct spelling of these headers is imperative to keep the link active; spelling errors are the most common mistake made when answer files are created.

THIRD-PARTY DRIVER INSTALLATION

Third-party drivers can be used to install an NIC during the unattended setup. The entry in the answer file is similar to that for the manually configured NICs. The additional information needed is the location of the driver files and the location of the `OEMSETUP.INF` file that contains the options name. The listing in Example 3.5 shows a possible configuration for a third-party NIC.

EXAMPLE 3.5 Network entries in the answer file for a third-party NIC driver

```
[Network]
InstallAdapters = AdaptersSection
InstallProtocols = ProtocolsSection

[AdaptersSection]
TRP = TRParamSection, C:\IBMTRP

[ProtocolsSection]
TC = TCParameters

[TCParameters]
DHCP = yes

[TRParamSection]
MaxTxFrameSize = 4096
DataRate = "M16"
```

The addition of the folder value highlighted in the preceding example denotes the location of the third-party drivers that are needed for the installation. You can add an extra entry in the batch file that runs the whole installation process (usually the `Autoexec.bat` file on the boot floppy) to copy these files to the local hard drive so that they are readily accessible. The additional lines to do this are highlighted in Example 3.6.

EXAMPLE 3.6 `Autoexec.bat` file on a network-enabled DOS boot floppy

```
echo on
cls
format c: /q /u < answer.txt
smartdrv c+
PATH=A:\;A:\NET
\net\net start
LOCK C: < answer.txt
C:
md ibmtrp
net use n: \\IBSNT04\TNetsys
copy n:\ibmtrp\*.* c:\ibmtrp\*.*
n:\i386\winnt /U:a:\unattend.txt /S:n:\i386
```

The commands highlighted in the preceding example create the local folder `C:\IBMTR` and copy the drivers from the network drive `N:`, which is connected to the server distribution point.

Windows 95/98 Answer File

The Windows 9x version of the answer file that provides input into the setup process is called `MSBATCH.INF`. This file is copied to the `C:\ZAK9x\Setup` folder during the ZAK setup phase. This file will require amending before it can be used to run a setup of Windows 9x. A separate file is included in the ZAK for both Windows 95 and Windows 98. The amendments required for these files are similar to each other and are shown below.

WINDOWS 95

- **ProductID**. Enter the product ID for the Windows 95 installation in this field. The product ID can usually be found on the back of the Windows 95 CD case.
- **ComputerName**. The computer name must be a valid NetBIOS computer name.

WINDOWS 98

- **ProductKEY**. Enter the product key for the for the Windows 98 installation in this field. The product key can usually be found on the back of the Windows 98 CD case and is in the format `00000-00000-00000-00000-00000`.

- **ComputerName**. The computer name must be a valid NetBIOS computer name.

The extract from a Windows 98 MSBATCH.inf file shown below highlights the changes you must make and also one of the changes made by the ZAK setup program.

```
[Setup]
Express=1
InstallDir="C:\Windows"
InstallType=3
ProductKey="xxxx-xxxxx-xxxxx-xxxxx-xxxxx"
EBD=0
ShowEula=0
ChangeDir=0
OptionalComponents=1
Network=1
System=0
CCP=0
CleanBoot=1
Display=0
DevicePath=0
NoDirWarn=1
TimeZone="Pacific"
Uninstall=0
NoPrompt2Boot=1

[NameAndOrg]
Name="ZAK Users"
Org="Microsoft"
Display=0

[Network]
ComputerName="ZAKComputer01"
Workgroup="ntdom01"
Display=0
PrimaryLogon=VREDIR
Clients=VREDIR
Protocols=MSTCP
Services=VSERVER
Security=DOMAIN
PassThroughAgent="ntdom01"
```

Summary

It is beyond the scope of this book to go into all of the different possibilities when it comes to building a network-enabled boot disk. The examples and definitions in this chapter worked for my own test configuration, but you will need to make adjustments to fit in with your own environment, especially the type of equipment you use.

As noted above, answer file section headers (represented in square brackets `[ ]`) can contain several keys. The keys in turn require values to be set. The values can be a simple boolean choice, such as 0 or 1, or they can be more complicated text strings. The values can also be the name of another section header. This protocol leads to a situation where section headers can be logically nested beneath another section header. Further nesting can take place so that the structure of the answer file can be quite complex.

An important point to remember when troubleshooting the unattended installation answer file is that for every value entered that refers to a logically nested section header, that section header must be defined in the file as well. Spelling is vitally important and a common cause of error.

It may take several attempts at running an unattended installation before you manage to include all of the relevant information in the answer file. To this end, you should set the `[Unattended]—FileSystem` key to a value of `LeaveAlone`, so that the FAT file system is used for the installation and can be easily formatted for the next test installation. When you have completed the answer file build, you can set this value to `ConvertNTFS` so that the file systems can be secured.

You have created a network share for the TaskStation files and the AppStation files. The boot disk should reference the correct network share (`Tnetsys` or `Anetsys`) so the correct installation takes place. It is during the Windows NT installation process that the computer is defined as either a TaskStation machine or an AppStation machine.

FOUR

What Happens During an Unattended Client Installation

In This Chapter

- Overview
- Script Files
- An Unattended Installation of Windows NT 4.0
- Manual Installation
- How the ZAK Helps with an Unattended Installation
- Summary

This chapter includes step-by-step instructions to complete an installation of a client PC that can be used by the ZAK task-based worker in the test environment. This installation involves running a near unattended installation of Windows NT 4.0 Workstation.

Almost all of the actual installation procedure for Windows NT is automated in this procedure, and that is why it is near unattended. Unfortunately, a task such as removing the boot floppy from the drive before the first soft reboot is a manual task.

This chapter is organized on two levels, almost two chapters in one. First, we discuss an installation as it would be seen or performed by the installation technician. Because of its very nature in not requiring much user intervention, the process appears to be quite short and uninvolved. However, the setup is actually quite complicated in the background, so you must understand what is happening here in order to be able to customize the installation procedure. This second level of discussion covers the background processes in detail.

Overview

You start the basic ZAK client setup by booting from the network boot disk created during the evaluation setup phase in Chapter Three.

In the batch file that you run from the boot disk, you map a network drive to the shared `\Netsys` folder that is the ZAK distribution point. You set up share names of `Tnetsys` and `Anetsys` for this purpose in the test setup build.

You then run the `Winnt.exe` 16-bit executable with parameters defining the location of the source files and supplying the name and location of the answer file to be used to streamline the process.

From an external point of view, the process now seems to move along swiftly and requires very little manual involvement.

The character-mode portion of the setup copies files and prepares for the graphical-mode setup phase.

The graphical-mode portion of the setup runs quickly through the options defined in the answer file and applies these options. A number of command files are run at this point to prepare the system for the final phase of the setup process.

The final setup phase then automatically logs on to the domain and runs a further set of script files. This is where the core system control features are applied to the machines and where a greater understanding of the process is required.

Script Files

Script files used during the unattended installation add an extra phase to the setup process. This *ZAK-mode* setup phase actually consists of an autologon sequence, which connects the newly configured computer to the domain, and then a series of nested script files run, to make system configuration changes. These changes must be made after the initial operating system installation. Table 4.1 lists and briefly describes the script files.

Except where indicated in Table 4.1, the script files are copied to the local hard drive of the computer on which you are performing the installation. Most of the files are copied into a folder structure below the `\%SystemRoot%` folder, (`C:\Winnt` in a default installation), into a folder named `\ZAK`. The only files in Table 4.1 that are not copied to the local system during the setup are the two logon files that must be copied to the `Netlogon` share by hand.

All of the files listed in this table are discussed fully in the sections that follow. File listing snippets are included in this chapter for reference during the discussion; the full listings are included in *Appendix E*.

TABLE 4.1 Script files used to complete the ZAK client setup

File Name and Location	Description
\%SystemRoot%\Cmdlines.txt	This file is called during the GUI setup phase and calls either Tskcmds.cmd (TaskStation) or Appcmds.cmd (AppStation).
\%SystemRoot%\Zak\Scripts\Tskcmds.cmd	For TaskStation only. This file is called by Cmdlines.txt to make registry changes, including setting the autologon feature and to apply a Service Pack.
\%SystemRoot%\Zak\Scripts\Appcmds.cmd	For AppStation only. This file is called by Cmdlines.txt to make registry changes, including setting the autologon feature and to apply a Service Pack.
\%SystemRoot%\Zak\Scripts\Zakboot1.cmd	This file is called by the Boot1cmd registry setting when the computer reboots. It calls the ZAK worker script file.
\%SystemRoot%\Zak\Scripts\Zakb1wrk.cmd	The main ZAK worker file. This file runs command files that install applications and clean up the system.
\%SystemRoot%\Zak\Scripts\Off97.cmd	For AppStation only. This file runs the setup program for Office 97.
\%SystemRoot%\Zak\Scripts\Cleanup.cmd	For AppStation only. This file removes any entries in the Startup folder on the local machine.
\%SystemRoot%\Zak\Scripts\Acls.cmd	This file applies Access Control Lists to the local file system. This file only works on an NTFS partition.
\%SystemRoot%\Zak\Scripts\Hide.cmd	This script sets the Hidden attribute on the file local file system.
\Applogon.cmd	For AppStation only. This is the logon script that all AppStation users run. This file is *not* copied to the local system during client setup.
\Tsklogon.cmd	For TaskStation only. This is the logon script that all TaskStation users run. This file is not copied to the local system during client setup.

An Unattended Installation of Windows NT 4.0

The Windows NT setup that we perform with the unattended installation methodology is basically the same as a manual installation. The basic requirements for a Windows NT installation are the same. The following list points out some of the requirements that should be fulfilled before you attempt an installation.

- You should be familiar with the manual Windows NT installation procedure. A brief synopsis of this procedure is included in *Appendix D*, but you should use the documentation that comes with Windows NT to become more familiar with the process. An unattended installation should not be your only experience of installing this operating system. Become familiar with the manual installation process first.
- Your hardware should meet the minimum requirements set out in the Windows NT installation guide that accompanies your distribution media.
- All of the hardware that will be used for the installation should be in the *Windows NT Hardware Compatibility List*. You can download this list from the Microsoft Web site at `http://www.microsoft.com/ntserver/hcl/hclintro.htm`.
- You should have all of the required third-party drivers that are not available on the Windows NT distribution media.

Manual Installation

The manual installation process for Windows NT 4.0 Workstation can be divided into two phases.

- **Character-mode**. This mode, also called the Text-mode, uses a basic installation of Windows NT to gather enough information about your computer to boot into the graphical-mode portion of the installation. The information includes processor type, motherboard information, hard drive controllers, and memory and disk space information.
- **Graphical-mode**. This mode, also called the GUI-mode, uses a setup wizard to gather more information about your required settings and to walk you through all of available options for completing the installation.

I have included an outline of the Windows NT Workstation 4.0 manual installation process in *Appendix D* as a reference point when you are looking at the unattended installation process. This synopsis is not intended as a replacement for the full installation guide for Windows NT, and it does not go through all of the possible variations that may be necessary for your individual needs.

You will find it useful to compare the stages listed in *Appendix D* to the unattended installation process that the ZAK uses. *Appendix D* will also be a useful reference point when we expose the ZAK installation components and discuss them in detail.

One thing of interest to note is that almost every step outlined in *Appendix D* requires input from the installer. Some of the steps included in *Appendix D* are concatenated and actually require multiple inputs.

How the ZAK Helps with an Unattended Installation

The unattended installation process completes all of the steps outlined in the manual process but with very little input required from the installer. The steps that require some manual intervention are marked with an asterisk (*) in the installation guide that follows.

An additional phase to this setup procedure is noted here as the *ZAK-mode* setup. This phase takes place after the basic Windows NT operating system setup and configures the system to be used by a task-based worker.

This section first describes the steps that would be apparent to anybody simply running the unattended installation process for a Windows NT client. Following this description is a discussion of what is really going on in the background. When you understand the real makeup of the ZAK process, you can begin to look at how to customize the process to fit the needs of your own organization.

The flowchart shown in Figure 4.1 shows the relationship between the command files and scripts used by the ZAK setup process to accomplish the required tasks. Use this in conjunction with the descriptions contained in the following sections to understand the interaction of processes that together make up the whole installation.

Character-mode Setup

Before you begin the installation ensure that the workstation meets the minimum required specification as listed in Chapter One. You should also remove all partitions from the drive and create and format a primary DOS partition. This partition should have at least 300 Mbytes of free disk space. Steps marked with an asterisk (*) require manual intervention.

- ***1.** Insert the network boot disk created for this installation. This boot disk should reference the correct network share (`Tnetsys` for TaskStation and `Anetsys` for AppStation), which is where the source files are stored.
- **2.** Restart the computer.
- **3.** Log on to the domain controller as an administrative user when prompted. A drive is mapped to the network share containing the distribution point, and any required network drivers are copied to the workstation.

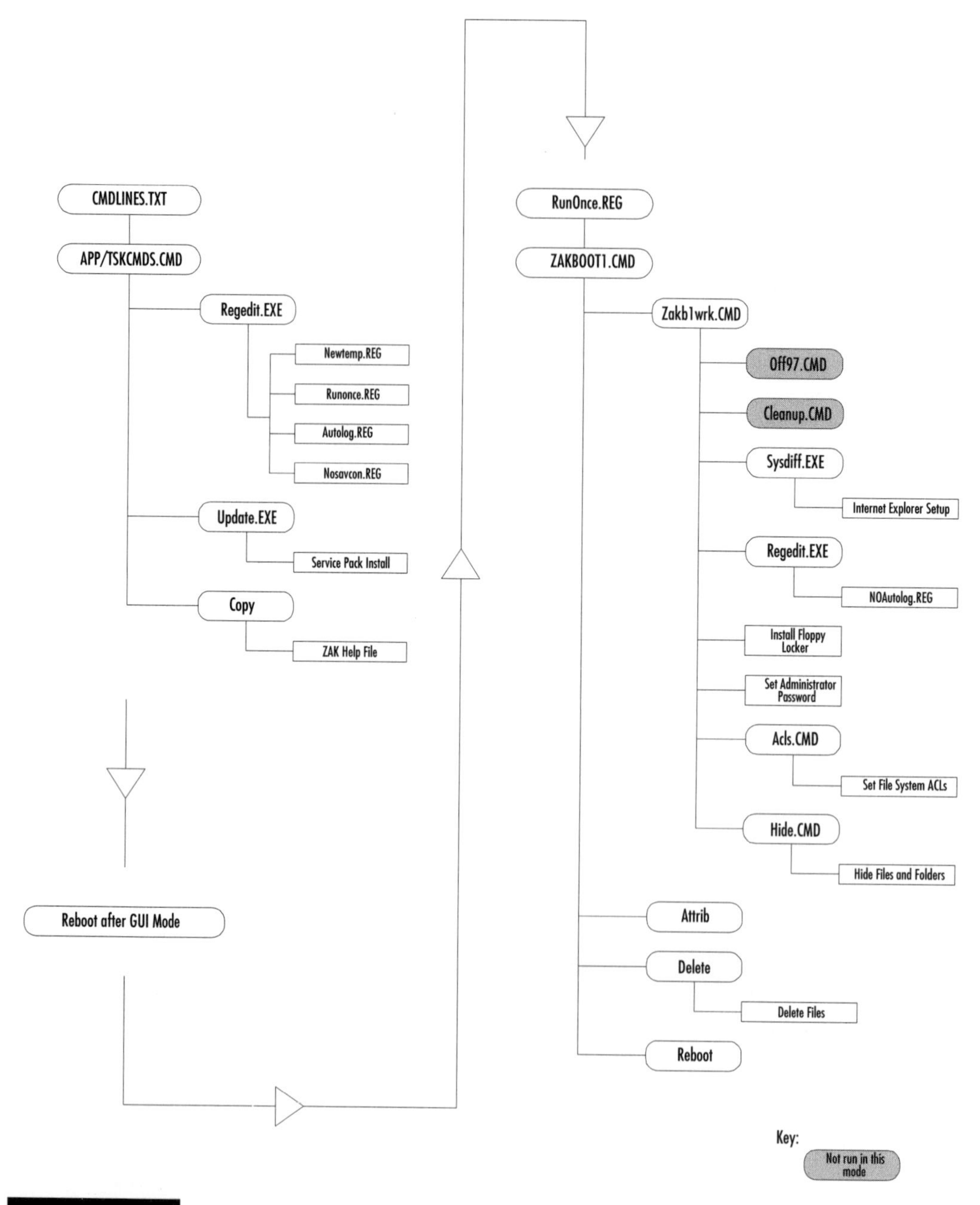

FIGURE 4.1 Road map of the Task/AppStation client setup background processes

4. The Windows NT 16-bit setup program (`Winnt.exe`) is called automatically from the `Autoexec.bat` file.
5. Initial Windows NT 4.0 setup files are copied. Setup parameters are read from the answer file on the boot floppy.
6. System files are now copied to disk. The inclusion of `Smartdrv` in the `Autoexec.bat` of the boot floppy reduced the time it took to copy the setup files from 18+ minutes to just over 8 minutes in a test installation. These times will vary depending on the configuration of the source computer, destination computer, and network.

*7. You can remove the boot disk from the drive as soon as the system files start to copy.

8. All of the information that the manual installation requires for the remainder of the character-mode phase is supplied by the answer file.
9. The file copy finishes and the system reboots. The local hard drive is checked for errors. At this point system files are expanded onto local hard drive.
10. The inclusion of the `NoWaitAfterTextMode = 1` entry in the answer file forces a soft reboot of the computer.

This is the end of the character-mode portion of the setup. The value-added of the ZAK at this point is simply to have answered all of the required questions to complete this installation phase. This makes the character-mode phase very uninvolved, and manual intervention is only required to remove the floppy disk from the drive before the first soft reboot. Compare this to the character-mode portion of the manual installation process contained in *Appendix D*. Almost every step outlined in the manual process requires user input. This intervention wastes time and therefore costs money. There is also more chance that the input is going to be different from installation to installation, thereby making it more difficult to manage the rolled-out platforms.

Graphical Mode: Part One

It is during the graphical-mode portion of the setup that the ZAK command files begin to be run.

1. The system reboots into a mini-single-processor version of Windows NT or multiprocessor version if your computer contains more than one processor.
2. The graphical portion starts from the soft reboot after the character-mode phase and setup files are loaded.
3. Windows NT setup initializes and starts to copy files.
4. The network is set up and started.

Up to this point, the way in which you can influence the course of the installation is through the answer file created for this machine. At this point, however, the default ZAK installation amends the setup process to facilitate the ZAK-mode portion of the setup.

CMDLINES.TXT

A script file named `Cmdlines.txt` is run. The `Cmdlines.txt` file is a simple command file that calls either the `Tskcmds.cmd` file or the `Appcmds.cmd`, depending on the client type. Example 4.1 lists `Cmdlines.txt` for TaskStation.

EXAMPLE 4.1 `Cmdlines.txt` for TaskStation

```
[commands]

;******************
;Run batch file that does all the cmdlines stuff
;******************
"cmd /c %SystemRoot%\zak\scripts\tskcmds.cmd"
```

APPCMDS.CMD AND TSKCMDS.CMD

For a TaskStation computer, the `Tskcmds.cmd` command file is called. For AppStation clients the `Appcmds.cmd` file is called. In reality, both of these files are exactly the same except for the name. The `Appcmds.cmd` file is listed in Example 4.2.

EXAMPLE 4.2 `Appcmds.cmd` file

```
@rem ******************
cmd /c %SystemRoot%\REGEDIT.EXE /S %SystemRoot%\zak\scripts\newtemp.REG
cmd /c %SystemRoot%\REGEDIT.EXE /S %SystemRoot%\zak\scripts\runonce.REG
cmd /c %SystemRoot%\REGEDIT.EXE /S %SystemRoot%\zak\scripts\autolog.REG
cmd /c %SystemRoot%\REGEDIT.EXE /S %SystemRoot%\zak\scripts\nosavcon.REG

@rem ******************
cmd /c %SystemRoot%\sp\update /u /n /z

@rem ******************
cmd /c copy %SystemRoot%\system32\windows.hlp %SystemRoot%\system32\windadm.hlp
cmd /c copy %SystemRoot%\zak\scripts\zak.hlp %SystemRoot%\system32\windows.hlp
```

The command file is split into three parts. The first section of these command files calls the registry editor program to amend four registry keys. The next section applies the Service Pack to the system. Finally, the default Windows help file is replaced by a dummy file provided with the ZAK. The default help file contains information that is mainly irrelevant to the task-based worker, so you can develop your own help files and use them as a replacement. The help files provided for the TaskStation and AppStation clients are actually identical.

NEWTEMP.REG

The values set for this registry key define the `Temp` and `Tmp` environment variables for the computer, as listed in Example 4.3.

EXAMPLE 4.3 Setting `Temp/Tmp` environment variables

```
[HKEY_LOCAL_MACHINE\System\CurrentControlSet\Control\Session Manager\
Environment]
"temp"="%SystemDrive%\\temp"
"tmp"="%SystemDrive%\\temp"
```

RUNONCE.REG

This setting runs the command file `Zakboot1.cmd` for one time only on the next reboot. This is set during the GUI portion of the setup, so the command file listed in Example 4.4 runs at the beginning of the ZAK-mode setup phase (after the autologon defined below).

EXAMPLE 4.4 Invoking the ZAK boot command file

```
[HKEY_LOCAL_MACHINE\SOFTWARE\Microsoft\Windows\CurrentVersion\RunOnce]
"boot1cmd"="cmd /c %SystemRoot%\\zakboot1.cmd"
```

AUTOLOG.REG

This key defines the required parameters for an administrative autologon. Autologon continues the unattended client installation after the normal end of the installation process, allowing the ZAK-mode setup phase to be processed. This file contains the user name an password of a *test* administrative user. These are the credentials you supplied during the ZAK installation and configuration portion of the test setup. During your customization process, you should consider setting up a nonadministrative user and applying the *Add workstations to Domain* user rights policy to enable this ordinary user account to add workstations as they are created. File and folder permissions would need to be set for this user to access the relevant network shares, but the process will mean that if the files containing the username and password are discovered, only the ZAK installation files are at risk. We discuss this idea further in Part Three, which covers customization.

The `Autolog.reg` file containing the user name and password is removed from the client at the end of the installation for security. The file is listed in Example 4.5.

EXAMPLE 4.5 Defining administrative autologon

```
[HKEY_LOCAL_MACHINE\SOFTWARE\Microsoft\Windows NT\CurrentVersion\Winlogon]
"AutoAdminLogon"="1"
;"DefaultDomainName"="Domain-Name"
;"DefaultUserName"="User-Name-Of-Administrative-Account-On-Domain-Name"
;"DefaultPassword"="Password-Of-Administrative-Account"
"DefaultUserName"="administrator"
"DefaultPassword"="password"
"DefaultDomainName"="NTDOM01"
```

NOSAVCON.REG

The value assigned to this key ensures that no network connections made during any of the setup phases are carried over to the next logon. See Example 4.6.

EXAMPLE 4.6 Removing network connection persistence across logons

```
[HKEY_CURRENT_USER\SOFTWARE\Microsoft\Windows NT\
CurrentVersion\Network\Persistent Connections]
"SaveConnections"="no"
```

Graphical Mode: Part Two

The graphical-mode portion of the setup does not appear to have two halves. The split between part one and part two is a logical one. Part two of the graphical-mode setup is where the ZAK-supplied command files are processed.

1. The `Cmdlines.txt` script file is run. In turn, it calls either the `Tskcmds.cmd` or `Appcmds.cmd` command file.
2. The Service Pack is applied in quiet mode.
3. The configuration is saved.

4. The inclusion of the `NoWaitAfterGUIMode = 1` entry in the answer file forces a soft reboot of the computer.
5. The installation of a base Windows NT system is complete.

ZAK Mode

The ZAK-mode portion of the setup runs automatically after the normal end of the Windows NT 4.0 setup process. At this point, the system reboots automatically and an autologon takes place to the domain. This autologon is facilitated by the registry setting made by the `Autolog.reg` file.

During a manual installation, the system would reboot at the end of the graphical-mode portion and the installation would be complete. The user would be presented with the *Press* <Ctrl> <Alt> <Del> *to logon* prompt. If you wished to install an application, you would have to log on to the system and follow the manual procedure for the application installation.

ZAK MODE STARTED (ZAKBOOT1.CMD)

During the graphical-mode setup, the file `Runonce.reg` was used to force the running of the command file `Zakboot1.cmd` at the next reboot. The `Zakboot1.cmd` file controls the ZAK-mode portion of the client setup. It calls the ZAK worker file named `Zakb1wrk.cmd`. It then removes the hidden attribute from the worker file and the `Autolog.reg` file, which contain username and password information for an administrative account. These files are then deleted for security. The `Zakboot1.cmd` file is listed in Example 4.7.

EXAMPLE 4.7 `Zakboot1.cmd` file

```
@REM   ZAKBOOT1.CMD

cmd /c %SystemRoot%\zak\scripts\zakb1wrk.cmd
cmd /c attrib -h %SystemRoot%\zak\scripts\zakb1wrk.cmd
cmd /c attrib -h %SystemRoot%\zak\scripts\autolog.reg
cmd /c del /f /q %SystemRoot%\zak\scripts\zakb1wrk.cmd
cmd /c del /f /q %SystemRoot%\zak\scripts\autolog.reg

@rem do the shutdown
shutdown.exe /C /R /T:20
```

As a result of the call to `Zakboot1.cmd`, the following sequence occurs.

1. Network drives are mapped, and the Office 97 installation starts for AppStation computers.
2. Internet Explorer is configured.

3. A cleanup takes place, and Service Pack source files are removed.
4. The local Administrator password is set.
5. Changes are made to the file system, such as hiding files, setting permissions on folders, etc.

The final command in this file is a shutdown command. Because there are nested command files called from within this file, the shutdown takes place at the end of all of the processing. This shutdown marks the end of the entire installation process.

APPLICATIONS CONFIGURED (ZAKB1WRK.CMD)

The `Zakb1wrk.cmd`, listed in Example 4.8, configures applications on the client such as SMS (if required), MS Office 97 (AppStation only), and Internet Explorer. SMS is set up by the `RunSMS.bat` file provided with the product. The Service Pack installation folder and files are removed during this command file run.

EXAMPLE 4.8 `Zakb1wrk.cmd` file

```
@rem uncomment the following line if you want sms
@rem cmd /c \\opktest3\sms_shr\runsms.bat
@net use O: \\IBSNT04\NETAPPS /user:NTDOM01\administrator password
**AppStation Only** cmd /c %SystemRoot%\zak\scripts\off97.cmd
**AppStation Only** cmd /c %SystemRoot%\zak\scripts\cleanup.cmd
@rem uncomment the following line if you want sms
@rem cmd /c copy %SystemRoot%\zak\scripts\smsrun32.lnk %SystemRoot%\
"profiles\All Users\Start Menu\PROGRAMS\STARTUP"
%SystemRoot%\zak\tools\sysdiff /apply /m %SystemRoot%\zak\scripts\msie302.dif
cmd /c rmdir /s /q %SystemRoot%\sp
REGEDIT.EXE /S %SystemRoot%\zak\scripts\noautolog.REG
%SystemRoot%\zak\tools\instsrv FloppyLocker %SystemRoot%\system32\
floplock.exe
@net user administrator password
cmd /c %SystemRoot%\zak\scripts\acls.cmd
cmd /c %SystemRoot%\zak\scripts\hide.cmd
```

OFFICE 97 CONFIGURED (OFF97.CMD)

The `Off97.cmd` file runs the setup of Microsoft Office 97 on AppStation computers in quiet mode. The file contains only one command line.

```
O:\Off97\msoffice\setup.exe /b3 /qnt /gc+ %SystemDrive%\temp\offlog.txt
```

You can use the /b*x* switch to specify which type of installation should be processed. Replace the *x* with 1, 2, or 3. Use number 1 to perform a *Typical* setup, 2 to perform a *Custom* setup, or 3 to perform a *Run from CD* or *Run from Network* setup.

The /qn[t] parameter forces the setup to run in quiet mode, suppressing all user input boxes as well as background and copy gauges. This switch also suppresses the message to reboot the computer after the installation.

The /gc[+] parameter causes a log file to be used. The logfile name must be an 8.3 format short name. The + specifies that an existing logfile will be appended to.

STARTUP MENU CLEANUP (CLEANUP.CMD)

The Cleanup.cmd file is run on AppStation computers. The file contains only one command line.

```
del /q "%SystemRoot%\profiles\All Users\Start Menu\PROGRAMS\STARTUP\*.*"
```

This delete command removes the contents of the Startup menu for an AppStation computer. The /q switch accomplishes this in quiet mode.

AUTOLOGON AFTER REBOOT REMOVED (NOAUTOLOG.REG)

The registry entries contained in the Noautolog.reg file overwrite the previous entries, set by the Autolog.reg file, which allowed for an autologon after the next reboot. This file removes the user name and password entries from the registry for security. This file is listed in Example 4.9.

EXAMPLE 4.9 Noautolog.reg file

```
REGEDIT4

[HKEY_LOCAL_MACHINE\SOFTWARE\Microsoft\Windows NT\CurrentVersion\Winlogon]
"DefaultUserName"=""
"AutoAdminLogon"="0"
"DefaultPassword"=""
```

ACCESS CONTROL LISTS SET (ACLS.CMD)

The Acls.cmd file applies access control list security to the file and folder structure on an AppStation or TaskStation client PC. This file is configurable to fit your own requirements and can be used to secure any folders that the ZAK client setup does not know about. This file is an important tool in the customization process to apply just the right amount of file security for your users.

The Acls.cmd file sample shown in Example 4.10 is a cut-down version of the actual file provided for AppStation and TaskStation file system security. The full file listing is available in *Appendix E*. This file is included here to show continuity in the process being described and to provide an example of the type of commands included in the full command file, which is more than 200 lines long.

EXAMPLE 4.10 Setting ACLs

```
@rem This script will put more stringent security on the local system files
@rem
pushd %SystemDrive%\
cacls.exe . /G administrators:f system:f everyone:r
<%SystemRoot%\zak\scripts\yesfile
cacls.exe * /C /G administrators:f system:f everyone:r
<%SystemRoot%\zak\scripts\yesfile

copy %SystemRoot%\zak\scripts\yesfile Temp\secure.dir
cacls.exe Temp\secure.dir /g administrators:f system:f
<%SystemRoot%\zak\scripts\yesfile
attrib +h Temp\secure.dir


cd %SystemRoot%
cacls.exe system32 /e /g everyone:c <%SystemRoot%\zak\scripts\yesfile
cacls.exe help /e /g everyone:c <%SystemRoot%\zak\scripts\yesfile
cacls.exe system32\viewers /t /c /e /g everyone:r
<%SystemRoot%\zak\scripts\yesfile
@rem OPEN UP SPECIFIC FILE EXCEPTIONS
cd %SystemDrive%\
cacls.exe explorer.exe /t /e /g everyone:r
cacls.exe newprof.exe /t /e /g everyone:r
```

LOCAL SYSTEM DRIVE HIDDEN FROM THE USER (HIDE.CMD)

The Hide.cmd file hides the entire local system drive from the user. You must remember that the user setup defined for the task-based worker is an extreme example of what the ZAK can be used for. This file, and many of those that have been discussed earlier, can be amended to fit the requirements of your organization. You may not wish all of the file system to be hidden, and so you can use the commands provided to achieve the results that best fit your needs.

This Hide.cmd sample listed in Example 4.11 is a cut-down version of the actual file supplied with the ZAK. The full version is listed in *Appendix E*.

EXAMPLE 4.11 Hide.cmd file

```
REM This is used to hide the files on the system
REM

attrib +h /s %SystemDrive%\*.*
For /R %SystemDrive%\ %%i in (.) do attrib +h "%%i"

attrib -h /s %SystemRoot%\profiles\*.*
For /R %SystemRoot%\profiles %%i in (.) do attrib -h "%%i"

REM Some directories and files don't get the right permissions because
REM they have already been marked as system. We cover them specially here
REM

attrib +h +s %SystemRoot%\fonts
attrib +h +s %SystemRoot%\tasks
attrib +h +s %SystemRoot%\wintrust.hlp
attrib +h +s %SystemDrive%\boot.ini

REM unhide the zak\scripts directory files, otherwise we won't be able to
REM continue

attrib -h %SystemRoot%\zak\scripts\*.*

REM unhide the exchange.prf file in the c:\temp directory. This is in case it
REM got left behind

attrib -h %SystemDrive%\temp\exchange.prf
```

SYSTEM SHUT DOWN (SHUTDOWN.EXE)

The system is shut down after a countdown of 20 seconds elapses. When the system reboots, the installation process is complete and the user can log on for the first time.

User Logon

When the user logs on to the system for the first time, the look and feel that is supplied by system policies is not fully in place—the policy is only downloaded from the network for the first time and some of the settings require the system to be rebooted before they become active.

After the computer is set up, you must log on to the machine with a user defined as a member of the relevant global group (TaskUsers for TaskStation installations, and AppUsers for AppStation installations). This logon ensures that the system policy is downloaded and the relevant registry settings are changed. All of the settings applied to the registry will become active after the next reboot.

Logon Scripts

The logon scripts for the two defined types of users are very simple. After either the TaskStation computer or AppStation computer has been set up, a user belonging to the TaskUsers or AppUsers global group will have to log on to the computer for the profile to download for the first time. Certain settings in the profile only take effect when the computer is restarted (such as hiding the Control Panel), and so after this initial logon, the machine should be rebooted. The next time the same user logs on to the machine the profile will have taken full effect and access will only be available where the profile dictates.

APPLOGON.CMD

This command file runs the logon script for all AppStation users.

```
net use O: \\IBSNT04\NETAPPS > %SystemDrive%\temp\logon.log
con2prt /f /cd \\IBSNT04\HPLASER152 >> %SystemDrive%\temp\logon.log
```

The commands contained in this file map a network drive to the network application share created for the Microsoft Office 97 installation and then replace any configured printers with one defined within the ZAK setup procedure.

TSKLOGON.CMD

This command file runs the logon script for all TaskStation users.

```
con2prt /f /cd \\IBSNT04\HPLASER152 >> %SystemDrive%\temp\logon.log
```

The command contained in this logon script is used only to connect to the printer defined within the ZAK setup process.

Troubleshooting

You may have to attempt the installations several time before you manage to complete one successfully, depending on the complexity of your computer configurations. If you are installing onto computers that contain only NT detectable hardware, then very few changes need to be made to the answer file. The most common problems with this installation procedure are listed below.

- **The system prompts for a Restart between modes**. The problem here is that either the `NoWaitAfterTextMode` or `NoWaitAfter-GUIMode` setting in the `[Network]` section header of the answer file is set to `0` or is missing.
- **NT Text-mode setup cannot find the answer file—Installation fails**. The answer file is most commonly placed on the network boot disk, and if this is removed from the drive too early, the settings will not have been read. Wait until the main system file copy indicator appears before removing the disk.
- **DetectAdapters error message during network setup**. The network card you are using may not be detectable during a manual NT installation. This should be tested. If the card is not detectable, then the relevant `[InstallAdapters]` section should be used, taking settings from a manually installed configuration. See Chapter Three for details.
- **The workspace isn't locked down when the user logs on**. This case would generally mean that the system policy has not been applied to the system. The policy is keyed on group names, so ensure that the user is a member of the correct global group and that the group name is spelled correctly. Reboot the system and try again. The first logon after installation will not have the policy applied correctly.

Summary

You should complete the unattended installations for the TaskStation and AppStation computers several times so that you can study them and use them as a base for customization.

The step-by-step installation points shown throughout the chapter allow you to see how the setup looks externally. Anybody running the installation process will see only these steps taking place. The background process holds the key to how the ZAK actually works and points to the areas where you can look to make customizations for your own requirements.

PART TWO

User Environmental Control

In This Part

The chapters in this section look at the tools and features provided by Microsoft to introduce an element of control of the desktop environment. The focus of these chapters is on user profiles and system policies.

User profiles are an integral part of Windows-based desktop environments and can be used with great success to introduce control to the desktop. You can provide a uniform look and feel to many users so that time is not wasted looking for application shortcuts or files. You can also introduce preventive measures aimed at stopping users from amending this look and feel, so every time a user logs on in a department the same desktop is presented.

System policies are also an integral part of Windows-based environments and can be used with great success to provide additional control over the users and computers. Policies can restrict access to desktop features such as My Computer, Network Neighborhood, and system tools such as registry editors.

When used together, user profiles and system policies can provide a formidable barrier against user-related problems and can implement a level of control to suit almost all environments. The ZAK uses these two tools and the methods surrounding them to implement all post installation control features. For this reason, a good understanding of these features is paramount.

The chapters in this second part of the book are structured as follows.

Chapter Five provides an in-depth view of user profiles and how they aid the control of a user environment. The different types of user profiles are discussed as well as the differences in profiles for the various Windows desktop operating systems.

Chapter Six looks at system policies and the template files that make up the exposed settings. The template files that are provided with Windows NT Server by default are looked at in this chapter. A good understanding of system policies is required before we look at the ZAK-supplied policy templates.

Chapter Seven looks specifically at the system policies that are provided with, and used by, the ZAK. System policies form the backbone of the lockdown procedures for ZAK clients, and when you fully understand the control structure provided by this tool, you can begin the customization process that will lead to a ZAK installation that fits your organizational needs.

Each of the three chapters outlined above finishes with lab exercises, which reinforce the topics covered in the chapter. You should work through these lab exercises to ensure that you understand the topic fully.

FIVE

User Profiles and Desktop Control

In This Chapter

- User Profile Defined
- Local User Profiles
- Windows 95/98
- Roaming User Profiles
- Mandatory Profiles
- NTuser.xxx Permissions
- Creating a Roaming Profile for Windows 95/98
- Summary
- Lab Exercises

This chapter looks at user profiles and how they can be used as a tool to lower the total cost of ownership of a distributed client/server network.

You can use these user profiles to control the look and feel of a desktop so that the many unnecessary problems caused by user interference with their own system can be avoided.

This chapter covers the different types of user profiles available and when you would use them. Also included in this chapter are step-by-step instructions on how to implement a user profile for a group of users. A good understanding of user profiles will help you to understand the power and scope of the ZAK and how you will be able to benefit from the collection of tools used by it.

User Profile Defined

A user profile is a group of settings that describe the look and feel of a user's environment on a Windows NT or Windows 95/98 computer. It can control what appears on a desktop or what applications are accessible. User profiles contain settings that can be applied to a user or group; they can be set up so that users can make changes and save them, or so that users cannot save any changes made.

User profiles were designed in part to answer the need for more control over the ever-growing complexity of the desktop and network systems. One of the main reasons that user profiles have never been a popular control method in the past is that they don't have an easy-to-use management tool. Microsoft has never delivered the control structure, and so the cost of installation (in terms of administrators losing sleep and hair) has never really been worthwhile. The ZAK goes some way to fulfilling this need for a control mechanism aimed at user profiles. It does not go all the way though, and the setup process for user profiles is quite involved.

With the help of the ZAK and with the help of the instructions included in this chapter, you can now deliver and manage from a central point the look and feel required by the enterprise workforce. Not all users have to have the same desktop look. This look can be tailored to specific needs. In addition, the profile can travel with the user so that the same look and feel can be provided in different locations with the minimum of administrative overhead.

User profiles can be used in conjunction with *system policies* to bring an even greater amount of control and security to the user environment.

User profiles can be shared among many users, but they are assigned individually with User Manager (for Domains). They cannot be assigned to groups (yet another failing of the design).

System policies control availability and access to resources and can be either set for users, groups, or the computer. System policies are discussed in Chapter Six.

You can configure the amount of control imposed, and granularity can be achieved by configuring this control for users and groups. User profiles have been with us since the introduction of Windows NT but are rarely exploited to their full potential because of the previously discussed difficulties concerning the lack of control mechanisms.

User Profile Types

The ZAK enables you to use profiles to help lock down the workstation environment, preventing unwanted interference with the local system by either well-meaning users or malicious third parties. Three types of user profiles are available today.

- **Local Profile**. A local profile is housed on the local workstation and is created automatically the first time a user logs on to a machine and then logs off. It is stored by default in the `\%SystemRoot%\Profiles` folder and contains all of the settings that were applied to the system while that user was logged on. If changes are made while a user is logged on, they are saved to the profile folder. A local profile only exists on the one workstation on which it was created and is not available if the user walks away and logs on locally to another machine.
- **Roaming Profile**. A roaming profile is the answer to some of the problems caused by users who log on to more than one machine. When users have the desktop look and feel of a machine set up just the way they like it or it has been optimized by IS personnel for their use, they should have those settings available if they move to another workstation. This is not possible with local profiles because they are only available on the single computer where they were created. Roaming profiles contain the same available settings as local profiles but are stored in a central point where they are available for downloading regardless of which workstation a user logs on to. In this way, the settings for that user can be available on all workstations.
  - These profiles must be downloaded across the network at logon time and changes are saved back to the central point across a network when the user logs off, so this approach can slow down the logon and logoff processes.
  - Roaming profiles can be shared among many users or groups, so the same desktop look and feel can be used for everyone in a department. The drawback here is that if one person makes a change (by deleting a shortcut, for example,) then this change will be saved to the central profile copy at logoff time. The next user to log on and download this profile will not have the shortcut available, and it will need to be recreated, usually resulting in a fault call to support personnel.

- **Mandatory Profile**. A mandatory profile is a type of roaming profile. It is set to be read-only so that it has all of the benefits of being available to many users, but none of the users can interfere with it or accidentally change it. In this way, you can control the look and feel of the desktop and also centrally control any necessary profile changes that user groups may require.

We look at the three different types of profiles in detail in the remainder of this chapter.

Structure and Location

A user profile is made up from the contents of a collection of special folders and a registry file, which combine to provide a means of applying and saving settings and user preferences on a desktop system. The settings and preferences contained in a profile are stored in two ways. Some of the settings are stored in a folder structure on either the local machine (local profile) or the validating server (roaming and mandatory profiles). The remaining settings are stored in system registry format in a file named `NTuser.xxx`. This file is stored in the profile folder structure for Windows NT, whereas a file named `User.xxx` is stored for Windows 95 and 98 machines. The `.xxx` suffix can be replaced with either `.dat` or `.man`. A mandatory profile has an extension of `.man`, and all other profiles have an extension of `.dat`.

The profile settings are split along two distinct lines. The profiles folder holds settings such as desktop icons, icons representing shortcuts to applications, user's links (generally as icons) and any other settings represented by visual objects such as folders, icons, files, etc. If you were to copy a file to your desktop for ease of access, it would be stored within the profiles folder structure. You use the registry hive containing user profile settings to hold less tangible environmental preferences such as wallpaper and background settings, international settings, and keyboard and mouse settings. Security-related settings such as the ability to run applications and access to system tools are also defined here. Tables 5.1 and 5.2 list the settings available in the two locations and briefly describe their use.

Local User Profiles

Local profiles are at the bottom end of the usefulness pile when it comes to controlling the desktop environment. Controls require a way to limit the user's ability to circumvent them, and this is not really practical with a local logon (although it is possible). However, the story of profiles and the ability to move on to the creation of roaming and mandatory profiles, first requires a discussion of the basics.

TABLE 5.1 Folder structure for Windows NT profiles

Folder Name	Description
Application Data	This content is defined by application programmers.
Desktop	Any items, such as shortcuts, to be displayed on the desktop.
Favorites	Shortcuts to the user's favorite locations. Used with Internet Explorer.
NetHood	Shortcuts to Network Neighborhood objects. A hidden folder by default.
Personal	Default storage location for files created by the user. Applications are specifically designed to save files here by default.
PrintHood	Shortcuts to printer objects. A hidden folder by default.
Recent	Shortcuts to the most recently used files and objects.
SendTo	Shortcuts to locations required for file placement. Referenced by the Explorer context menu for files.
Start Menu	Shortcuts to applications. Newly installed applications should place shortcuts here.
Templates	Shortcuts to template objects. A hidden folder by default.

TABLE 5.2 `NTuser.xxx` registry hive contents

Item	Description
Windows NT Explorer	Persistent network connections and user defined explorer settings.
Taskbar	Taskbar settings and personal program groups and properties.
Printers	Networked printer connections.
Control Panel	User-defined settings made in Control Panel.
Accessories	User-defined settings for all applications within the Accessories group such as those for Clock, Paint, and Calculator.
Help Bookmarks	All bookmarks placed in Windows NT help.

Creating a Local User Profile

The creation of a local user profile is an automated process. When a user logs on to a Windows NT system locally for the first time, a profile is created for him and saved under the `\%SystemRoot%\Profiles` folder in a subfolder named after the user. If a subfolder of that name already exists, then a folder of the same name with an extension of `.000` is used. If this folder already exists, then a folder of the same name and an extension of `.001` is used, and so on. Folders with the same name can exist for many reasons, including the user name having been used before.

Before we continue this discussion, a brief introduction to the system identifier (SID) is called for. A SID is an identifier, created when a new user or group is created, that represents that user or group. The SID is guaranteed to be unique within a domain. When permissions are set for a folder, the username is not actually stored as the owner of the permissions; rather the SID that represents the user is stored as the owner of the permissions. Now, when a user is created, you can delete that user and create another with the same user name. These two accounts are not linked in any way because of the unique nature of the system identifier (SID), which sits behind the user account. However, if the first (deleted) user had a local profile, then when the new user logged on, the profile folder would already exist (and be permissioned for the SID representing the deleted user), so a new folder with an incremented extension number would be created.

An entry is made for the user in the local registry, linking that user to the profile folder that contains his settings. Profile link entries do not exist in the local registry for users who only log on to a machine remotely. The registry key used for this link is `HKLM\Software\Microsoft\Windows NT\CurrentVersion\ProfileList`. Listed under this key are the system identifiers of all users who have logged on interactively to this machine. One of the values stored under each SID entry is the `ProfileImagePath`, which holds the location of the profile used by that user. This value could be edited to point the user account to a profile in another location.

Browsing Local Profiles

Local profiles are important because you can use them to create your own roaming or mandatory profiles. You can see a list of the profiles known on your local machine.

1. Log on locally as Administrator on the local machine.
2. Select **Settings** from the **Start** menu and choose **Control Panel**.
3. Double-click on the **System** application.
4. Select the **User Profiles** tab.

Figure 5.1 shows the resulting list of profiles for a sample machine.

Profile Maintenance

In Figure 5.1, the first account name is "Account Deleted." The local profile still exists for a user account that has been removed from the system. You should perform maintenance on your user profiles to ensure that the disk space used does not become excessive. Remember that if a user copies a 20 Mbyte file to his desktop, it becomes part of the profile and is stored in the `\%SystemRoot%\Profiles` folder. Temporary Internet files are stored here by default as well, so disk space usage can grow quickly. You can delete a profile by simply selecting it in the **System Properties** screen shown in Figure 5.1 and pressing the **Delete** button. Answering **Yes** to the confirmation deletes the profile.

A command-line utility also exists that enables you to remove profiles from a local system. The `DelProf.exe` tool is available as part of the Windows NT Resource Kit and can be used to clean up your user profiles. See the Resource Kit documentation for usage instructions.

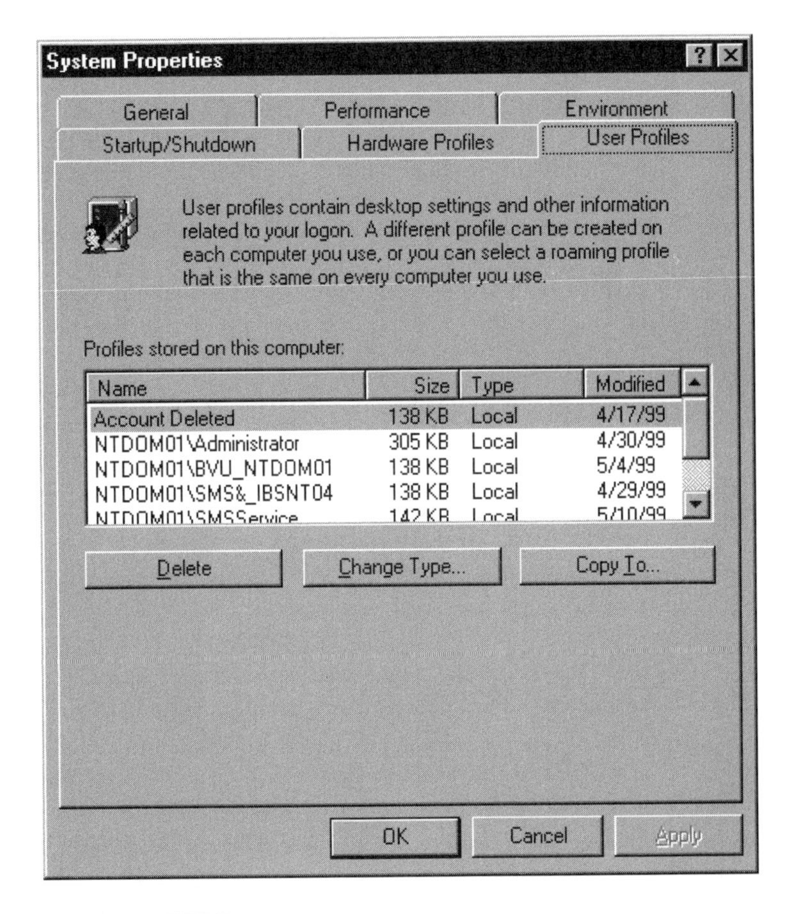

FIGURE 5.1 User profiles listed on a Windows NT computer

Permissions

User profiles are protected by up to three sets of permissions.

- **Network share permissions**. You can use network share permissions to protect user profiles, but they can add difficulty to the process of troubleshooting if you need to find out where permissions are being derived. If at all possible, you should avoid using share permissions in favor of NTFS file and folder permissions.
- **NTFS file and folder permissions**. You can use NTFS permissions to protect user profiles. When you copy a user profile and set the *Permitted to Use* flag, you are actually setting NTFS permissions on the destination folder structure, as well as registry permissions in the `NTuser.xxx` file. You can easily change NTFS permissions to further restrict access to a profile folder if necessary.
- **Encoded permissions contained in the NTuser.xxx file**. The permissions set with the *Permitted to Use* flag when a user profile is copied are also set in the `NTuser.xxx` file, which is a binary representation of a registry hive. These permissions can only be changed with the registry editor, so if you need to make permissions more restrictive, it is easier to use just NTFS permission. If you need to make permissions less restrictive or need to set them for extra users, then you must set them in the `NTuser.xxx` file as well as at the NTFS level. The steps required to change permissions for the registry portion of the profile are described in the next section.

When applying permissions, consider replacing all references to the Everyone group with Domain Users. This approach will afford you better control over who gains access to your resources. You cannot control the Everyone group membership, but you can control Domain Users.

Default User Profile

The Default User profile is created during the Windows NT setup process; it is a base profile that contains shortcuts to programs and accessories loaded during the system setup. Programs such as Calculator and Notepad, residing in the *Accessories* group are examples of these.

When a user logs on locally to a Windows NT machine for the first time, the Default User profile is copied into a newly created subfolder of `\%SystemRoot%\Profiles` named after the user. (The rules for the naming of this folder are discussed earlier in this section.) When the user makes changes to the machine, the changes are saved to this new folder, because the user now has his own profile distinct from the Default User profile.

The Default User profile can be useful if you have applications on your system that all local users would need to access. You can simply create the correct shortcuts in this user profile, and every new user to log on to the machine will automatically have a profile created that matches the Default User profile. The usefulness is limited because the profile can only be used locally on each machine and an update to the Default User profile would not be reflected in any user profiles already created.

All Users Profile

The All Users profile is created at setup time as is the Default User profile. The All Users profile is a stripped-down version of a profile containing a Desktop folder and a Start menu folder and stores icons and program shortcuts that are made available to *all users* who log on interactively to the machine. The logon can be to the local machine or to the domain. The user will always receive the contents of the local All Users folder structure.

To ensure that everyone who logs on to a particular machine has access to a program, place the shortcut within the All Users profile structure, making it available for everyone to use.

Although we refer here to the All Users profile, you may consider this not to be a real profile because it does not have all of the folders found in other profiles and does not have an `NTuser.xxx` registry file.

Windows 95/98

The user profile structure and behavior differs slightly between Windows NT and Windows 9x systems.

Table 5.3 shows the main differences between the way in which user profiles are applied and stored for Windows 95/98 systems and Windows NT systems.

User profiles are handled in a different manner for Windows 95/98 than for Windows NT. You must understand how these work if you attempt to bring some elements of control into this environment.

When a user logs on to a Windows 95/98 machine, the local registry key `HKLM\Software\Microsoft\Windows\CurrentVersion\ProfileList` is checked to see if this user has an entry. If the user has an entry, the system checks to see if there is a locally cached version of the profile. The system also checks the user's home directory to see if a profile exists there. If a profile is found in both locations, the newest version is used. If a profile is found in only one of the locations, then it is used. If no profile is found, then the Default User profile from the local machine is used. This is different from Windows NT, where the Default User profile can be set to be on the server.

TABLE 5.3 Comparison of Windows NT and Windows 95/98 profiles

Windows NT	Windows 95/98
The `NTuser.xxx` file used to store settings in a registry format.	The equivalent file is `User.xxx`.
The `NTuser.dat.log` file is a transaction tracker for fault tolerance. It provides the support to roll back a transaction when a profile recovery is attempted.	The `User.da0` file stores a full copy of the profile when the user logs off and the profile is saved. This file can be used as a complete backup of the last-saved profile.
Common group support is included.	Common group support is not available.
The user profile default location is in `\%SystemRoot%\Profiles` (local profile) or where the Profiles path is directed.	A user's home directory is the default location for the user profile. This location can be changed.
All shortcuts, files, folders, and contents of the profile folders are copied to the local machine when a logon is made with a roaming profile.	Can be configured so that only shortcuts (`.lnk`) and program information (`.pif`) files are copied locally.
The Default User profile can be stored centrally.	The Default User profile can only exist locally.
The `\Applications` profile folder is used by developers for such things as storing custom dictionary files.	The `\Applications` folder does not exist.

All of the attempts listed above to find a profile depend on there being an entry in the local registry for this user. If there is no entry, then the user has not been set up to use a profile on this machine.

Changes in the profile are made in the location from which it was read. If the profile was built from the Default User profile, then a folder is created on the local machine named after the user and located under the `\%WinDir%\Profiles` folder. This folder is updated at logoff.

Roaming User Profiles

Roaming user profiles are a much more useful tool for presenting a uniform look and feel to the desktop for users. A roaming profile is similar to a local profile, except that it is available to users at any configured domain computer. Availability is accomplished by storing the profile in a central location instead of on the local drive. The profile is downloaded every time the network user logs on to the domain, and it is uploaded at logoff time.

Roaming profiles can be shared among many users, facilitating the uniform desktop look and feel that leads to better control of the desktop arena.

Locally Cached Copy

The process of downloading a profile every time a user logs on to the network can be costly in terms of network bandwidth, so if a slow network connection is detected, a locally cached copy of the profile can be used.

The locally cached copy of the profile is the same as the copy that was last saved to the central storage point. When a slow network is detected, the user can stop the download and use the local copy.

The locally cached copy of the profile is what the user interacts with once logged on to the domain. When the roaming profile is downloaded, it overwrites the locally cached copy. Desktop settings are directly linked to that local copy until logoff. If the user creates an icon on the desktop, it is stored in the `\%SystemRoot%\Profiles\%Username%\Desktop` folder. If a file is copied directly into this folder, it would instantly appear on the desktop. It is changes in this locally cached copy that are copied to the roaming profile location on the network.

Creating a Roaming Profile for NT 4.0

You create a roaming user profile by following the instructions contained in this section. The process is broken down into the following steps:

- Choose a Central Location.
- Create the Network Share.
- Create a local Template User.
- Create a Base Profile.
- Copy the Base Profile to the Central Server.
- Set up users to access the new Base Roaming Profile.
- Amend the copies of the Base Profile as necessary.

CHOOSE A CENTRAL LOCATION

Roaming profiles need to be accessible to the users, so you should store them on a high-availability central server. Consider two main factors when deciding where to locate the user profiles for your organization.

- **Storage space**. User profiles can range in size from hundreds of Kilobytes to many Megabytes. If a user copies a file to the desktop and then saves the roaming profile at logoff, the file is transferred with the rest of the profile information to the network share and back when the user logs on again. The location needs to have enough free disk space to be able to store all of the profiles used in your organization. You can also divide your users and store the profiles in more than one location.
- **Network speed**. As mentioned above, the profile can be quite large, and it needs to be downloaded at logon time and uploaded at logoff time. This can cause severe delays for the user at these times if the link speed between the share location and the workstation is slow. Slow link speeds can be accommodated in system policy settings, as described in Chapter Six.

A common location for roaming user profiles once they are implemented is on the primary domain controller; in most cases, this is not a good idea. You should consider user profiles as an application and ask yourself if you would like the user to be running an application from this point. The answer will almost invariably be no.

Consider placing user profiles on an application server to offload some of the strain from the authentication servers.

For permissions to be applied to profiles, the profiles should reside on an NTFS partition.

CREATE THE NETWORK SHARE

When you have chosen the location for the centrally stored profile, you must prepare the network share. For the purposes of the examples in this chapter, we use the following information.

- The profiles folder resides on an application server named **IBSNT04**.
- The network share used to house the profiles is called **NetStore**.
- A user account named **TstUser1** is created to use the profile.

You can substitute more relevant information from your own organization for the information listed above.

1. Use Microsoft Explorer to create a folder called **NetStore** on the server.
2. Right-click the new folder to display the context menu.
3. Select **Sharing**.
4. In the sharing dialog box, select the **Share As** radio button. Figure 5.2 shows the network share dialog box.

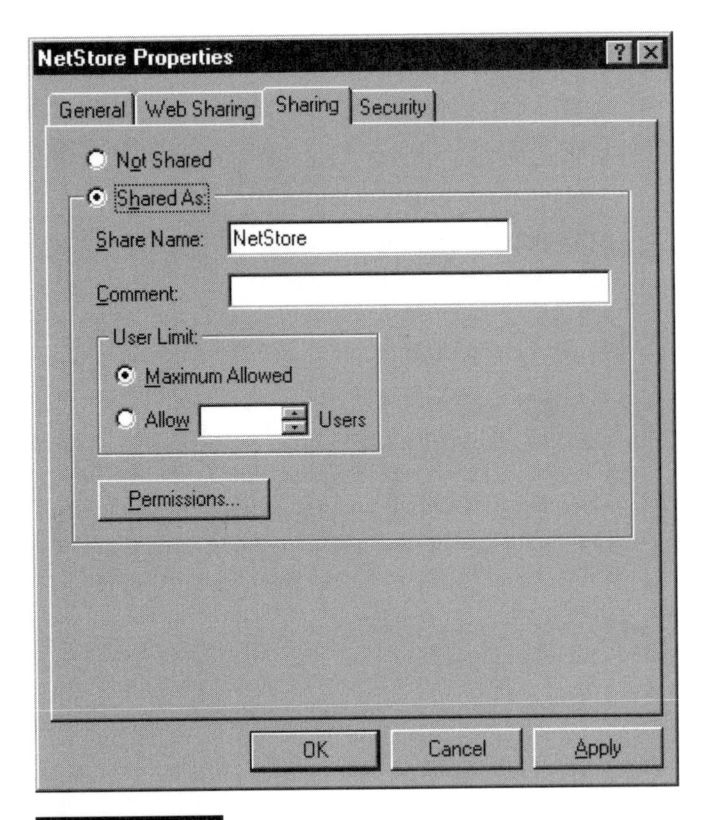

FIGURE 5.2 Sharing a folder on the network

5. Accept the default share name of **NetStore**.
6. Select the **Permissions** button and remove the **Everyone** group from the **Access Through Share Permissions** dialog box.
7. Set the permissions to be **Domain Users** - **Full Control**.
8. Select **OK**.

The folder is now shared on the network with the share permissions set as described. Ensure that the NTFS permissions on the folder structure are set to **Domain Users—Full Control**. When subfolders are created here, the user must have Full Control permissions. Individual permissions are then set on these subfolders to deny access to all other users.

CREATE A LOCAL TEMPLATE USER

You should have a test user account for the roaming profile setup procedure. This user account can be created specifically for testing, or it can be an existing account amended to fit the profile outlined below. Create the user account locally on a system as opposed to creating a domain user.

1. Start up **User Manager** on a workstation that can be used to build the profile.
2. Select **New User** from the **User** menu.
3. Enter the username **TstUser1** and password details for the new user.
4. Select the **Profiles** button.
5. Ensure the **Profiles Path** remains empty.
6. Select **Add** to add the user.
7. Select **Close**. The user **TstUser1** is added to the accounts database on the local machine.

The *Profiles Path* was intentionally left blank in step five. When no location for a user profile is entered, the local Default User profile is copied and stored in a folder below the local profiles folder, named after the user. In this case, when this user logs on to the local system, a profile folder named `\%SystemRoot%\Profiles\TstUser1` will be created. This newly created profile is the base for the roaming profile that we wish to create.

CREATE A BASE PROFILE

One of the ways in which the ZAK brings an element of order and control to the desktop is to use the same profile for one particular job-type. The defined task-based workers are split into two groups, TaskStation and AppStation users. These groups are the basis for which profile is used for which type of user.

This thinking can be extended and adapted to fit your own organization. You can define a profile for each of your user departments or some other grouping within your enterprise. In fact, the ZAK is built on the understanding that this profiling will be done.

You may find it useful to create a base profile that is common to all users. IT policies within large organizations often mandate that everybody use the same basic applications. E-mail, word processing, and spreadsheet applications are often licensed per enterprise, and all staff should have access automatically. A base profile would support a common desktop look, which would include shortcuts to all of these applications.

Other applications, such as graphics applications for the Marketing department and number-crunching applications for the Accounts department, are less widely used and would not necessarily appear on the base profile.

Once you have created the template user, you can create a base user profile.

1. Log on locally to the workstation used in the previous step as **TstUser1**. The default user profile on the machine is used to populate the desktop at this time.

2. Make any changes to the desktop look and feel that you find necessary. These changes should include shortcuts to all applications that are common to everyone, as well as any other desktop settings common to all. For this example, place a text file named `App.txt` on the desktop to simulate an application shortcut.
3. Install any applications that you wish to use locally, or set shortcuts to point to the network share where these applications reside. The use of network-based applications can add an extra piece of control to the system.
4. Logoff. The new profile is stored in the `\%SystemRoot%\Profiles\TstUser1` folder.

The base profile is now created and is ready to be copied to the `NetStore` share for use by different users. At this point, make a copy of the base profile (a full copy of the contents of `\%SystemRoot%\Profiles\TstUser1` folder), and keep it safe. You should not be logged on as the TstUser1 account when you copy the profile because you will have files open and cause a sharing violation.

The base profile consists of the folders shown in Figure 5.3. Note the attributes of the folders. Some are hidden; we show them in the figure by setting the Options from the View menu.

COPY THE BASE PROFILE TO THE CENTRAL SERVER

Once you are happy with the contents of the base profile, you should log off to ensure all files are closed and copy the profile to the central storage point. You should be able to use this base profile in its present state as the starting point for all user profile builds within the enterprise. By making copies of the profiles for the different users or groups, you can have this profile loaded as a starting point and then amended to fit the more specific requirements of individual users or groups.

There are two main methods used for distributing a base profile: manual distribution and Default User distribution.

MANUAL DISTRIBUTION

For manual distribution of the profile, use the System Properties dialog screen to copy the local profile to a central server and to give permissions to use the new profile.

1. Log on locally as Administrator on the machine that stores the base profile.
2. Select **Settings** from the **Start** menu, and choose **Control Panel**.
3. Double-click on the **System** applet.
4. Select the **User Profiles** tab.

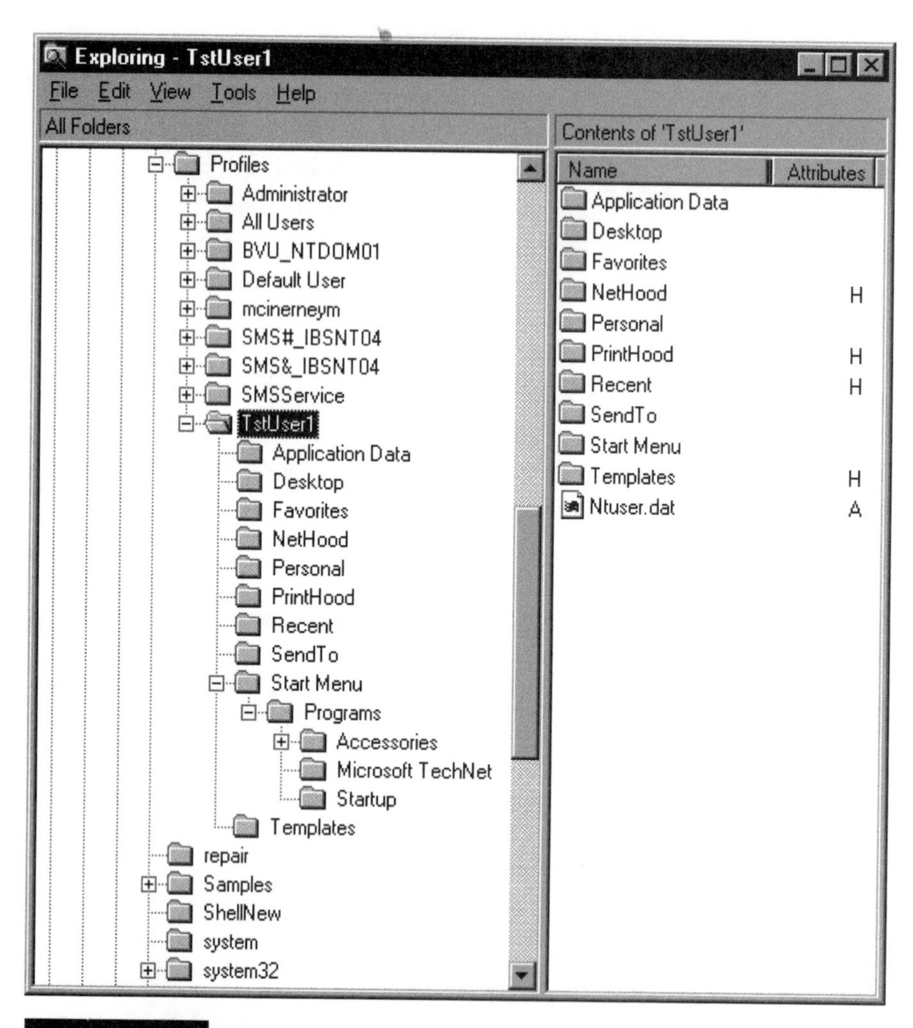

FIGURE 5.3 Folder structure of a newly created profile

5. Select the **TstUser1** profile and choose **Copy To**.
6. Enter the path to the **Netlogon** share on the primary domain controller, and append the folder name **\TstProf**. This name can be in UNC form or can be a previously hard-coded drive letter, for example, **\\IBSNT04\NETLOGON\TstProf**.
7. Select the **Change** button in the **Permitted to use** box.
8. Select the **Domain Users** group.
9. Select **Add** > **OK**.
10. Select **OK** to begin copying the profile.

You can repeat this distribution method to make multiple copies of the base profile that can then be amended to cater to individual or group preferences. If your organization has departments named Accounts, Sales, and Marketing, then you can create global groups within the domain for each one of these and make a profile copy for each, assigning the correct permissions. We explore more fully the possibilities of the ZAK customization procedures in Part Three.

DEFAULT USER DISTRIBUTION

One of the differences between the functionality of Windows 95/98 profiles and profiles for Windows NT is that the Default User profile can be stored centrally for Windows NT. The Default User distribution method can supply the base profile as the first profile downloaded by new users logging into the domain. The users can then make changes as permitted, saving the profile when they log off. Follow these instructions to set the base profile as the Default User profile.

1. Log on locally as Administrator on the machine that stores the base profile.
2. Select **Settings** from the **Start** menu, and choose **Control Panel**.
3. Double-click on the **System** applet.
4. Select the **User Profiles** tab.
5. Select the **TstUser1** profile, and choose **Copy To**.
6. Enter the path to the **Netlogon** share on the primary domain controller, and append the folder name **\Default User**. This name can be in UNC form or can be a previously hard-coded drive letter, for example, **\\IBSNT04\NETLOGON\Default User**.
7. Select the **Change** button in the **Permitted to use** box.
8. Select the user or group permitted to use this profile in the final location. These permissions are difficult to change, so unless you have a good reason for protecting the profiles at this point, choose the **Domain Users** group.
9. Select **Add** > **OK**.
10. Select **OK** to begin copying the profile.
11. Repeat steps 5 through 10 for each validating server (backup domain controllers) or use the Replication service to replicate the profile to these BDCs.

With the Default User profile located on the authentication servers, you are ready to distribute profiles. When a user logs on to the domain for the first time, the system checks for a profile setting in his user account. If one doesn't exist, the system checks for a Default User profile on the `Netlogon` share of the authenticating server. If this exists, then it is used to populate a local profile for the current network user. If a Default User profile does not exist in the `Netlogon` share, then the local machine Default User profile is copied and used to populate a new local profile for the user.

This procedure works for domain users. Local user logons are handled by the local machine, and the local copy of the Default User profile is used to populate new profiles.

The result of the procedure is that a local profile is created from the centrally stored Default User profile. You now have to follow the instructions in the section *Manual Distribution* to copy this local profile to the central storage area. Obviously, this is a more cumbersome process than the first method and is not widely used.

SET UP USERS TO ACCESS THE BASE ROAMING PROFILE

Users must be assigned a profile before they can load it. Profiles are assigned to users only and cannot be assigned to groups (another example of excellent Microsoft design?), although they can be shared amongst many users. Using User Manager for Domains, you can assign a profile to a user by entering the profile folder in the *Profiles Path* box. The next time the user logs on, he will download the new roaming profile as long as it exists in the specified location and he has the correct permissions.

You can share a single profile among many users, but you must set up all users to use it in the same manner. The permissions must be set to allow all of the assigned users to access the profile.

AMENDING THE BASE ROAMING PROFILE

At this point you have created a local profile, amended it to reflect your profile needs, copied it to a central server, and given permissions for all Domain Users to use the profile. Consider the fictional domain user **SmythJ**. He has been set up so that he will download and use a new roaming profile named **TstProf**. Let us assume that SmythJ is a member of the Accounts department and performs the same job function as all other users in this department.

You can now amend the new roaming profile called TstProf to reflect any required differences between the base profile and a profile for the Accounts department. If there is an application for sole use by the Accounts department, then you can create a shortcut on this desktop for user SmythJ; that change will be uploaded at log off to be included in the profile. In this way, you can amend the profiles to more closely suit the needs of the user community. Remember that even though you want the whole of the

Accounts group to use the same profile, you must assign the profile to each user on an individual basis in User Manager for Domains.

The basic way in which you amend a roaming profile is simply to log on as the user who is using the profile and make any changes at the desktop that you require. For example, you may wish to add a program to the Start menu by using the Taskbar editor, or you may wish to create a shortcut on the desktop pointing to a particular application. When you have amended the desktop, you simply log off the machine. At logoff time, the locally cached profile is copied up to the central location and overwrites the stored copy. The locally cached copy is already updated, as the desktop changes you made were actually made in the locally cached profiles copy. When the user next logs on (or when any user authorized to use this profile logs on), the saved profile containing the changes is downloaded to the local machine, overwriting the locally cached copy.

You can encounter problems that may not allow you to upload the changed profile to the server. These problems can be out of the control of the local system, such as server failures or network problems. When you log off under these circumstances, you receive a message stating "The System failed to update your centrally stored profile." This means that the locally cached copy of the profile may contain changes and the central copy does not reflect this. User profiles are timestamped, and this timestamp is checked when the user logs on to see which one of the central or local profiles is newest. Under normal circumstances, the central copy is the newest because it is updated last. In the specific circumstance mentioned above, the local copy is newer. The next time the user logs on, a message is displayed stating "Your locally cached profile is newer than the centrally stored copy, do you wish to use the local copy?" During a countdown of 30 seconds (by default), you must choose which copy to use. Regardless of your choice, the upload procedure at log off will work normally and the central copy will be updated (as long as the network problems do not recur).

You've Heard the Good News... Now for the Bad News

This ability to change the roaming profile as easily as changing the desktop look can cause problems with desktop management. Imagine the scenario where you set the whole of the Accounts department to use a single roaming profile. The positive aspect of this action would be that any of the Accounts users could log on at any machine and get the same desktop look. Everything goes well for awhile until one user, while working late, decides that he doesn't require a shortcut to one of the accounts packages on his desktop because his job responsibility doesn't require him to use it. He deletes the icon. He is the last person in the department that night, and when he logs off, the changes he has made (deleting the icon) are copied to the roaming profile used by everybody in Accounts (because it only exists as a single entity). When the users arrive the next day, they all download the profile, which is missing the icon, and nobody knows how to access the package anymore.

This can be a common problem when sharing a roaming profile among multiple users. The problem is exacerbated if your users are prone to tinkering with their systems. I have worked in environments where technical call centers have been housed and so the user base has been prone to "enhancing their system." This is an environment where the total cost of ownership is greatly increased because of the numbers of faults introduced unnecessarily into business systems.

All users have the same rights to the profile folder, and any changes made to the local desktop are replicated to the centrally stored (single) copy. Even if you intend a change to be made, you could make a local change and log off to replicate the change to the central copy. If another user is logged on using that profile when you perform the change, it will be overwritten when that user logs off and automatically copies the profile to the server.

The solution to this problem comes in two forms. You can create a profile for every user, based on a profile template. This template is simply a saved copy of a base template generic enough for all to use; then, you add extra facilities depending on the user's needs. The overhead in managing this type of installation is quite large and it is not recommended for anything except the smallest of installations. The second way of tackling the problem is to use *mandatory profiles*. These profiles can be shared among many users and are basically read-only for these users.

Mandatory Profiles

You can allow an entire department to use the same roaming profile, as discussed in the previous section. As we saw, if a user accidentally makes a change to settings contained in the profile and logs off, the change is replicated to the server copy of the profile and all users have the change when they next log on. This process can introduce an amount of uncertainty into the management of user desktops and adds a level of complexity that you really don't need. IT systems are already complex enough, and one of the benefits of user profiles is supposed to be to "bring some order to desktops and to reduce management cost." This statement can be true, but only after you have put many hours into the correct design and implementation process.

Enter the mandatory profile. A mandatory profile is a roaming profile that is set so that the user cannot save any changes to the settings contained in the profile—in essence, a read-only roaming profile. To change a roaming profile into a mandatory profile you simply rename the `NTuser.dat` file, which contains the registry hive portion of the profile, to `NTuser.man`. This makes the profile read-only from that point on. If a user is already logged on to the system and using the roaming profile when you make this change, the update of the roaming profile will fail at user logoff because the profile is now read-only but the system was not expecting this. If a user logs on to the system and the profile is already mandatory, then no attempt to update the profile is made at logoff time and so no error is generated.

Mandatory profiles can be taken one step further. Not only can you make them read-only so that changes are not saved, but you can also set up a user so that if the mandatory profile is not available, the user cannot log on to the domain. This would mean that if the server holding the profile was not available, then the user couldn't access the system.

Normally, if a user attempts a domain logon and the profile named in the user account setup cannot be found, the system will attempt to log the user on by using the locally cached copy of the profile (whether it is a roaming profile or mandatory). If this is not successful, the local Default User profile is used. This procedure could present an ingenious user with a way to circumvent the control mechanisms that you have in place.

To avoid this possibility, you can opt to lock out the user if the profile is unavailable. To do this, you rename the profile folder so that it has an extension attached of `.man`. This would mean that a profile folder named `\\IBSNT04\NetStore\UserProf1` would be renamed to `\\IBSNT04\NetStore\UserProf1.man`. You must also change the profile path for the user in User Manager for Domains so that the `.man` extension is included.

The net result of setting up a user in this manner is that if the profile is not available for any reason, a message appears on the workstation screen at logon time saying that "the operating system is not able to log you on because your roaming mandatory profile is not available. Please contact your network administrator." The login attempt then ends.

Mandatory profiles can be useful if you need to use a common desktop for many users and the users do not need to make changes of their own. A word of caution, though. Some application programmers write their applications to hold user-dependent information in the registry. An example is a word processing application that stores the user's preferred settings (file locations, etc.) in the registry. Because the user cannot save any of the settings stored in a mandatory profile, an error is produced when he tries to save these settings (usually at program exit time). This can lead to loss of functionality, so before a wide-spread roll-out, you must fully test all applications that are going to be included in a mandatory profile. Microsoft Office 97 is one such application.

NTuser.xxx Permissions

You can easily adjust the portion of the profile stored in the folder structure by simply adding shortcuts to the folder representing the functionality you wish to achieve. If you want to place an application icon on the desktop, then you can just add the icon to the `\Desktop` folder within the profile structure. The new icon will appear immediately if you add it to the \Desktop folder in the locally cached profile, or it will appear the next time the user logs on if you add it to the folder in the centrally stored profile copy (as long as it is not removed by users logging off and overwriting the central copy). Take care when adding shortcuts to the centrally stored copy of the profile. Shortcut targets are stored as fully qualified names. The UNC form of the path is used and not a hard-coded drive letter. This can mean that a shortcut intended to point to a user's local hard drive may point to the central server's hard drive when the shortcut is downloaded in the profile. For all shortcuts that point to the user's local drive, ensure that you place them in the locally cached profile so that they are sent to the central store at logoff.

The profile attributes held in the binary `NTuser.xxx` file are a little more difficult to get to. To make changes to these settings, you must use the registry editing tool `Regedt32.exe` for Windows NT 4.0 profiles. Remember that you should not make profile changes while the user is logged on unless the profile is mandatory. Roaming profile changes will be overwritten when the user logs off if the profile is already in use when the changes are made.

Permissions are set in the registry portion of the user profile in two ways. First, NTFS file and directory permissions need to be set so that the authorized users can gain the correct access. Second, permissions are set by the registry editor in the same way as any other registry hive. To view or change the permissions set in the registry file, follow the instructions for the example, which takes you through some sample changes to the user profile, *TstProf*, created in the *Manual Distribution* section.

1. Log on to the profiles server with administrative permissions and Full Control permission to the **\TstProf** profile folder on the **Netlogon** share.
2. Select **Run** from the **Start** menu.
3. Enter **Regedt32** and select **OK**.
4. Select **Load Hive** from the **Registry** menu.
5. Navigate to the **\\IBSNT04\Netlogon\TstProf** folder (or the folder holding the profile that you wish to amend).
6. Choose the **NTuser.xxx** (`.dat` or `.man`) file, and select **Open** to display the **Load Hive** dialog box. The **Key Name** being asked for is a unique name that you can use to distinguish it as the loaded hive. This is important because the hive needs to be unloaded after the changes are made.
7. Enter a unique key name. For this example, enter **TestLoad**.
8. Select **Open**. The **TestLoad** hive is added to the currently selected registry hive. This hive contains the settings from the **NTuser.xxx** file.
9. Select the root of the **TestLoad** registry hive or the hive that you have loaded.

10. Select **Permissions** from the **Security** menu.
11. Change the permissions to match your requirements.
12. Select **OK** to confirm the changes.
13. Select the root of the **TestLoad** hive.
14. Select **Unload Hive** from the **Registry** menu to unload the hive and save the settings to the original **NTuser.xxx** file.

When the registry hive is unloaded, it is written back to the `NTuser.xxx` file that opened during the *Load Hive* process.

Creating a Roaming Profile for Windows 95/98

You can allow Windows 95/98 users to use roaming profiles similar to those in use on Windows NT machines.

The first step is to perform the client workstation setup which you do in two stages. First, enable profiles for the workstation by using the **Passwords** applet in **Control Panel** on the workstation in question. The **User Profiles** tab allows you to set the **Users can customize their preferences** flag, and this enables the use of profiles on the workstation.

After profiles are enabled, set the **Primary Network Logon** to **Client for Microsoft Networks**. You do this from the **Networks** applet of **Control Panel** by scrolling through the options and selecting **Client for Microsoft Networks**. Of course, *Client for Microsoft Networks* has to be installed as a known client first.

The next step in performing the client workstation setup for Windows 9x users is to create the user account in the domain and set it up with a home directory. The steps taken to create the user account are the same as for any other domain user. Use **User Manager for Domains** at the NT Server to create an account.

The main difference between Windows NT roaming profile users and Windows 9x roaming profile users is that the Windows 9x users store their profile in their home directory on the network by default. You can change this behavior by using the `HKLM\Network\Logon\UseHomeDirectory` registry key to redirect the location.

To make profile locating work for the home directory, do not put an entry in the *Profiles Path* in the user's account setup. Instead, set up the home directory by selecting a drive letter in the **Home Directory** section and entering the path to the target network share. Append the variable `%Username%` to the end of the share name. Figure 5.4 shows the completed profile page for a Windows 9x domain user.

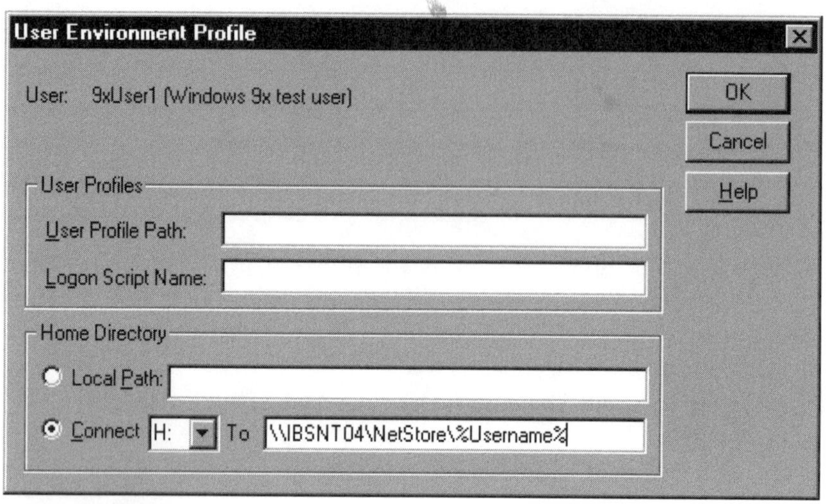

FIGURE 5.4 Windows 9x user profile setup

The next stage in the process is to create the profile for the Windows 9x user. This is accomplished on the Windows 9x workstation. When the user logs on to the domain from the workstation for the first time, he is asked whether or not he wants to save individual settings. The answer must be **Yes**. The local `\Profiles` folder is created under the `\%Windir%` folder as a result of the first profile-enabled user answering this question. The user's individual profile is saved in the usual way, as a subfolder of the main local `\%Windir%\Profiles` folder. When the user logs off, any settings are saved to the local copy of the profile. At this point, the server copy is created. The profile in its entirety exists as the folder structure and files within `\%Windir%\Profiles\%Username%`. This folder structure (starting from and including the `\%Username%` folder) is copied automatically to the network share that was entered as the user's home directory in *User Manager for Domains*. When the user next logs on, he will receive the copy of the profile stored on the network share; any changes made to the profile from this point on will be saved back to the network share.

Making the Windows 95 Profile Read-Only (Mandatory)

The Windows 95 roaming profile that you have just created can be made into a mandatory profile in a similar manner to the Windows NT profiles. A file named `User.dat` exists in the user's profile folder. Change the extension of this file from `.dat` to `.man` to make it a mandatory profile.

Summary

User profiles are a useful and often overlooked tool that can bring an element of order to the desktop environment. The management of user profiles has never been a simple task, largely because a real management tool for the feature is lacking.

On their own, user profiles do not form the formidable barrier that would be required to completely lock down the desktop, but they play an important role along with system policies in the overall strategy that you can use to control the desktop look and feel.

User profiles help to lower the total cost of ownership by providing users with an environment containing access to all of the applications and system facilities required for their job. The presentation of these facilities is uniform and configurable, so training costs are reduced for end users and unnecessary distractions are removed.

Central configuration and manipulation of desktops saves time and lowers costs through reduced administration overheads. This saving may be offset in the early stages, however, by the administrative effort required for the initial setup of user profiles.

Lab Exercises

Use the lab exercises that follow, progressively, to step through the whole process of profile building and maintenance.

Prerequisites

You should set up the environment for the labs in advance so that the processes can run smoothly. Some of the tasks required to build the lab environment may be well known to you, but look closely at the instructions to ensure that your environment is set up as required.

EQUIPMENT

- One NT 4.0 domain controller with 100 Mbytes of free disk space. The domain controller name for this lab will be **IBSNT04**.
- A network share created on the domain controller. Name this **NetStore**, and ensure that the group **Domain Users** has **Full Control** NTFS and share rights.
- One newly installed NT 4.0 Workstation. This should be a domain member. The name for our purposes will be **ZAKpc02**.

If the workstation is not newly installed, there may be already existing profiles, which may cause different results to be displayed for these labs than the ones included here.

USERS

- Administrator access to the domain controller.
- Administrator access to the local workstation.
- User account DomUser1 created on the domain.
- User account LocUser1 created on the local workstation. Leave the *Profile Path* empty.
- User account LocUser2 created on the local workstation. Leave the *Profile Path* empty.

OPTIONAL

If you are going to perform the Windows 95/98 profile setup, you will need to ensure the following:

- The ability to create a domain user named 9xUser1. Do not create the user at this point.
- A Windows 95 and/or Windows 98 installed computer.

Lab 1: Local Profiles

In this exercise, you will create a local profile on a workstation and make changes to the profile to see how they affect the desktop appearance. You will expose the effects that the Default User and the All Users profiles have on the desktop.

LOCAL PROFILE CREATION

1. Log on to the workstation **ZAKpc02** locally as user **LocUser1**. The user should receive a plain desktop environment that was copied from the local Default User profile.
2. Log off the local workstation to save the new local profile to a folder named **\LocUser1** located beneath the **\%Windir%\Profiles** folder.

CHECK THE LOCAL PROFILE

1. Log on to workstation **ZAKpc02** as Administrator.
2. Select **Settings** from the **Start** menu, and choose **Control Panel**.

3. Double-click on the **System** application.
4. Select the **User Profiles** tab. The list of profiles will include **LocUser1**.
5. **Exit** the **System Properties** screen.
6. Start Windows NT Explorer.
7. Navigate to the **\%Windir%\Profiles** folder (usually `C:\Winnt\Profiles`).
8. Look at the folders that exist here. Figure 5.5 lists the `\Profiles` folder containing the LocUser1 profile. Explorer is set to show hidden files in Figure 5.5.

AMEND THE LOCAL PROFILE

1. Log on to workstation **ZAKpc02** as **LocUser1**.
2. Open **Windows NT Explorer** so that the view is the same as that shown in Figure 5.5. You will have to set the Explorer viewing options to show hidden files.
3. Right-click on the computer's desktop, and select **New** > **Text Document**.
4. Enter the name of the new document as **TestDoc1.txt**.
5. Press Enter to confirm the name. As you do this, the document should appear in the **Desktop** folder under the **LocUser1** profile. You may have to select <F5> to refresh the view to see this.

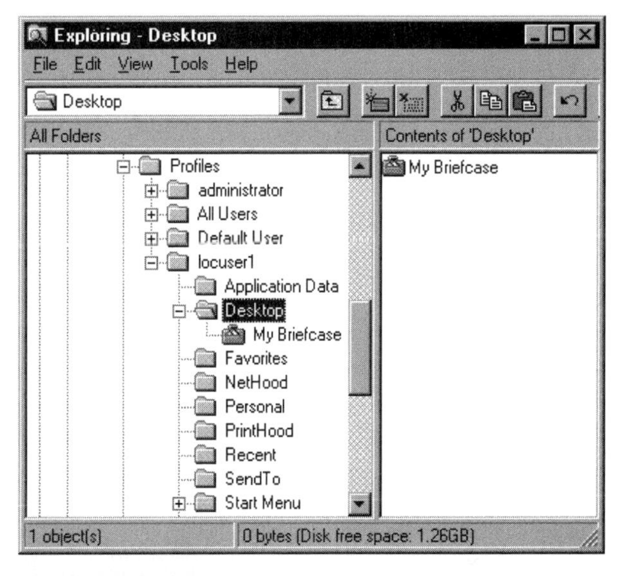

FIGURE 5.5 The local `\Profiles` folder now contains a `\LocUser1` subfolder

6. In Windows NT Explorer, double-click the **\LocUser1** folder in the node pane (left-hand side).
7. Select the **\Desktop** folder in the contents pane (right-hand side), then select **New** > **Text Document** from the **File** menu.
8. Name the new document **TestDoc2.txt** and confirm the name. The new document will appear on the user's desktop.

The link between the profiles folder structure and the look and feel of the desktop is demonstrated. There are no mysteries here; when you make changes to the desktop or the Start menu, you are actually making changes in the profiles folder structure.

DEFAULT USER PROFILE

1. Log on to workstation **ZAKpc02** as Administrator.
2. Open **Windows NT Explorer** and navigate to the **\%Windir%\Profiles** folder.
3. Delete the **LocUser1** profile folder structure.
4. Expand the **Default Users** profile structure and create a new text document in the **Desktop** subfolder. Call this document `This came from the Default User.txt`.
5. Log on locally as user **LocUser1**.

Note that the previously created document (`TestDoc2.txt`) is no longer on the desktop (it was removed along with the profile), and the document placed in the Default User profile is now on the desktop. Remember that the Default User profile is used to populate all new profiles, so any shortcuts, files, or documents placed in this folder structure will be used whenever a new profile is created. The Default User profile is copied at profile creation time only. If you were to go back and place another file in the `\Desktop` folder of the Default User profile, it would not appear in the LocUser1 profile. But don't take my word for it, try it yourself.

ALL USERS PROFILE

1. Log on to workstation **ZAKpc02** as Administrator.
2. Open **Windows NT Explorer** and navigate to the **\%Windir%\Profiles** folder.
3. Expand the **All Users** profile folder. The contents here are limited to **\Desktop** and **\Start Menu** subfolders.
4. Create a text document in the **\Desktop** folder named `This came from the All Users profile.txt`. When the name is confirmed, the document will appear on the desktop for the logged-on user (Administrator).
5. Log off and log on as **LocUser1**.

Note that the same document exists on the desktop of this user as well. All users logged on at the local machine will have access to this file, regardless of whether they are authenticated locally or logged on to the domain. The file is not duplicated; rather, the single copy is reflected on all desktops. If one user deletes the file, then it is gone for all users. A significant difference between this profile and the Default User profile is that the Default User profile is used once only, when a profile is created. The All Users profile is used constantly by all users who log on to the machine.

LAB 1 SUMMARY

Take some time to experiment with the possibilities that user profiles provide. Install some applications and see how the menu structure on the Start menu is reflected in the structure contained in the user's profile. Some applications developers place the shortcuts to programs in the All Users profile so that anyone can use them. Others place the shortcuts in the user's profile, and so they would not be available to the next person who logs on to the system.

Important: When you have finished experimenting with this profile, log on as Administrator locally on computer ZAKpc02 and delete the LocUser1 profile folder structure. Log back on locally to the workstation as LocUser1 to create a fresh profile for the next lab.

Lab 2: Roaming and Mandatory Profiles

In this exercise, you will convert a local profile into a roaming profile. You will then create a user and assign the profile to that user. In the last part of the lab, you will change the roaming profile to a mandatory profile, looking at how this change affects the user.

CONVERT A LOCAL PROFILE TO A ROAMING PROFILE

1. Log on to the domain as Administrator from **ZAKpc02**.
2. Select **Settings** from the **Start** menu and choose **Control Panel**.
3. Double-click on the **System** application.
4. Select the **User Profiles** tab.
5. Select the **LocUser1** profile and choose **Copy To**.
6. Enter **IBSNT04\NetStore\RomProf1**.
7. Select the **Change** button in the **Permitted to use** box.
8. Select **Domain Users**.
9. Select **Add** > **OK**.
10. Select **OK** to begin copying the profile.

The local profile has now been copied to the server and is available as a roaming profile for all members of the Domain Users group because of the permissions set here. The local profile structure is mirrored on the server; you can check by using Windows NT Explorer. At this point, you have a roaming profile that has not been assigned to any users.

ESTABLISH A USER ACCOUNT TO ACCESS A ROAMING PROFILE

1. Log on to the domain controller locally as Administrator and start **User Manager for Domains**.
2. Double-click the user **DomUser1**.
3. Select the **Profiles** button.
4. In the **Profile Path** box, enter **IBSNT04\NetStore\RomProf1**.
5. Select **OK** to confirm the changes.
6. Log on to the domain from computer **ZAKpc02** as user **DomUser1**. The loaded profile should contain the document `This came from the Default User.txt`. This document was added to the local profile previously from the Default User profile and was copied to the roaming profile along with all other local profile settings. The file `This came from the All Users profile.txt` should appear on the desktop as well because anybody logged on locally will receive it.
7. Log on to the domain from another PC as user DomUser1. The file `This came from the All Users profile.txt` should *not* appear; it is provided locally from ZAKpc02 and so is not available here. The file `This came from the Default Users profile.txt` will appear because it was incorporated into the user's profile at creation time and then sent up to the roaming profile location. Figure 5.6 displays the resulting look.

MAKE A ROAMING PROFILE READ-ONLY (MANDATORY)

1. Log on to the domain controller as Administrator.
2. Using Windows NT Explorer, navigate to the folder **IBSNT04\NetStore\RomProf1**.
3. Select **Folder Options** from the **View** menu.
4. Select the **View** tab.
5. Make sure that the **Hide file extensions for known file types** button is *not* selected to ensure that all file extensions are shown in Explorer.
6. Select **OK**.
7. Right-click the file **NTuser.dat**, and select **Rename**.
8. Change the file extension from **.dat** to **.man**. When the rename is committed, the profile becomes read-only (mandatory).

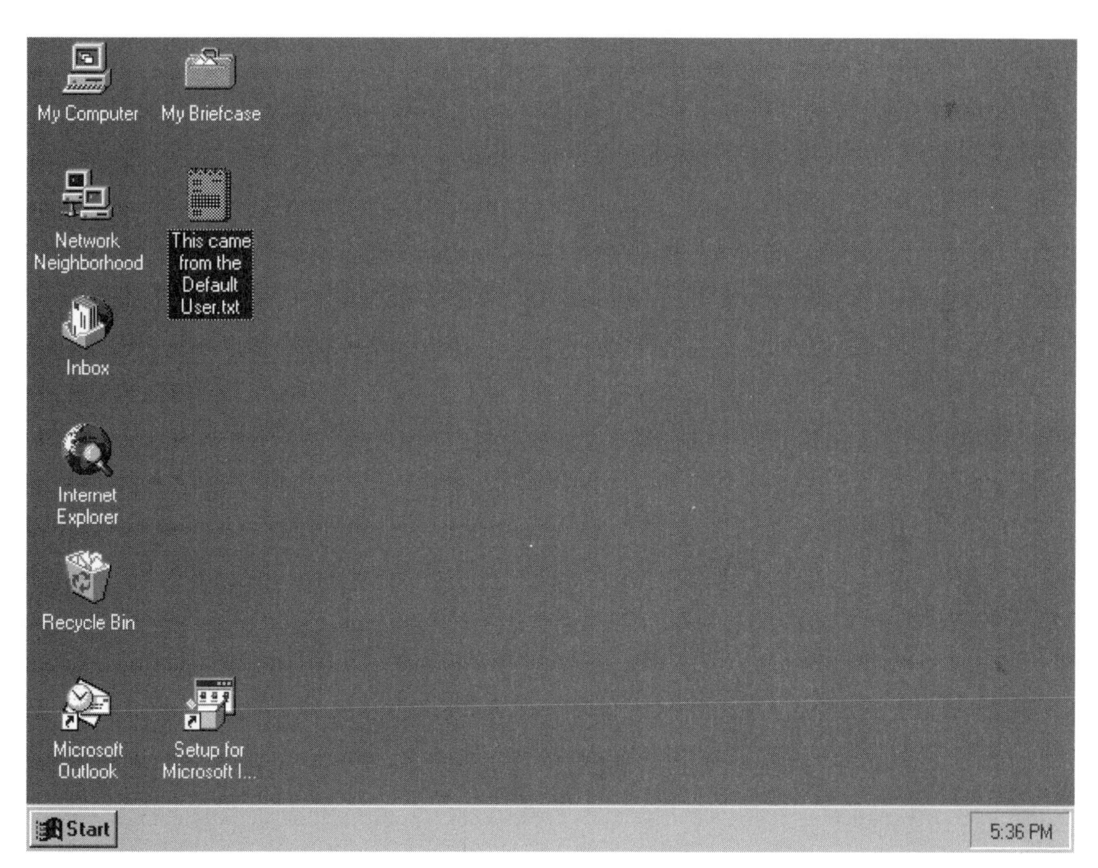

FIGURE 5.6 Profile for DomUser1 displays only the Default User text file on all other machines

9. Log on to the domain from computer **ZAKpc02** as user **DomUser1**.
10. Add a text document to the desktop.
11. Log off, and log back on to the domain from computer **ZAKpc02** as user **DomUser1**. The text file is not displayed.

The text file does not appear when you log off and log back on because changes to the desktop look and feel are not saved when a profile is mandatory.

At this moment, if the read-only profile was not available for some reason, you would still be able to log on, using the locally cached version of the profile.

MAKE A ROAMING PROFILE REQUIRED (MANDATORY)

1. Log on to the domain controller as Administrator.
2. Using Windows NT Explorer, navigate to the folder **\\IBSNT04\NetStore**.
3. Right-click the **RomProf1** folder, and select **Rename**.
4. Add the file extension **.man** to the folder name. The resulting folder name is **\\IBSNT04\NetStore\RomProf1.man**.
5. Start **User Manager for Domains**.
6. Double-click user **DomUser1**.
7. Select the **Profiles** button.
8. In the **Profile Path**, enter **\\IBSNT04\NetStore\RomProf1.man**.
9. Select **OK** and then **OK** again to confirm.
10. Log on to the domain from computer **ZAKpc02** as user **DomUser1**. The logon will be successful, and the desktop will look as it did in Figure 5.6. Log off again.
11. On the domain controller, rename the **\\IBSNT04\NetStore\RomProf1.man** folder to **\\IBSNT04\NetStore\RomTest1.man**.
12. Log on to the domain from computer **ZAKpc02** as user **DomUser1**. The logon will fail with the message `the operating system is not able to log you on because your roaming mandatory profile is not available. Please contact your network administrator.`
13. Rename the profile on the domain controller so that it is back to **\\IBSNT04\NetStore\RomProf1.man**.

The logon failed in this case because the user account has been set up to *require* a profile. When the defined profile is unavailable for any reason (in this case it was renamed), the user is refused permission to log on to the domain. It is the action of placing the `.man` extension to the **Profile path** in *User Manager for Domains* that specifies "this is the profile path; if this path is unavailable, do not allow the user to log on."

LAB 2 SUMMARY

The main difference between local profiles and roaming profiles is the availability of a roaming profile at any domain computer. Settings held within the two types of profiles can be exactly the same.

Mandatory profiles can be useful if you need to place severe restrictions on the desktop environment. Using mandatory profiles, you can make the profile read-only or both read-only and required.

Lab 3: Windows 9x Profiles

In this exercise, you will enable a Windows 95 machine to accept user profiles from a central storage point. In the final part of the exercise, you will create the profile itself.

ENABLE WINDOWS 9X PROFILES

1. Select **Settings** from the **Start** menu.
2. Select **Control Panel**.
3. Run the **Passwords** applet.
4. Select the **User Profiles** tab.
5. Select the **Users can customize their preferences** radio button.
6. In the **User Profiles Settings** box, choose the options that you wish to enable.
7. Select **OK** to confirm the settings. You must reboot the system before profiles are enabled.

The ability of the local computer to use profiles must be switched on for Windows 9x machines, where they are disabled by default.

SET THE PRIMARY LOGON

1. Select **Settings** from the **Start** menu.
2. Select **Control Panel**.
3. Run the **Networks** applet.
4. Ensure that the **Primary Network Logon** is set to **Client for Microsoft Networks**.
5. Double-click the **Client for Microsoft Networks** service, and ensure that the radio button **Log onto a Windows NT Domain** is checked and the correct domain name is entered.
6. Select **OK**. If changes were made, you must reboot to enable them.

You must direct the Windows 9x machine to the authentication domain and ensure the correct client software is used during the logon process.

USER SETUP IN THE DOMAIN

1. Log on to the domain controller as Administrator and start **User Manager for Domains**.
2. Select **New User** from the **User** menu.
3. Enter the username **9xUser1** and password details for the new user.
4. Select the **Profiles** button.

5. Ensure the **Profiles Path** is empty.
6. In the **Home Directory** section, select a drive letter for a home directory. Use drive **H:** for this lab.
7. For the home directory location, enter the path to the network share `\\IBSNT04\NetStore`. Append the user name to the end of the path. The resulting entry should be **\\IBSNT04\NetStore\%Username%.**
8. Select **OK**.
9. Select **Add** to add the user. The home directory should be created automatically. Under certain circumstances, this will not happen and a message will ask you to create it manually. Remember to give the correct permissions if you have to create the home directory.
10. Select **Close**.

CREATE THE PROFILE

1. Log on to the Windows 9x workstation as user 9xUser1. The following is displayed: `You have not logged on here before [since the profile settings were enabled], would you like to retain individual settings for use later.`
2. Answer **Yes**. The local `\%Windir%\Profiles` folder is created along with the user's local profile.
3. Enter the password confirmation if this is the first time this user has logged on to this machine.
4. Make any required changes to the profile.
5. Log off; the changes will be saved to the local profiles folder.
6. Use Windows Explorer on the workstation to copy the entire **\%Windir\Profiles\9xUser1** folder and contents to the **H:** drive.

The next time the user logs on, he will receive the profile copy that is stored on the `H:` drive. All updates will be copied to this profile at logoff time.

LAB 3 SUMMARY

Windows 9x profiles are not compatible in any way with Windows NT profiles. Superficially the folder structure may look similar, but the real difference is in the registry structure contained in the (NT)`user.xxx` files. Registry structures are completely incompatible between Windows 9x and Windows NT, so profiles from one system cannot be used on the other.

S I X

System Policies

In This Chapter

This chapter looks at system policies. These policies control the look and feel of a desktop and also control system settings on a per-machine basis. This functionality complements similar functionality drawn from user profiles.

The ZAK uses a combination of system policies and user profiles to bring control to the user desktop. This control enables you to reduce costs by reducing the chances for user-caused problems to occur. The downside of this type of control is the initial overhead of implementation.

The chapter looks at system policies in general with no specific reference to the policy files and templates provided with the ZAK. It is important to have an overall view and understanding of what can be accomplished with system policies and the default offering of Windows NT before looking at the specifics of the ZAK. All of the behind-the-scenes portions of the policy editor such as template files and group priorities are discussed.

Introduction

System policies are made up from a set of registry entries that control the computer resources available to a user or group of users. These registry entries can be applied to individual users, groups of users, or individual machines regardless of the logged-on user.

System policies can control access to many different resources on the local machine. Desktop settings and user access to resources can be controlled easily. Settings, such as the contents of the *Start* menu, and access to system tools, such as registry editors, are examples of the controls you can apply.

System policies are defined with the Policy Editor tool, `Poledit.exe`. This program is not installed on an NT system by default and needs to be loaded according to the instructions in the next section. `Poledit.exe` is a graphical user tool that presents an easy-to-use browser list of available settings.

You may be forgiven for wondering about the differences between user profiles and system policies. In reality, many of the settings that can be controlled by user profiles can also be set in system policies. System policies can contain far more machine-specific settings than user profiles. Another difference between the two methods of system control is the way in which they are applied.

When a user profile is applied, registry settings are changed in the `HKEY_USERS` registry hive for any portions relevant to the user. The system policy settings are made to the same registry hive for users, and to the `HKEY_LOCAL_MACHINE` hive for computer-specific settings. When you apply a system policy that contains settings that may conflict with profile settings, the policy settings overwrite the profile settings in the registry. This gives the ultimate control of the available settings back to the Administrator, even if users are allowed to change their own user profile settings.

System policies can be applied to all users, individual users, groups of users, all computers, and individual computers.

Policy Editor Installation

The system policy editor is shipped on all Windows NT 4.0 Server CDs, although it can be installed on Windows NT 4.0 Workstation as well. A policy editor is provided on the Windows 9x CD media also.

For a Windows NT 4.0 Server installation, copy the template files (`.adm` files) found on the Server CD in `\Clients\Srvtools\Winnt\I386` to the `\%SystemRoot%\Inf` folder, which is a hidden folder by default. Copy the `Poledit.exe` file to the `\%SystemRoot%` folder, and copy the `Poledit.cnt` and `Poledit.hlp` files from the same source to the `\%SystemRoot%\Help` folder. Once you have created a shortcut for the program on your desktop, you are ready to use it. Note that the files do not need to be copied to the exact locations shown above and can even be used from a remote location, but a nondefault installation may need further changes, such as environment variables.

For a Windows NT 4.0 Workstation installation, you follow the same procedure as that shown above for Server. The files are copied locally to the workstation. You can also run a batch file from the Server CD, which is \I386\Clients\Srvtools\Winnt\Setup.bat. Use this file to install the client-based server tools locally to the workstation. The tool set includes the policy editor. Again, once a shortcut is created to the Poledit.exe program, you are ready to use it.

The Windows 9x policy editor installation is slightly more involved than the previous two. Files cannot simply be copied. The installation process must be run in its entirety. You must run the Windows setup process to add a program; use the Add/Remove Programs applet of Control Panel. Select Have Disk, and select the X:\Admin\Apptools\Poledit option, where X: is the drive letter for your Windows 9x media. To get full functionality, select both Group Policies and System Policy Editor when prompted. When you select Install, files are copied and the installation is complete.

The system policy editor that is shipped with Windows 95 is not capable of loading more than one template file at a time. To get this increased functionality, use the policy editor program files from a Windows NT machine. You also need to run the files locally because the local operating system determines which type of policy file is created. Policy files are not compatible between Windows 9x and Windows NT.

Policy Editor Modes

There are two different ways to use the policy editor; registry mode and file mode. The most common method for using the policy editor is in file mode.

Registry Mode

In registry mode, the policy editor acts as a user-friendly interface into the registry settings exposed by the tool. Changes made in this mode are made directly into the registry. So, you could use the tool as a means of exposing only those settings that you wish to modify and then use the tool in place of the more powerful registry editor.

File Mode

File mode uses a safer method of achieving the same results as registry mode. File mode allows you to change registry settings but does not implement them in real time. Instead, the changes are saved to a policy file, which can be applied to any number of machines at a later date. A default policy file can be saved on a domain controller (and replicated to all other validating servers) so that it is loaded as users log on to the domain. Windows 9x machines have a different registry format that is not compatible with Windows NT machines. The Windows 9x policy file is saved in ASCII format, and the Windows NT 4.0 policy is saved in Unicode format. Therefore, any policy file created on a Windows 9x machine cannot be applied to a Windows NT machine (and vice versa), and you must use the policy editor natively on the target operating system to manipulate policy files on each of the two systems.

Exposed Settings Types

The types of settings exposed by the policy editor can be grouped into two main categories: those applied to users regardless of the machine logged on to and those applied to computers regardless of the logged-on user. There is an area of crossover where the same setting can be made for both user and computer. In this case, the settings applied to the user take precedence.

User-Related Settings

The settings applied to users allow registry entries to be made to control such things as system display settings, control panel availability, wallpaper settings, and use of the registry editor. These settings can be applied for all users, for a single user, or for groups of users. The settings are applied after the computer-specific settings.

Computer-Related Settings

The computer settings grouping allows registry entries to be made to control such things as Custom Shared Folders, SMMP settings, Remote Access settings, and Logon banner settings. These are all made on a computer-by-computer basis and are not affected by the user logging on to the machine. These registry settings are applied before the user gains control of the system and so cannot be affected by the user.

An Overview of the Policy Editor Tool

The policy editor for Windows NT and Windows 9x presents a graphical interface into many of the areas of the registry that control the look and behavior of the desktop environment. The registry editing tools that can be used to accomplish the same tasks as the policy editor do not provide the user with a friendly interface and are more difficult to use in general. Still, be careful when using the policy editor. A change committed here may be applied to a production system, and, as with any registry change, you should be aware of the effect before applying it.

Before the policy editor can be used it must be installed correctly. The installation is discussed above; the discussion is continued in the lab exercises at the end of the chapter.

To start the policy editor, simply double-click on the policy editor shortcut or choose **Start** > **Run** > **Poledit.exe** after you have installed the program. The policy editor starts up, but no policy is loaded. Figure 6.1 shows the system policy editor at startup and the available File menu options.

Figures 6.2 and 6.3 show the available options in the Edit and Options menus, respectively.

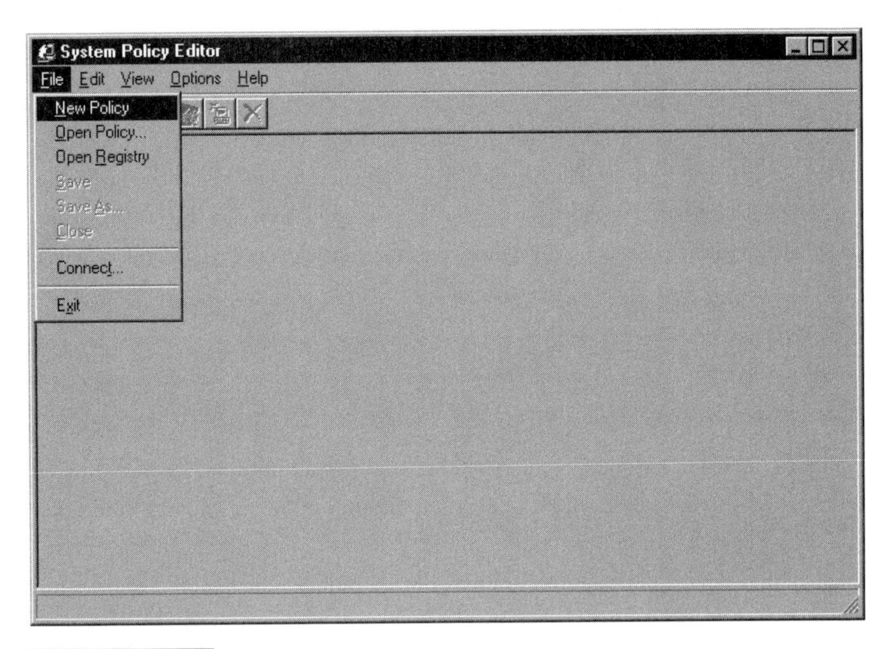

FIGURE 6.1 System policy editor and the available File menu options

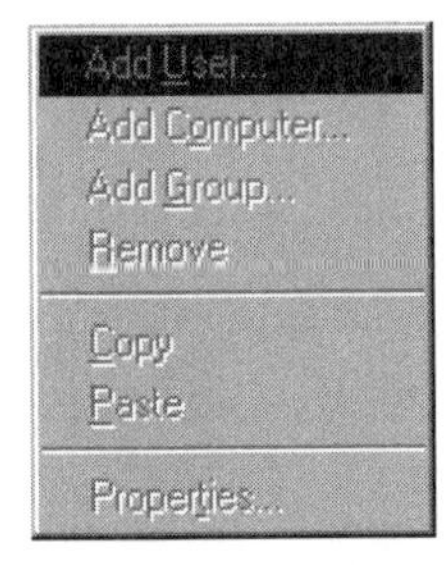

FIGURE 6.2 System policy editor available Edit menu options

FIGURE 6.3 System policy editor available Options menu options

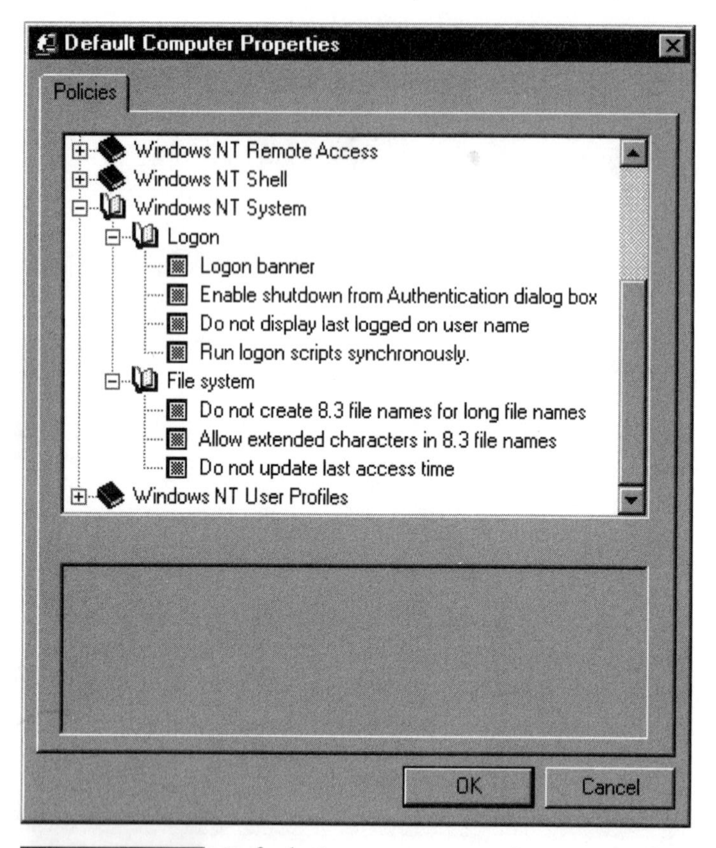

FIGURE 6.4 Default Computer properties page in the system policy editor

Categories

Each portion of the policy that you are configuring is made up from parts known as Categories. These are headings and subheadings that logically group similar available settings. Each main category contains one or more subcategories or one or more actual available settings. Figure 6.4 shows the *Default Computer* portion of a policy with the *Windows NT System* category expanded to show two subcategories (Logon and File system) and seven available policy settings.

Policy Settings

The policy settings contained within the categories described above actually map to one or more registry keys, where the setting of registry values takes place. You enable the policy value by selecting the square check box preceding the policy description. The three available settings are:

- ☑ **Checked box**. Activates the setting in the policy that you are configuring. The registry key is activated (or added and activated if it does not already exist).
- ☐ **Blank box**. Deactivates the setting from the policy that you are configuring. The registry key is added if it is needed and set to off.
- ▩ **Grayed box**. Excludes the setting from the configuration. Whatever the current setting in the registry is (at the time that the policy is implemented on a machine) remains the same. If the key doesn't exist, it is not created. If the key exists, the setting is not changed.

It is important to understand the difference between deactivated and excluded. When policies are applied, a user can take settings from many different sources. If a user belongs to a group that has a defined policy, and there is also a defined Default User policy then settings may conflict. If this happens, the policies are applied in a specific order, as described later in the chapter. If a key in the first applied policy is set as activated and the second applied policy has the key set to deactivate, then the key will be deactivated, overriding the first setting. If, however, the second policy had the key set as excluded, this would leave the setting as activated because the excluded setting leaves the key untouched. Remember this distinction and think about what you are trying to achieve. Do you care what a key value is set to? If not, leave it as excluded. If you do, specifically set it to activated or deactivated as necessary.

Template Files

Template files are text-based files that gather together similar groups of registry settings and expose these settings in a user-friendly interface. The template files govern how the categories, subcategories, and policy keys are displayed. They govern the order in which items are displayed as well as the connection between a setting entry shown in a category and the actual registry key(s) manipulated when the setting is amended. These template files are named in a `*Filename*.adm` format and are usually placed in the `\%SystemRoot%\inf` folder (which is hidden by default). Part of the manual installation procedure for the policy editor is to copy the template files from the source to this destination folder.

Default NT Templates

Windows NT comes with a set of default template files—`Winnt.adm`, `Windows.adm` and `Common.adm`—that can be loaded and used to build policy files for your organization.

WINNT.ADM

The default `Winnt` template file contains computer and user categories and keys that can be set only for a Windows NT 4.0 system. This file is loaded by default when the Windows NT version of the policy editor is first started up. This template file and custom template files are discussed later in this chapter.

WINDOWS.ADM

The default `Windows` template file contains computer and user categories and keys that can only be set for a Windows 95 system. This file is not loaded by default in the Windows NT version of the policy editor and is not covered in any more detail in this chapter.

COMMON.ADM

The default `Common` template file contains computer and user categories and keys that are common to both of the operating systems mentioned above. To be included in this template file, a registry key must have exactly the same name in both systems and have the same supported values.

The support for common registry entries is a throwback to the desire to synchronize the two registry structures in the Windows 95 and Windows NT operating systems. This goal was never achieved, and so you are left with two registry structures that are completely incompatible but have entries with the same name, that control the same feature, and that have the same available settings.

File Structure

Policy editor template files are flat ASCII files that can be opened and edited with a text editor such as Notepad or Wordpad. The key to how registry information is exposed is contained in the structure of the template files. Simple mistakes such as spelling errors can render a template file unusable until the error is corrected. Syntax errors will prevent the template file from loading at policy editor startup time when the structure is checked for consistency. Figure 6.5 shows an example of this type of error.

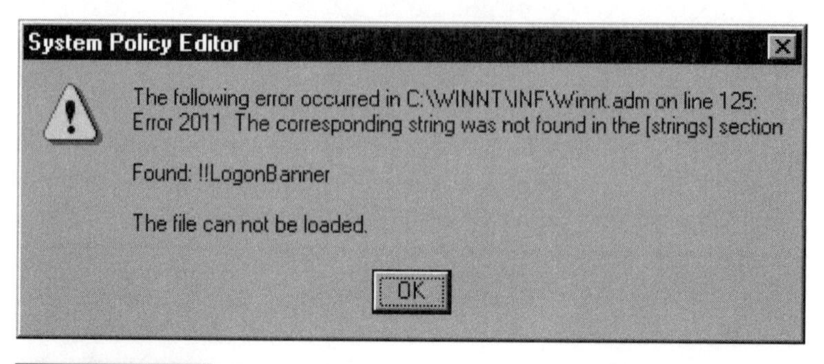

FIGURE 6.5 Syntax errors are a common problem in user-created template files

The error messages in the policy editor do give you sufficient information to find the problem and fix it.

Example 6.1 is an edited extract from the `Winnt.adm` template file.

EXAMPLE 6.1 Extract from the `Winnt.adm` template file

```
CLASS MACHINE


CATEGORY  !!Printers
KEYNAME System\CurrentControlSet\Control\Print
          POLICY !!PrintManager_Browser_Restrict
          VALUENAME  DisableServerThread
          PART !!Disable_Server_Tip1                   TEXT
          END PART
          PART !!Disable_Server_Tip2                   TEXT
          END PART
          END POLICY

          POLICY !!Scheduler_Thread_Priority
          PART !!Scheduler_Priority                    DROPDOWNLIST
          VALUENAME SchedulerThreadPriority
             ITEMLIST
                NAME "Above Normal"  VALUE NUMERIC  1
                NAME "Normal"        VALUE NUMERIC  0
                NAME "Below Normal"  VALUE NUMERIC  -1
             END ITEMLIST
          END PART
          END POLICY

          POLICY !!Beep_Enabled
          VALUENAME BeepEnabled
                VALUEOFF NUMERIC 0
          PART !!Beep_Tip1                             TEXT    END PART
          PART !!Beep_Tip2                             TEXT    END PART
          END POLICY
END CATEGORY

[Strings]
Printers="Windows NT Printers"
PrintManager_Browser_Restrict="Disable browse thread on this computer"
Disable_Server_Tip1="When this box is checked, the print spooler does not"
Disable_Server_Tip2="send shared printer information to other print servers."
Scheduler_Thread_Priority="Scheduler priority"
Scheduler_Priority="Priority"
```

```
Thread_Priority_Above_Normal="Scheduler priority above normal"
Thread_Priority_Below_Normal="Scheduler priority below normal"
Thread_Priority_Normal="Scheduler priority normal"
Beep_Enabled="Beep for error enabled"
Beep_Tip1="A check in this box enables beeping (every 10 seconds) when a remote"
Beep_Tip2="job error occurs on a print server."
```

The extract from the template file shown above can be used to expose registry settings in the policy editor. If the extract were to be placed in a text file named with a `.adm` extension and loaded into the policy editor, the settings would look like those in Figure 6.6.

Keywords and values make up the first part of the template file. While discussing the different sections of the template file, we refer to the screen shot in Figure 6.6 and the extract in Example 6.1.

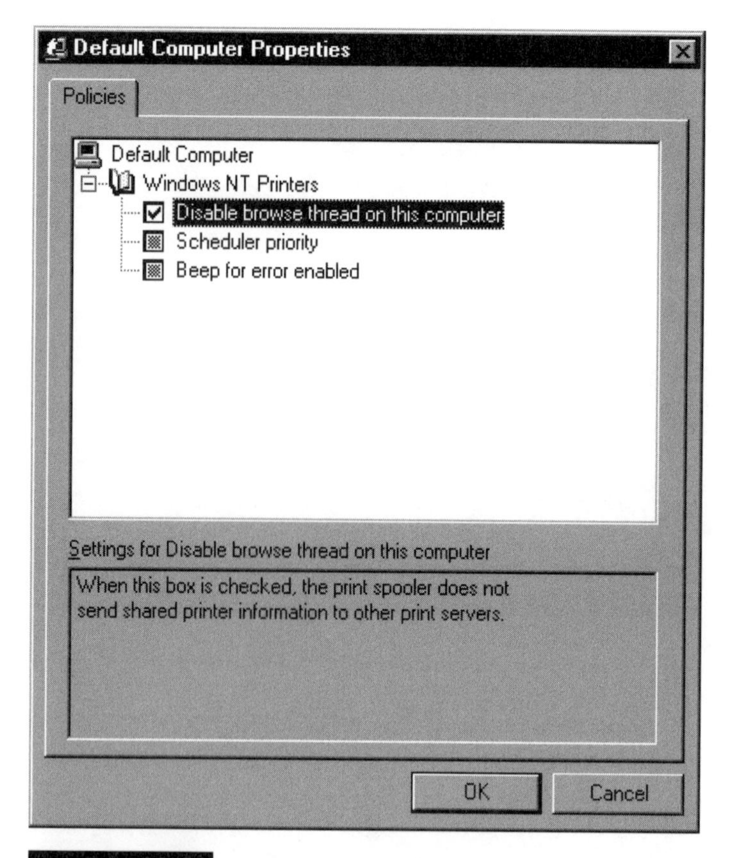

FIGURE 6.6 The corresponding policy exposure for Example 6.1

CLASS

The first entry in the file is the `CLASS` keyword. This keyword can only be set to one of two values, `MACHINE` or `USER`.

`MACHINE` is used as the class when you want all of the entries that follow to be part of a Computer policy. `USER` is the class when all of the entries that follow are part of a User policy.

Once a `CLASS` statement has set the focus, all following statements are set to be part of that particular class. You can change the focus by adding a further `CLASS` statement.

CATEGORY

The `CATEGORY` keyword opens a new section in the policy properties screen or further subdivides a section already opened. In Example 6.1, the `CATEGORY` keyword `!!Printers` corresponds to the *Windows NT Printers* category shown in Figure 6.6. Categories can have more categories nested within them in a familiar programming structure. The main rule with categories is that they should all have a corresponding `END CATEGORY` statement.

TEXT STRING

If you look at the text string that immediately follows the `CATEGORY` keyword in Example 6.1, you will see that it is `!!Printers`. The `!!` symbols signify that there is a string definition for this entry in the `[Strings]` section. Follow the listing down to the `[Strings]` section, where you will see the entry: `Printers="Windows NT Printers"`. This is where the `Windows NT Printers` category title comes from in Figure 6.6. Text strings localize the definitions to one area so that the programming portion of the file is less complex to look at. Also, when you make changes to text strings, they only have to be changed once in the `[Strings]` section to be reflected throughout the exposed template, centralizing one component of the maintenance.

KEYNAME

The `KEYNAME` points to the registry key that corresponds to the setting that is exposed. The policy editor makes changes in only two registry hives, and the definition of the `CLASS` keyword points to which hive should be amended, so the `KEYNAME` does not contain a hive name.

POLICY

The `POLICY` keyword provides an option in the policy screen that can be selected for configuration. It is identified with another text string that translates in the `[Scripts]` section to a meaningful label. As with the `CATEGORY` keyword, `POLICY` keywords require a corresponding `END POLICY` statement.

VALUENAME

The VALUENAME keyword contains the actual name of the registry value that should be amended for this option, as it appears in the registry.

PART

The PART keyword places text information, drop-down lists, or dialog boxes in the lower part of the policy editor screen. These can convey context-sensitive help or can accept user input when registry values are required. The PART keyword for drop-down lists and input values comes before the corresponding VALUENAME keyword and must finish with a corresponding END PART statement.

In Figure 6.6, PART keywords are used to display the two lines of text in the bottom half of the policy editor screen.

PART *VALUE*

Value is a flag that is placed on the end of a PART statement to denote the type of information contained in PART. Several options are shown below.

TEXT • The TEXT flag only displays text and can be used as context-sensitive help. The text can be displayed when the option is highlighted.

NUMERIC • The NUMERIC flag causes the value to be written to the registry with the data type of REG_DWORD. You need to know what data type the registry value can hold before setting these flags.

DROPDOWNLIST • The DROPDOWNLIST flag provides exactly what you would expect. The list syntax is shown below in an extract from the fuller listing provided at the beginning of this section.

```
PART !!Scheduler_Priority                               DROPDOWNLIST
       VALUENAME SchedulerThreadPriority
              ITEMLIST
                     NAME "Above Normal"                VALUE NUMERIC  1
                     NAME "Normal"                      VALUE NUMERIC  0
                     NAME "Below Normal"                VALUE NUMERIC  -1
              END ITEMLIST
       END PART
```

The text for the drop-down items is defined by the NAME statement. The data values that would be entered into the registry are associated with each option: in this case, the numbers 1, 0, and -1.

EDITTEXT • The EDITTEXT flag denotes that the data type for the selected registry value is REG_SZ.

REQUIRED • The REQUIRED flag does not allow the option to be selected without a corresponding value being entered. An error message is generated if no value is entered; the user must either enter a value or deselect the option.

EXPANDABLETEXT • The EXPANDABLETEXT flag denotes that the data type for the selected registry value is REG_EXPAND_SZ.

MAXLEN • The MAXLEN flag specifies the maximum length of a text input.

DEFAULT • The DEFAULT flag specifies the default value for numeric or text input.

MIN AND MAX • The MIN and MAX flags denote the minimum and maximum values allowed for a numeric field.

VALUEOFF

The VALUEOFF keyword is used in conjunction with the VALUE keyword and provides the actual registry value when the corresponding policy option is set to OFF. In code Example 6.1, the Valuename !!Beep_Enabled represents the registry value \HKLM\ System\CurrentControlSet\Control\Print\Beep_Enabled. The VALUEOFF keyword is set to 0 for this VALUE. Therefore, this keyword is set so that if the setting is disabled, the value 0 is placed in the registry.

VALUEON

The VALUEON keyword is used in conjunction with the VALUE keyword and provides the actual registry value when the corresponding policy option is set to ON.

[STRINGS]

The template file ends with a section where all string definitions are made. For every entry in the template file preceded by double exclamation marks (!!), there should be a corresponding definition for the string value. More string values can be defined here to correspond with entries made previously in the file.

Building Custom Template Files

You can build your own template files to expose registry settings that are not normally available to the policy editor. You may wish to do this so that you can include extra security-related settings in a policy that can be implemented across the domain, or you may wish to include registry settings for an application that does not have its own policy template. An outline for creating your own template files is set out below. Make sure you are comfortable with the layout of the template files and the keyword uses before proceeding.

- Make a list of the registry key that you want to include in your template, along with all supported values and data types involved.
- Start a new template file in Notepad, or open a *copy* of an existing file and remove most of the entries, leaving just enough information to help you lay out the file properly.
- Enter the required information in the proper format. This is by far the most difficult part of building the template file.
- Test the template file by trying to load it into the policy editor. Do this often and fix problems before adding more functionality.
- Build up the functionality of your policy template step by step and test the template in between each stage.
- Test the finished, loaded policy on the local registry of a machine that you can afford to destroy. This is no idle statement. Mistakes in syntax are found by the policy editor at load time. Mistakes in registry settings are not found until they are applied and possibly kill the system.
- Last but not least, make sure you understand the registry before attempting this type of exercise. A custom-made policy can bring great benefit to your organization by allowing you to apply controlled measures to restrict unwarranted activity. If it exists as a registry key in the `HKEY_LOCAL_MACHINE` or `HKEY_USERS` registry hives and it can be amended with `Regedt32.exe`, then it can be controlled by this program with a custom template file. Take some time to browse through these registry hives and look at the number of entries here.

NTconfig/Config Policy Files

Recall that the most common mode of operation for the policy editor is file mode. When you use the editor in this mode, you will eventually have to save the settings to a file. You can use the resulting policy file to apply settings to any user logging on to the domain or any Windows NT machine being used to log on to the domain.

Both Windows NT 4.0 systems and Windows 9x systems that connect to the domain receive policy updates by default in what is known as *automatic mode*. This means that they automatically look for a policy file on the `Netlogon` share of the validating server with a file name of `NTconfig.pol` for NT systems and `Config.pol` for Windows 9x systems. If you are using any of the standard domain structures, this setting will work well. All Windows NT or 9x workstations that belong to a domain go to this network share by default to look for a policy. Some circumstances may require the use of another location (such as applying a policy to a machine that is part of a workgroup and so doesn't use an authenticating server), so *manual mode* is available where the location and file name for the policy files can be redefined.

If you choose to leave the policy update mode as automatic, then you must ensure that the policy file is replicated either automatically by the replication service or manually to all validating servers. If the policy file is not available for some reason, you may find that a user profile overrides a previously set policy definition and the resulting user access could cause problems.

Individual User and Group Policies

You can apply policy settings to individual users and groups of users instead of to all users by defining a user or group with the **Edit** > **Add User** or **Add Group** options in the policy editor and defining the details of the policy assignee. All settings are defined in the same way; the only difference is that settings defined here only apply to the one named user or group. When using groups as the assignee, you must either browse for a group that exists in the domain or enter the name exactly as defined in the domain. Figure 6.7 shows the Add User dialog box for the policy editor.

Prioritizing Between Multiple Groups

Group priorities help resolve conflicts that may arise when a conflicting setting is made in multiple groups and a user belongs to all of those groups. To assign priorities, you arrange the groups that have defined policies in some

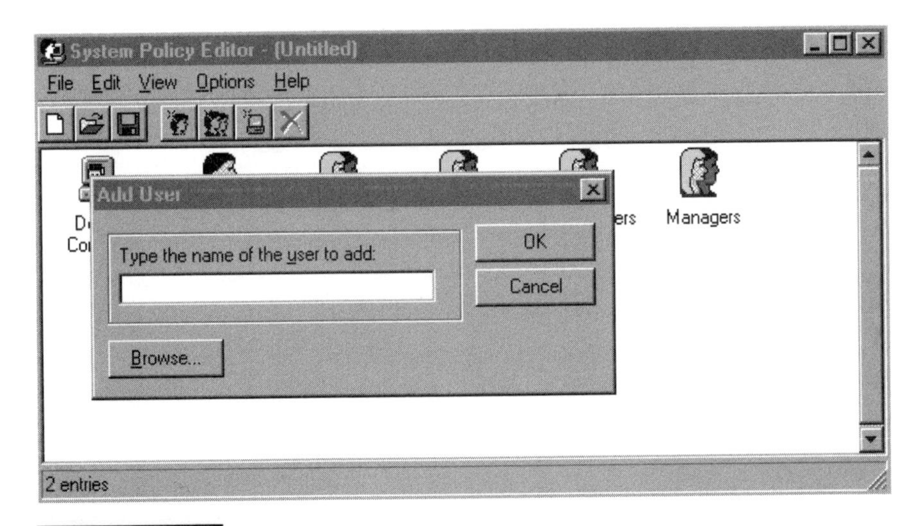

FIGURE 6.7 Add User dialog box in `Poledit.exe`

sort of hierarchical order by using the **Options** > **Group Priority** setting in the policy editor and by moving groups up or down the hierarchy. The group policy that is at the foot of the list is applied before other group policies, and the list is ascended until the highest-priority group policy is applied. This means that any conflicting settings may be overwritten by the next policy in the list to be applied. Figure 6.8 shows the group priority dialog box for a sample policy file.

Saving the Policy

While you are making changes to the policy file, you may want to save the policy file regularly. Simply use the **File** > **Save** or **Save As** options to place the settings in a policy file. The name and the location of the policy file depend on how you have decided to apply the file to your users. The default name for a Windows NT policy file is `NTconfig.pol`, and for Windows 9x it is `Config.pol`. The files are placed on the domain `Netlogon` share so that they are available to all users as they logon.

Use the second option for saving the files when you set the policy to be updated in manual mode. If this is the case, then you should name the policy file to meet your needs and place it in the location defined as your manual update folder. Manual mode is rarely used for policies; avoid it unless your needs are specific enough to require its use.

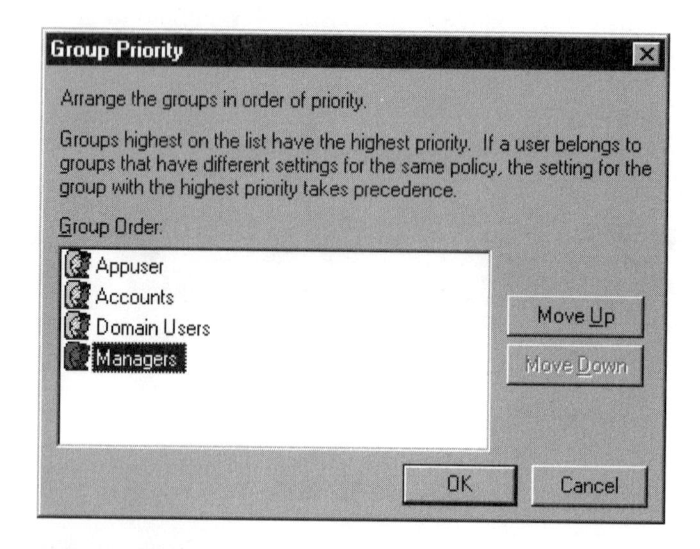

FIGURE 6.8 Group priority dialog box

How Policy Conflicts Are Resolved

System policies offer a flexible means of applying registry settings. The same setting may be available for both computer and user applications. You may decide to apply settings to individual users, to groups of users, and also to all users. Settings could be applied to individual computers as well as all computers. With these various options at hand, some settings can be applied more than once. For example, you may apply a setting that bars all users from running registry editing tools. You may also make the setting for the individual Administrator user but set this so the registry editing tools are allowed. These settings may also be set in the user profile. So you need a hierarchy to ensure that the settings you intend to be applied are actually made and not overwritten.

Computer Policies

Policy settings can be implemented for computers in one of two ways. They are applied either through a Default Computer policy or through a named computer policy. This is best illustrated by the example setting shown in Figure 6.9, *Do not display last logged on user name*.

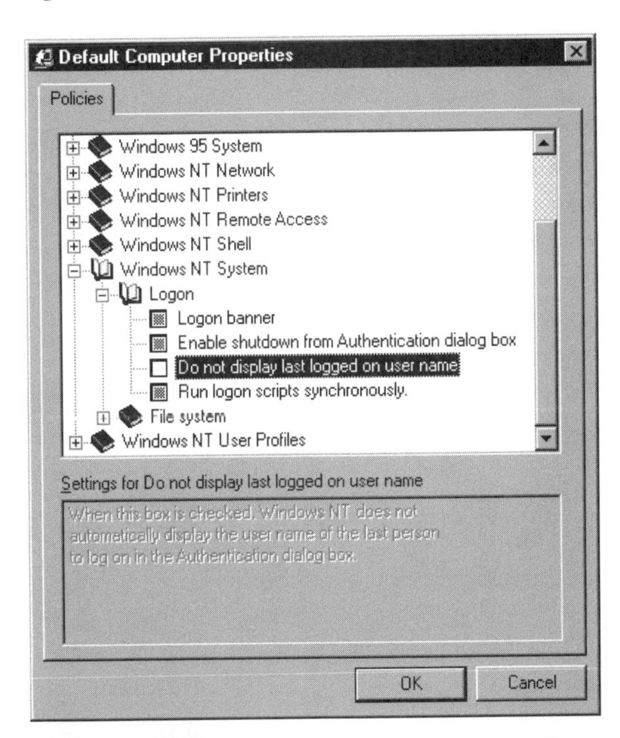

FIGURE 6.9 Default Computer settings allow the last logged on user name to be displayed

The setting in Figure 6.9 is set in the Default Computer Properties screen. This setting will be applied to all machines logging on to the authentication server that houses the policy file (this should be all authentication servers).

Now, a similar entry is made in an individual computer policy that is defined only for computer IBSNT04. The entry for this setting is set to be enabled (white check box with a check mark), as shown in Figure 6.10.

When the policies are applied, they are applied in the priority order shown in Figure 6.11.

The computer policy settings contained in Default Computer are applied if no named computer policy exists. In this particular case, the server IBSNT04 has a setting applied that will *not* display the last logged-on user name. This is so because the Default Computer policy (which allows the display of user names) is not applied and the setting in the named computer policy is applied.

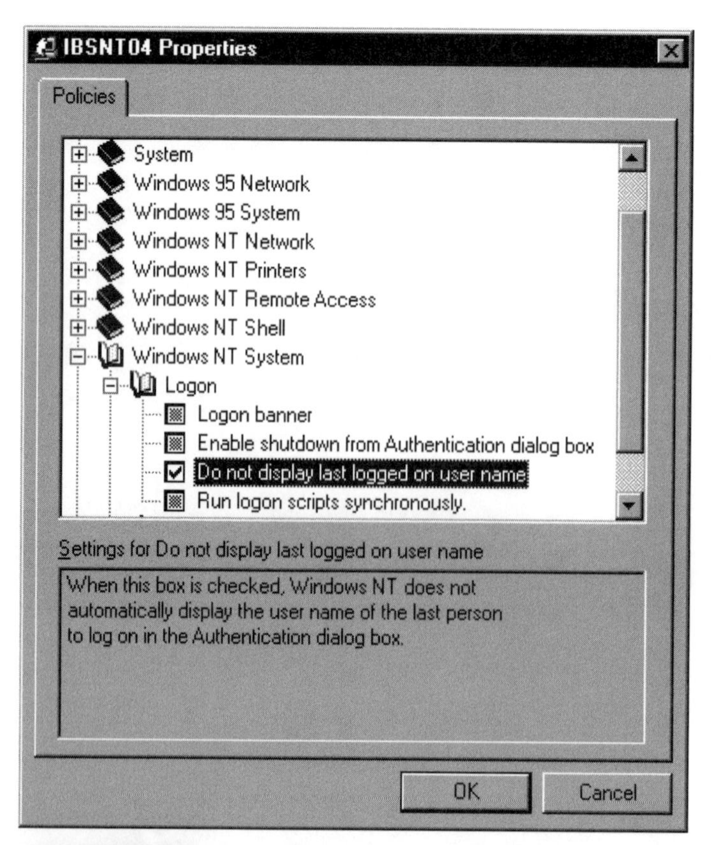

FIGURE 6.10 Individual policy for IBSNT04 prevents the last logged on user name from being displayed

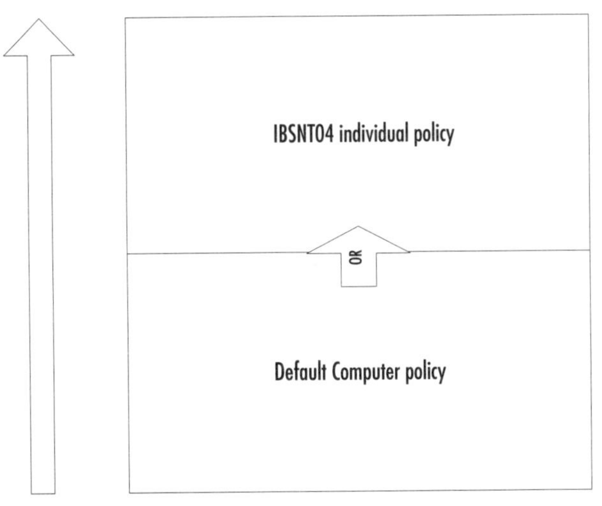

FIGURE 6.11 Application of computer policies performed on an "Either / Or" basis

User Policies

In a similar yet more complex fashion, user policies can be applied in various ways. They could be applied to all users or to individual users who could be members of one or more groups where the same setting is applied. Group priorities come into play when you are defining user policy settings.

When the policies are applied, they are applied in the priority order shown in Figure 6.12.

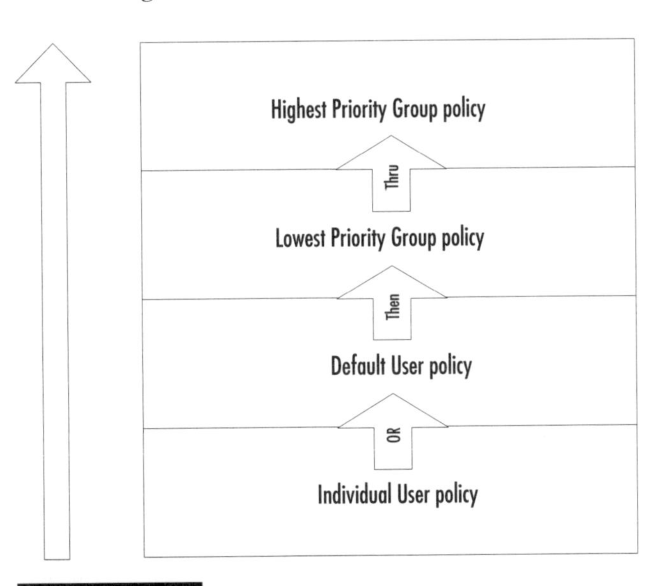

FIGURE 6.12 Group priority helps resolve conflicts for User Policies

If an individual user policy exists, then it is applied first. All other user-related policies are ignored under these circumstances. The settings applied in the Default User policy are applied if no individual user policy exists. Group policies are then applied in the order defined by their respective group priorities. Again, if a named user policy exists, the group policies are not applied. So, if a named user profile exists, the settings are always applied. If none exists and there are multiple group policies, then only the group order is important. The settings in the highest-priority group always win in this scenario.

Policy Application Flowchart

The flowchart shown in Figure 6.13 will help you to see which policies will be applied and in which order.

As you can see from the flowchart, the computer-related policy is applied after the user-related policies. This means that any conflicting settings between computer-related and user-related policies are always set from the computer-related side.

Application of Policy Settings

The main danger when applying conflicting settings is that you may leave a setting ignored (grayed-out) in the higher-priority policy, expecting the existing setting to remain in place. If one of the stages of policy application (such as from group membership) alters the existing setting, then this new setting is passed through the higher-priority policy and the result is not what you expected. If a setting is important to you, set it as enabled or disabled. Do not leave it grayed-out unless you are certain of the underlying logic of policy structure (including group membership).

This same warning applies to a slightly lesser extent to computer policies as well. For these policies, you can only receive setting from one of two places (Default Computer and named computer), so the chances for confusion are lessened.

Policy Implementation vs. User Profiles

If you look at some of the settings exposed by the policy editor, you can see that there are other ways of putting the setting in place. A user can change his wallpaper on his own local machine using **Control Panel** > **Display**. As an administrator, you can set the wallpaper in a roaming profile or you can set it in a mandatory profile. The system policy also allows this setting to be implemented. Where there are conflicts in system or user settings, a hierarchy must be in place to resolve any problems.

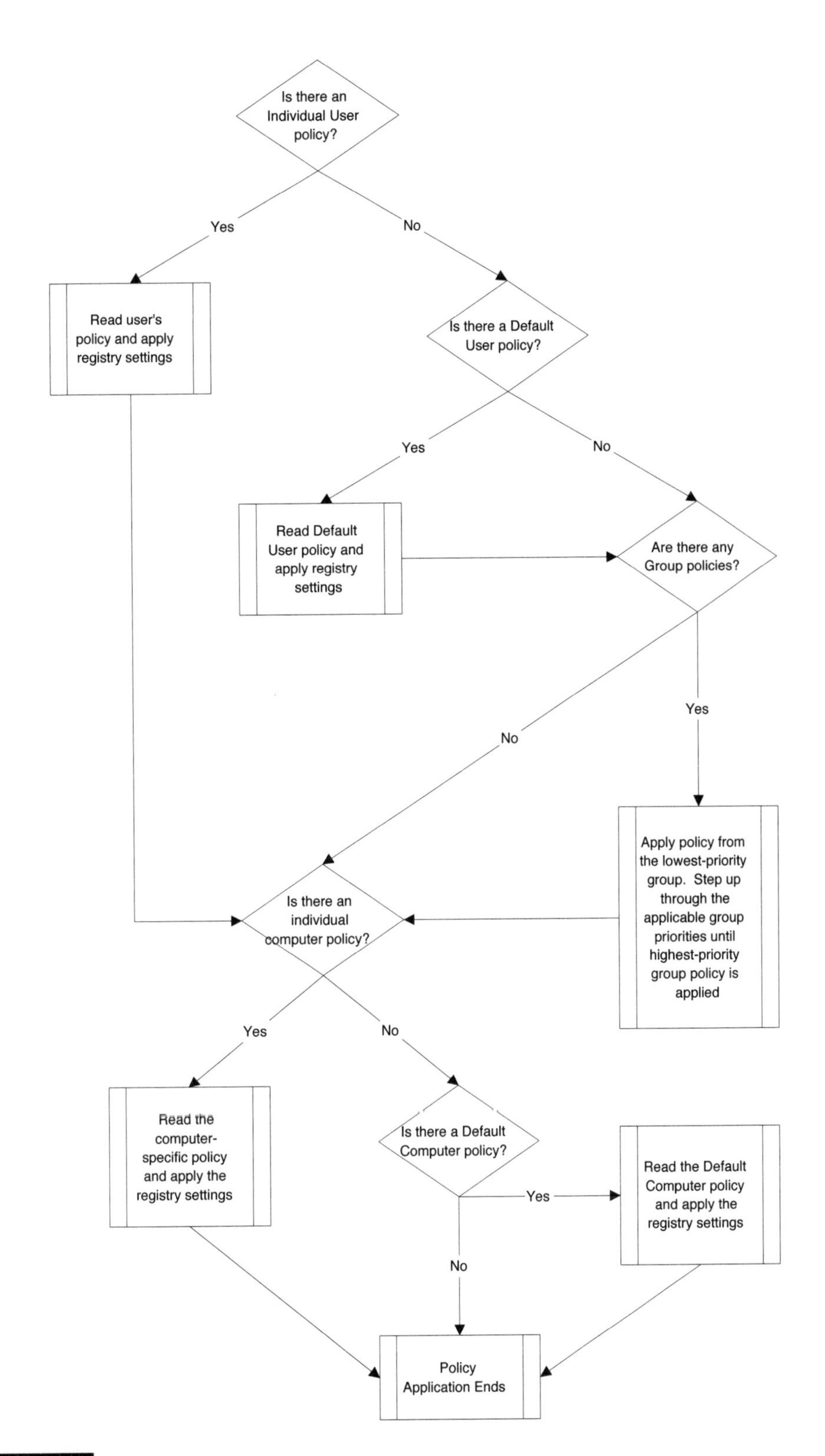

FIGURE 6.13 Policy application flowchart

The order in which these settings are implemented is defined in Windows NT. Figure 6.14 shows a graphical representation of the implementation of these settings.

The order of precedence is as follows:

- Original registry settings and any user-defined registry settings are applied to the machine.
- Registry settings defined in user profiles are applied to the machine when the user logs on. These settings can come from a local profile, a roaming profile, or a mandatory profile. The settings contained in the profile overwrite any existing registry settings.
- The system policy is applied next and overwrites any conflicting settings in the registry. The policy is applied according to the conflict resolution rules discussed earlier. This means that even if the user set preferences for wallpaper settings locally and saved them to his roaming profile, the introduction of a system policy stipulating that all users must display the company logo as wallpaper would overwrite the local settings. If the profile is a roaming profile, then these settings would be uploaded and would overwrite the profile settings. If a mandatory (read-only) profile is in use, then the settings would not be saved to the profile but would still be overwritten every time the policy file is read. The user could change these settings (if the policy allows), but the next time the user logs on the policy settings appear.

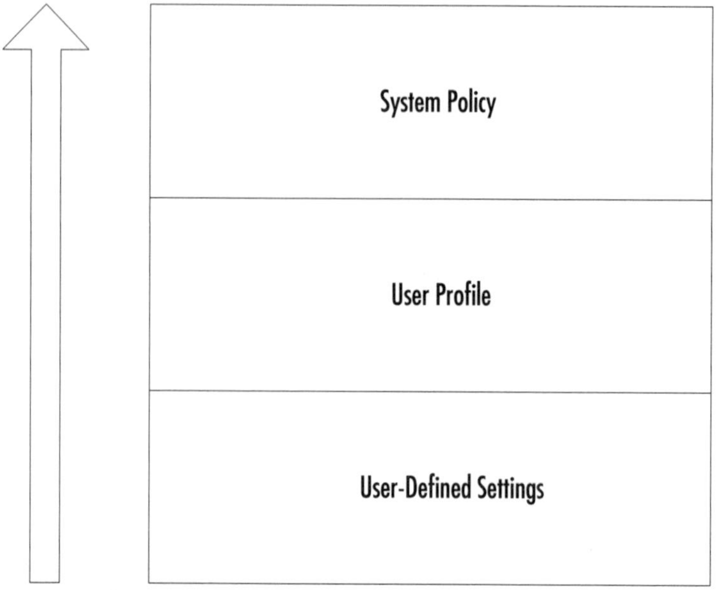

System Policy

User Profile

User-Defined Settings

FIGURE 6.14 Policy settings put in place last take precedence over other methods

Summary

System policies make registry settings for the computer or user logging on to the domain. They apply controls to the user environment, and when used successfully, they provide administrators with an easily used tool that can apply settings to vast numbers of users or computers.

The registry hives that are exposed with system policies are `HKEY_LOCAL_MACHINE` and `HKEY_USER`. Although only a select number of registry values are exposed with the default template files supplied by Microsoft, you can manipulate the files or create new ones that expose any value in these registry hives.

Because settings are exposed from the loaded templates, all user-related policies contain the same available categories and values. The Default User policy, an individual user policy, and all group policies have the same default look as each other. Default Computer policies and named computer policies have the same default look as each other.

Lab Exercises

The lab exercises that follow work together in progression through the whole process of profile building and maintenance. Some of the labs are progressive, so they should be completed in order.

Prerequisites

The prerequisites for the labs that follow are the same as for the labs in the previous chapter. The same server and computer names will be used, as well as the same users and groups. One further user should be created for this lab. Create **DomUser2** with settings similar to those of DomUser1. The only additional requirement is that the policy editor is installed according to the instructions below.

1. Log on to the domain controller as Administrator.
2. Load the **NT Server CD** into an available drive.
3. Copy the files **Common.adm**, **Windows.adm**, and **Winnt.adm** to the server's **\%SystemRoot%\inf** folder, which is usually **C:\Winnt\Inf** (a hidden folder by default).
4. Copy the **Poledit.exe** file to the server's **\%SystemRoot%** folder.
5. Copy the **Poledit.cnt** and **Poledit.hlp** files to the server's **\%System-Root%\Help** folder.
6. Create a shortcut to the **Poledit.exe** program in the **Administrative Tools** folder.

You install the system policy editor on an NT Server by simply copying the necessary files to the server and creating a shortcut for ease of use.

Lab 1: Create a Policy File

In this exercise, you will create a policy file and save it in the default location. The policy file will contain default settings for single users, all users, two global groups, and all computers.

OPEN AND SAVE THE POLICY

Follow the steps below to open a new policy file and save it as the default NT policy file for the domain.

1. Start the **System Policy Editor**.
2. Select **Options** > **Policy Template**. Note the loaded templates are **Winnt.adm** and **Common.adm**. `Windows.adm` is not loaded by default because it contains settings for Windows 9x computers only. Select **OK**. If the policy editor has been used before and different templates were loaded, unload all templates and reload those specified above.
3. Select **File** > **New Policy** to start a new policy file. This file will contain the Default Computer and Default User icons by default.
4. Select **File** > **Save**.
5. Navigate to the server's **Netlogon** share folder. This is usually **\%SystemRoot%\System32\Repl\Import\Scripts**.
6. Enter the file name **NTconfig.pol**.
7. Select **Save**.

This procedure has opened a new policy file based on the default templates provided with Windows NT. The file is saved with the name `NTconfig.pol` and placed in the default location for policy files, which is the `Netlogon` share of all authenticating servers.

ADD A SINGLE USER TO THE POLICY

1. Start the **Policy Editor**.
2. Select **File** > **Open**, and select the **NTconfig.pol** file from the server's `Netlogon` share.
3. Select **Add User** from the **Edit** menu.
4. Browse and select the **DomUser1** user name. You can enter the user name by hand, but be aware that there is no spell checker here.
5. Select **OK**. A single-person icon, named after the user, is added to the policy file desktop.
6. Repeat steps 3 through 5 above, replacing the user name with the **Administrator** user.

ADD GLOBAL GROUPS TO THE POLICY

1. Open the policy file **NTconfig.pol**.
2. Select **Add Group** from the **Edit** menu.
3. Browse and select the **Domain Users** group.
4. Select **OK**. A group icon, named **Domain Users**, is added to the policy file desktop.
5. Browse and select the **Domain Admins** group.
6. Select **OK**. A group icon, named **Domain Admins**, is added to the policy file desktop.

Two groups have been added to the policy file so that the effect of group priorities can be looked at.

SET GROUP PRIORITIES

1. Start the Policy Editor and open your policy file.
2. Arrange the order of the defined groups so that **Domain Users** is on top of **Domain Admins**. This arrangement places Domain Users as the highest-priority group.
3. Select **OK**.
4. Select **File** > **Save** to save the policy file.

Lab 2: Make Policy Settings

In this exercise, you will make some simple changes to the default policy so that you can see the effects of the policy setting and look at how conflicts are resolved. The policy editor should be started and the `NTconfig.pol` file opened for these exercises. Before continuing, make sure that your policy file is similar to the one shown in Figure 6.15.

DOMUSER1: SINGLE USER SETTINGS WITH NO CONFLICTS

1. Log on to the domain as **DomUser1** from **ZAKpc02**, and look at your Start menu. Two items on this menu are **Run** and **Find**. These will be removed by application of the policy.
2. On the server, double-click the **DomUser1** icon in the **NTconfig.pol** policy file.
3. Expand the **Shell** > **Restrictions** categories. All values by default in this screen have grayed-out boxes.
4. Place a check mark in the **Remove Run command from Start menu** option and the **Remove Find command from Start menu** option.
5. Select **OK**.
6. Select **File** > **Save** to save these changes to the policy file.
7. Log off as DomUser1 on ZAKpc02, and log back on to the domain as the same user. Figure 6.16 displays the resulting Start menu.

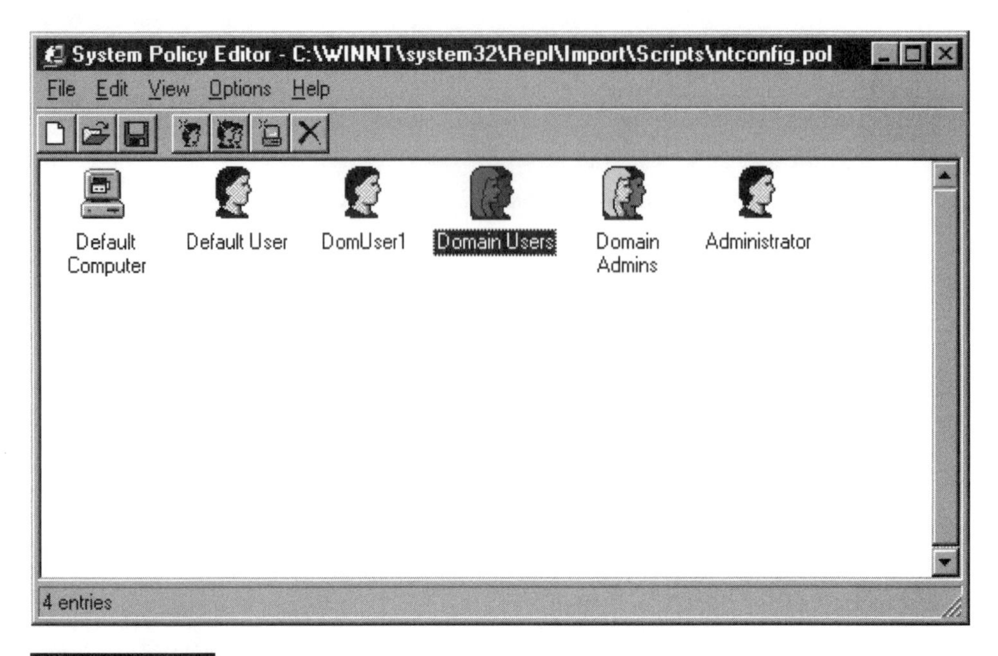

FIGURE 6.15 The `NTconfig.pol` file when the exercises in lab 1 are complete

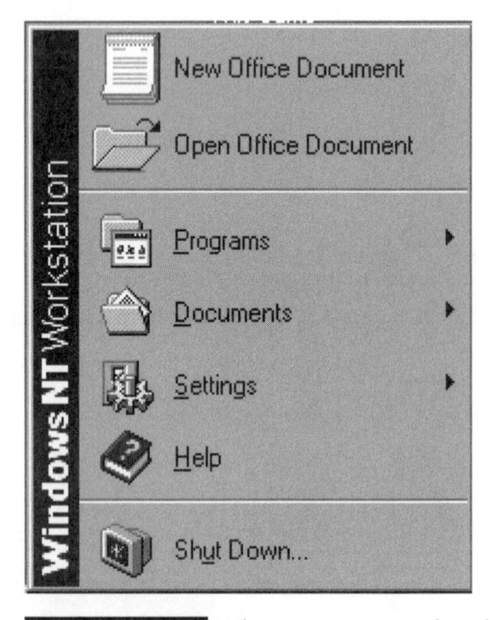

FIGURE 6.16 The Run command and the Find command have been removed from the Start menu

The policy contained in the `NTconfig.pol` file was applied to user DomUser1, and the result was to remove the two command functions from the Start menu. Logging on to the domain as any other user will show that these functions are still available for everybody else.

DOMAIN USERS: GROUP SETTINGS IGNORED

1. Log on to the domain as **DomUser1** from **ZAKpc02**.
2. Select the **Display** applet from **Control Panel** and note that the **Settings**, **Screen Saver**, **Background**, and **Appearance** tabs are available. There may be others depending on your video display settings.
3. Log off, and log on as the domain administrator to look at the same items. The same tabs should be available.
4. On the server double-click the **Domain Users** icon in the `NTconfig.pol` policy.
5. Expand the **Control Panel** > **Display** categories.
6. Place a check mark in the **Restrict Display** option. This makes the settings in the bottom pane of the editor screen available.
7. Place a check mark in the **Hide Background tab** option and the **Hide Settings tab** option.
8. Select **OK**.
9. Select **File** > **Save** to save these changes to the policy file.
10. Log off as **DomUser1** on ZAKpc02, and log back on to the domain as the same user.
11. Select the **Display** applet from **Control Panel** to verify that all tabs are still visible.
12. Log off, and log back on to the domain as **Administrator** from the same machine. Note that the same tabs are seen by this user. The individual user policies preclude the settings from being made from the Domain Users policy.
13. Now log on as user **DomUser2**. The two tabs are not visible for this user. Figure 6.17 shows the Display applet as it looks to DomUser2.

The tabs were hidden in the Display applet for all members of the Domain Users global group except those that have their own individual policies. The policy setting from the Domain Users group option was carried through for user DomUser2 because no other setting of a higher priority was set to interfere in any way.

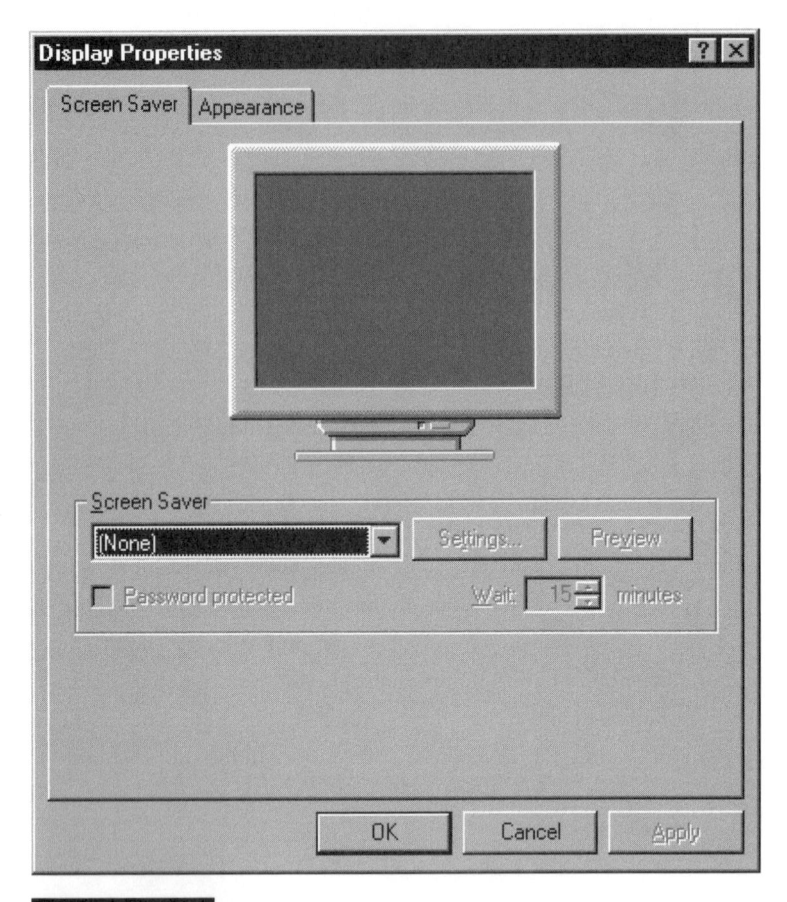

FIGURE 6.17 The Display applet has a restricted number of tabs visible

ADMINISTRATOR: GROUP PRIORITIES AND CONFLICTS

1. On the server, double-click the **Domain Users** icon in the `NTconfig.pol` policy.
2. Expand the **Control Panel** > **Display** category.
3. Ensure the **Restrict Display** option is grayed-out.
4. Double-click the **Default User** icon in the **NTconfig.pol** policy.
5. Expand the **Control Panel** > **Display** categories.
6. Place a check mark in the **Restrict Display** option.
7. Place a check mark in the **Deny Access to the display icon** option, but leave all of the other options with no check mark.
8. Select **OK**.

9. Single-click the **Administrator** icon in the **NTconfig.pol** policy, and select **Edit** > **Remove** to remove the named policy for Administrator.
10. Select **Yes**.
11. Double-click the **Domain Admins** icon in the `NTconfig.pol` policy.
12. Expand the **Control Panel** > **Display** categories.
13. Place a check mark in the **Restrict Display** option.
14. Place a check mark in the **Hide Appearance tab** option, but leave all of the other options with no check mark.
15. Select **OK**.
16. Select **File** > **Save** to save these changes to the policy file.
17. Log off, and log back on to the domain as Administrator from ZAKpc02. Look at the Display applet appearance.

The Appearance tab is hidden, and all other tabs are visible for Administrator. The policy is applied as shown in Figure 6.18.

First, the Default User policy is applied because the individual user policy has been deleted. The net effect at this moment is that all users are denied access to the Display applet of Control Panel. Next, the Domain Admins group policy is applied (for members of this group only) because it has the lowest group priority. The net effect is that for members of this group, the Display applet is available again, but the Appearance tab is hidden and all other tabs are visible. Then, the Domain Users policy is applied as the next highest priority group.

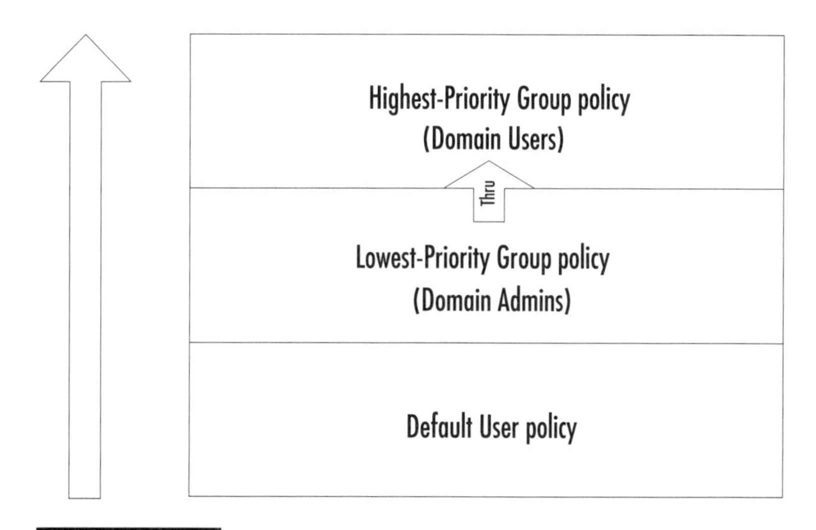

FIGURE 6.18 Administrator user policy applied through the various stages

The net effect is to leave all Display settings as they are for members of this group because of the grayed-out setting in the group policy. The Appearance tab is still hidden for members of Domain Admins.

When multiple groups are used in a more realistic corporate environment, the resulting complexities can be overwhelming. Everything can be running quite well, and then you add a user to a group to give file and directory access through group membership. If this group has a policy set and is a high-priority group, you may inadvertently change the policy application order as well. So, Administrator beware!

SEVEN

ZAK-Supplied System Policies

In This Chapter

- Introduction
- ZAK-Related Policy Template Files
- ZAKconfig.pol/ NTconfig.pol Files
- Default Computer Policy
- Default User Policy
- TaskUsers/AppUsers Policies
- Policy Categories
- Summary
- Lab Exercises

This chapter looks specifically at the template files and policies that are provided as part of the ZAK. These ZAK-specific files create the controlled user environment that leads to lower administration and management costs.

The chapter looks at the structure of these files and the controls that each of the portions provides at the desktop. At the end of this chapter, you should have a sound understanding of the control principles involved in presenting the user environment that was seen when you made the first installations of the TaskStation and AppStation computers. The settings exposed by the ZAK policies will help with customization and should give rise to thoughts on how your own organization can benefit from these settings.

Introduction

The user profiles and system policies discussed in the previous chapter are the basis for the ZAK-specific templates and files that provide several layers of control to prevent unwanted accidents at the desktop.

Moving forward from the basic templates and files provided with the retail versions of Windows NT, the ZAK presents a more advanced set of files that are aimed specifically at desktop control (and therefore lowering ownership costs).

ZAK-Related Policy Template Files

The ZAK provides its own template files specifically designed to produce maximum control over users and so limit associated costs. The template files are derived from those that accompany the retail version of NT 4.0, from the Office 97 Resource kit and from the Internet Explorer Resource kit.

The system policy files provided in the ZAK are:

- `Access97.adm.`
- `Off97NT4.adm.`
- `Query97.adm.`
- `*Common.adm.`
- `Ieak.adm.`
- `Outlk97.adm.`
- `*Winnt.adm.`
- `*ZAKwinnt.adm.`

The template files listed above can be found in the `C:\ZAKadmin\Policy Templates` folder.

The resource kits for Office 97 and for Internet Explorer contain full details of the system policy files provided in these kits. The remainder of this chapter looks at the actual settings used by default for the TaskStation user and AppStation user and at the three template files indicated in the above list that are either related to the Windows NT system or provided by the ZAK.

ZAKconfig.pol/NTconfig.pol Files

The `ZAKconfig.pol` file is the default policy file provided with the ZAK for NT. The file contains policies based on the templates listed above. Copy the file found in the `C:\ZAKadmin\Policy Files` folder to the `Netlogon` share of the domain controller. You will also have to rename the file as `NTconfig.pol` so users can use it. During the remainder of this chapter we refer to the file as `ZAKconfig.pol.`

When looking at policy files, you should ensure that all relevant templates are loaded into the policy editor before you open the policy file. Do this by closing any open policy files and then using the **Options** > **Policy Template** > **Add** command.

Template files are always loaded in alphabetical order, so changing a file name may alter the order in which the categories are loaded and the settings applied.

You can look at the policy file and its exposed settings by loading the file into the policy editor, using the File > Open Policy menu after loading the template files. Figure 7.1 shows the ZAK policy file, which includes the two global group policies.

The order in which system policy template files are loaded is important when it comes to template files with conflicting registry settings. The same registry value can be set by different template files; when this happens, the setting that appears lowest in the policy layout always takes precedence. When using the policy editor, make sure that you do not change template file names once they have been used for a policy. If a setting is applied in two different places for the same policy and then the load order of the policy

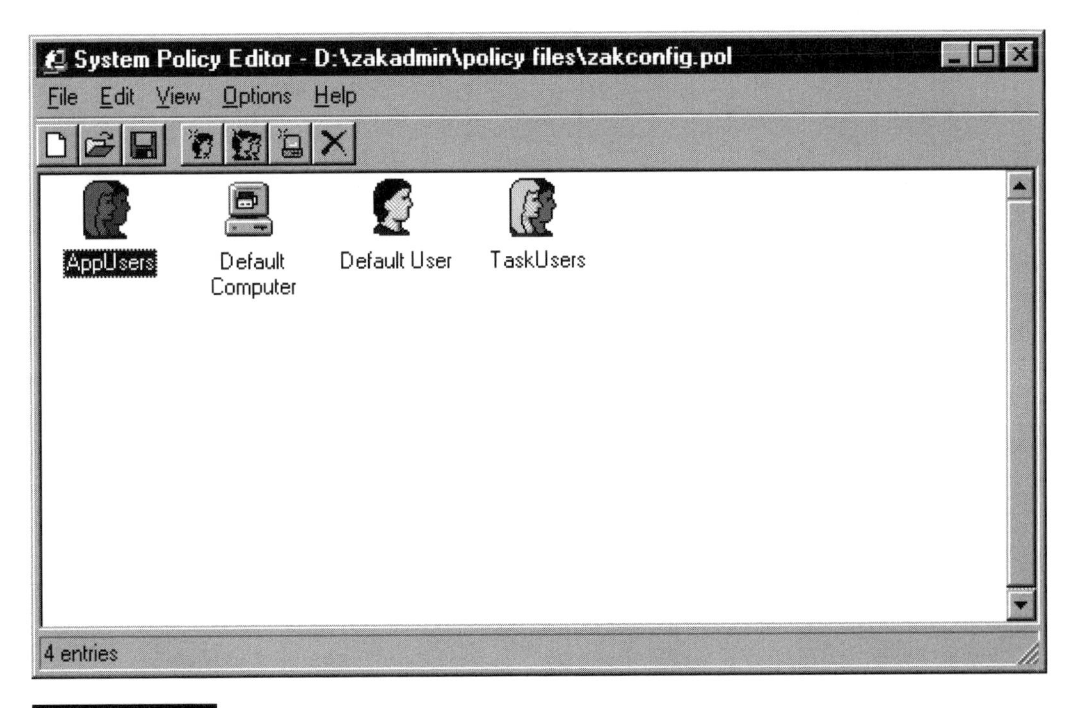

FIGURE 7.1 The `ZAKconfig.pol` file with two predefined global group policies

templates is changed, then the result can be different because of the new application order. Template file categories are loaded from template files opened in alphabetical order. If you load three templates, `Common`, `Winnt`, and `ZAKWinnt`, then those categories from `Common.adm` are loaded first, those from `ZAKwinnt.adm` last. This load order would change if you rename `Common.adm` to be `Zcommon.adm`.

If you want to know what is defined by each individual template file, then load them into the editor one by one and load the policy file. Only the settings exposed by the single loaded template will be visible.

Default Computer Policy

The Default Computer policy is loaded if no named computer policy exists for the machine from which the user is logging on. The Default Computer policy is not widely used in the ZAK implementation. Most of the control comes from the user-based policies. Table 7.1 lists all settings in the Default Computer policy that are set to any state other than grayed-out (which means ignore this setting).

TABLE 7.1 Activated Default Computer settings for the ZAK

Category	Setting	Value	Template
Windows NT System—Logon			`Winnt.adm`
	Logon Banner	Deactivated	
	Enable Shutdown from Authentication dialog box	Deactivated	
	Do not display last logged-on user name	Activated	
	Run logon scripts synchronously	Ignored	

As you can see from Table 7.1, the Default Computer policy is not used widely for ZAK control purposes. The control theory behind the ZAK is based mainly on who the user is rather that where the user logs on from.

Default User Policy

The Default User policy is loaded only if a policy does not exist for the individual user. The policy is loaded before any group policies that overwrite the settings of the Default User policy if a conflict exists. It is not extensively used by the ZAK for control purposes by default. The default ZAK settings are based on the two task-based worker definitions, which are related to global groups in Windows NT. Most of the control is applied from these group policies. The Default User policy is a good place to make settings that should apply to all users. If you wish to implement a base standard of control for all users and then vary this control per group, the starting point should be the Default User policy.

Table 7.2 shows the few registry settings that are set by default through the Default User policy.

TABLE 7.2 Activated Default User settings for the ZAK

Category	Setting	Value	Template
Windows NT System			Winnt.adm
	Parse Autoexec.bat	Ignored	
	Run logon scripts synchronously	Activated	
	Disable Task Manager	Ignored	
	Show welcome tips at logon	Deactivated	

As with the Default Computer policy, very few registry settings are set by the Default User policy.

The setting *Run logon scripts synchronously* is an example of a possible policy conflict. In this case, the Default Computer policy has the setting grayed-out (ignored), and it is activated in the Default User policy. Computer settings are applied last, so the activated setting of the user policy will take precedence only because the Default Computer setting ignores this option.

TaskUsers/AppUsers Policies

The TaskUsers and AppUsers policies are applied to any member of the TaskUsers or AppUsers global groups, respectively. These groups were defined during the evaluation system setup. The exploration of the TaskUsers and AppUsers policies contained in this section concentrates on the settings provided by the three policy files that are associated with the NT system and the ZAK configuration:

- Common.adm.
- Winnt.adm.
- ZAKwinnt.adm.

These three template files provide all of the ZAK control mechanisms that are not directly related to either Internet Explorer or Microsoft Office. Information on the other template files and template files for other applications can be found in the relevant resource kit, so for our examination of the TaskUsers and AppUsers policies, only the three template files named above have been loaded. This approach provides a clear view of the policy editor screens and the exposed settings.

To follow along with this discussion, load the policy file (`ZAKconfig.pol`) that is provided with the ZAK and the three template files listed above.

To start looking at the TaskUsers policy, double-click the TaskUsers icon when the policy file is opened. The policy should look like that shown in Figure 7.2.

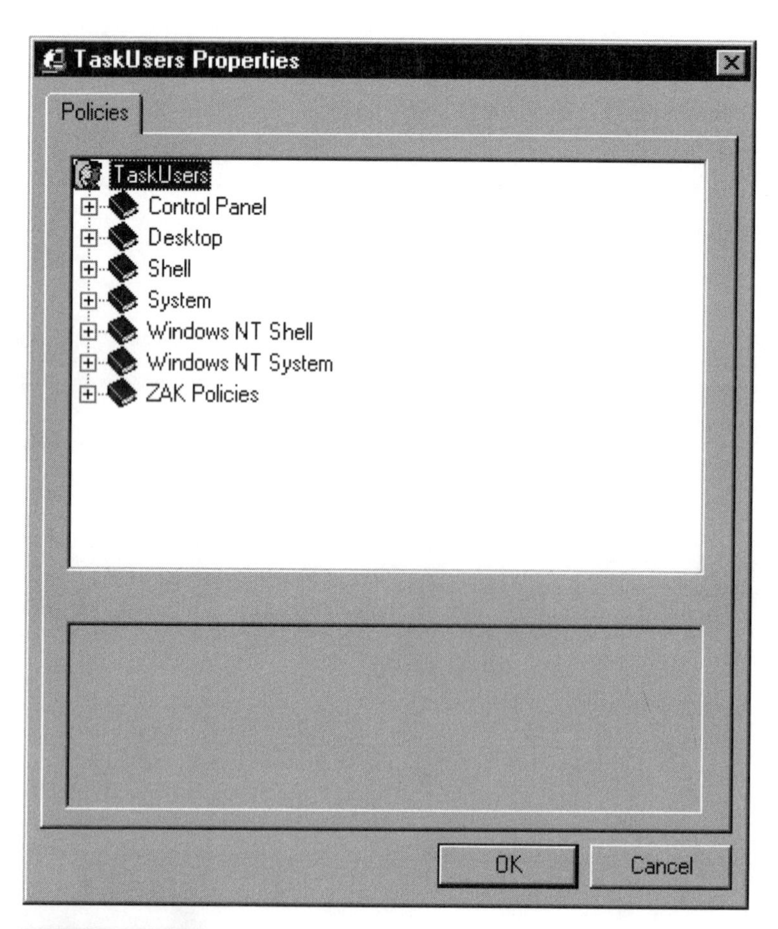

FIGURE 7.2 Fewer categories are available because of the number of templates loaded

To look at the AppUsers policy, select Cancel to close the TaskUsers policy, and double-click on the AppUsers icon. You will see that the AppUsers policy has the same settings exposed as the TaskUsers. Regardless of how many group policies or individual user policies are defined within the one policy file, the exposed settings for the User class are the same and the exposed settings for the Machine class are the same. The list of exposed settings is derived from the templates that are loaded and cannot be changed within the same policy file for different groups or users.

Extra registry keys can be exposed by the policy editor. The template files can be added to and amended to fit your own requirements. However, policy editor will only expose the same settings for all users and groups or all computers. It is an all or nothing situation.

Policy Categories

The exposed settings are contained within Categories. These categories can contain one or more settings, or they can contain further categories. This section lists the first level categories, subcategories, and any settings contained in these. The comparison tables list the default ZAK state for the TaskUsers and AppUsers global group policies. For clarity, differences between the two policies are highlighted.

Control Panel

		TaskUsers	AppUsers
Display	Restrict Display.	Ignored	Ignored

The Control Panel category of the TaskUsers and AppUsers policies has no settings in use. The one setting in this category is ignored.

Desktop

		TaskUsers	AppUsers
Desktop	Wallpaper.	Ignored	Ignored
	Color Scheme.	Ignored	Ignored

The Desktop category of the TaskUsers and AppUsers policies has no settings in use. The two settings in this category are ignored.

Shell

		TaskUsers	AppUsers
Restrictions	Remove Run command from Start Menu.	Enabled	Enabled
	Remove folders from Settings on Start Menu.	Enabled	Enabled
	Remove Taskbar from Settings on Start Menu.	Enabled	Enabled
	Remove Find command from Start Menu.	Enabled	Enabled
	Hide drives in My Computer.	Enabled	Enabled
	Hide Network Neighborhood.	Enabled	Ignored
	No Entire Network in Network Neighborhood.	Enabled	Enabled
	No workgroup contents in Network Neighborhood.	Enabled	Enabled
	Hide all items on desktop.	Enabled	Enabled
	Disable Shut Down command.	Enabled	Enabled
	Don't save settings at exit.	Enabled	Enabled

The Shell category is where a large part of the user control is applied for both the TaskUsers and AppUsers groups.

The scale of the desktop lockdown presented by these options is huge. Almost all options are removed from the Start menu. All items are hidden on the desktop. If you could find My Computer, all drives have been hidden within it. If a TaskUsers member could find Network Neighborhood, then there would be no content. AppUsers members can find Network Neighborhood, but still there is no content. The Shut Down command is not available, and when the system is shut down (via <Ctrl Alt Del> secure attention sequence), settings are not saved. A large amount of the task-based workers control is presented here.

System

		TaskUsers	AppUsers
Restrictions	Disable registry editing tools.	Ignored	Ignored
	Run only allowed Windows applications.	Ignored	Ignored

The System category does not have any settings activated for the TaskUsers or AppUsers policies.

Windows NT Shell

		TaskUsers	AppUsers
Custom User Interface	Custom Shell.	Enabled	Ignored
Custom Folders	Custom Programs folder.	Ignored	Enabled
	Custom desktop icons.	Ignored	Ignored
	Hide Start menu subfolders.	Ignored	Enabled
	Custom Startup folder.	Ignored	Ignored
	Custom Network Neighborhood.	Ignored	Ignored
	Custom Start menu.	Ignored	Enabled
Restrictions	Only use approved shell extensions.	Ignored	Ignored
	Remove File menu from Explorer.	Enabled	Enabled
	Remove common program groups from the Start menu.	Enabled	Enabled
	Disable context menus from the taskbar.	Enabled	Enabled
	Disable Explorer's default context menu.	Enabled	Enabled
	Remove the Map Network Drive and Disconnect Network Drive options.	Enabled	Enabled
	Disable link file tracking.	Enabled	Enabled

The Windows NT Shell category contains three subcategories.

- **Custom User Interface**. Custom User Interface presents the user with an alternative shell to Windows Explorer. The shell of choice for the TaskUsers group is Internet Explorer and is defined through the Custom Shell setting. When a member of the TaskUsers group logs on to the domain, he is presented with Internet Explorer as the running application. The approach could be replaced with any productivity tool. If a number of users should only have access to a mainframe application through a terminal emulator, then this application could be set up as the single application to run for this group of users. This setting is not used for AppUsers group members. AppUsers members by definition are required to run a number of applications, so the restriction to one application running as the shell would not allow these users to perform their jobs.

- **Custom Folders**. The Custom folders category presents customized application access to AppUsers members. A customized Start menu and Programs menu are presented from a network share. This approach centralizes the administration of the available applications. The local Start menu is hidden. The Custom Folders category is not used by the TaskUsers policy because only one application is presented to this type of user.
- **Restrictions**. The Restrictions category applies further control to the desktop environment. This category removes the final items from the Start menu so that only the Help and any custom menus are available. Taskbar access and context menus are removed. The settings in this category complement the previous settings in the Shell–Restrictions category.

Windows NT System

The Windows NT System category has two settings in use.

		TaskUsers	AppUsers
Windows NT System	Parse Autoexec.bat.	Ignored	Ignored
	Run logon scripts synchronously.	Ignored	Enabled
	Disable Task Manager.	Enabled	Disabled
	Show welcome tips at logon.	Disabled	Disabled

The Disable Task Manager setting is enabled so that TaskUsers cannot start the Task Manager program and use it to spawn other processes.

The Show Welcome Tips setting is disabled.

ZAK Policies

The ZAK policies category has a number of subcategories defined, but for the TaskUsers group, only one setting is operational. This setting is contained in the **ZAK policies—Windows NT—Drives—Restrictions** category; the setting is **Show only selected drives**.

Use this setting to limit the scope for local system damage by the user. You can amend the setting from the default allowable values to cover the entire range of available drive letters. With this setting, you can hide any number of local or network drives while still allowing applications to run from these drives. The setting and how to amend it is covered in the practice labs at the end of the chapter.

		TaskUsers	AppUsers
Windows NT– User Profiles through System Policies	AppData Folder.	Disabled	Disabled
	Favorites Folder.	Disabled	Disabled
	NetHood Folder.	Disabled	Disabled
	PrintHood Folder.	Disabled	Disabled
	Recent Folder.	Disabled	Disabled
	Recent Folder.	Disabled	Disabled
	SendTo Folder.	Disabled	Disabled
Windows NT– Internet Explorer Security	Active Content.	Disabled	Disabled
	Active Content Security Level.	Disabled	Disabled
Windows NT– Drives–Restrictions	Show only selected drives.	Enabled	Enabled
Windows	Load.	Ignored	Ignored

Summary

The largest part of desktop control exercised by the ZAK is done through system policies. System policies are easy to amend and are managed centrally, so the overhead in maintenance is limited.

User policies are the other main method of control and can be used successfully to provide a standard environment without implementing what some people may consider to be draconian control methods.

You can reach a middle ground by using parts of each method to present your own users with the best working environment possible while controlling what is done in that environment.

Lab Exercises

The lab exercise that follows explores some amendments to the default ZAK-supplied policy. This exercise highlights some of the control features and shows how they are enabled (or disabled).

Prerequisites

The prerequisites for this lab are twofold: a preinstalled AppStation computer, as defined in Part One; the ability to log on to the domain with the account name AppUser1, as created in Chapter 2. The correct policy implementation requires that all of the preliminary test system build covered in Chapter 2 was completed.

You should log on with user AppUser1 and take a look at the user's environment. Note the menus available from the Start menu; note also the drives you can see when you attempt to open a file from Microsoft Word or Excel. The AppUser1 user must log on to the workstation at least once before you proceed to make sure the policy has been applied.

As this exercise requires a policy file to be in use, the live policy file (`NTconfig.pol`) is referred to throughout the lab. This should be a copy of the `ZAKconfig.pol` file copied to the `Netlogon` share of the server.

Lab 1: Environmental Changes

In this exercise, you will make changes to the AppUsers and Default User policies and note the results.

OPEN THE POLICY

1. Log on to the server as Administrator.
2. Start the Policy Editor.
3. Ensure all eight of the ZAK-provided templates are loaded.
4. Select **File** > **Open Policy,** and select the **NTconfig.pol** file from the `Netlogon` share. This share points to `\%SystemRoot%\System32\Repl\Import\Scripts`.

SHELL RESTRICTIONS

1. Double-click the **AppUsers** icon.
2. Expand the **Shell—Restrictions** category. Note that on the workstation the AppUser1 user only has the Help, Documents, and Programs options available on the Start Menu.
3. In the policy, remove the check mark from the following items:
   - Remove **Run** command from Start menu.
   - Remove **Taskbar** from Settings on Start menu.
4. In the policy, change the setting to "ignore" (grayed-out) for the following items:
   - Hide all items on the desktop.
   - Disable Shut Down command.

5. Save the Policy file.
6. Log AppUser1 off the workstation, and log back on as AppUser1 again.

If you look at the Start Menu presented to AppUser1 after these changes have been made, you see the following results. The Run command has returned. The Settings folder has returned because the Taskbar has been put back in place. The settings folder was hidden by virtue of its contents being removed.

The second set of changes made above have no effect. As the user has logged on at least once with these settings enabled, then all desktop items were hidden and the Shut Down command removed. The grayed-out setting allows the current status to remain unchanged.

POLICY CONFLICTS

1. Double-click the **Default User** icon.
2. Expand the **Shell—Restrictions** category.
3. In the policy, change the setting from ignored to disabled (white box, no check mark) for the following items:
   - Hide all items on the desktop.
   - Disable Shut Down command.
4. Save the Policy file.
5. Log AppUser1 off the workstation, and log back on as AppUser1 again.

The result of the last set of changes was implemented for AppUser1. The desktop icons appeared and the Shut Down command is now available. This will come as a surprise to some people. The settings applied to the Default User are put in place first if no individual user policy exists. Then, group policies overwrite conflicting settings. Because the settings in the AppUsers group policy were set to "ignore," then those from the Default User policy carried through.

LAB 1 SUMMARY

The policy settings exposed by the ZAK-related template files could also be changed by the registry editors. The policy editor is a type of registry editor, providing a user-friendly interface. The exposed settings all have a purpose, and time spent now making test changes to the policies and looking at the results will pay dividends when you look at customizing the ZAK for your own requirements.

PART THREE

ZAK Customization

In This Part

The chapters in this part look at the tools, techniques, and methods that can be used to customize the default behavior of the ZAK. This customization process is absolutely essential for getting the most out of the ZAK. The default behavior will rarely fit the needs of any organization; to maximize the benefit, you must take time to compare the offerings of the default behavior and carefully manipulate the parts that will be of use to you.

Chapter Eight concentrates on changes that can be made to the default Windows NT setup. Included in the first portion of this chapter is a look at reducing the number of files copied during an installation by excluding unwanted system components. Other topics covered include amending the default behavior to customize the optional components that are installed, allowing multiple installations of the operating system using a Uniqueness Database, and coverage of the tools used by the ZAK to perform the installation.

Chapter Nine looks at two possible customization scenarios and the steps necessary to reach a defined goal. The goals are clearly defined at the beginning of each of the projects, then the techniques and methodologies to make the required changes to the base ZAK configuration are shown. The two projects included here contain real examples of how you can change the ZAK to fit your own needs.

EIGHT

Customizing the Windows NT Unattended Setup

In This Chapter

- Introduction
- Installation Size Reduction
- Optional Installation Features
- Uniqueness Database Files
- System Tools

This chapter looks at ways to make changes to the Windows NT unattended setup process described in Chapter 4. Customization processes and tips covered in this chapter enable you to make changes to the default unattended setup so that the resulting installation meets the needs of your organization. Also discussed in this chapter are the tools provided with the ZAK and how they can be used to amend the default behavior of the ZAK installation.

Introduction

The Windows NT unattended setup process described for task-based user workstations in Chapter 4 was based on simply turning a manual process, which requires a large amount of user intervention, into an automated process. The Windows NT setup itself was a Typical setup, producing a workstation that might or might not have all of the facilities and OS-supplied applications that you require on your desktops.

You can tune the Windows NT setup process by using manual mode. You can choose to install a Custom setup, select the facilities you wish to include, and ensure that unwanted options are not used. You can make the same choices in an automated setup procedure by manipulating the setup files that are used during a setup to decide which features to install. The first part of this chapter concentrates on the Windows NT setup portion of the client installation.

Many tools included in the ZAK enable us to customize the way in which the kit is applied after the initial NT setup has completed. These customization tools are all used by the ZAK in some way, and we can use these tools to produce whatever results we need. The second part of this chapter looks at the ZAK-mode portion of the client setup where these tools are used.

Installation Size Reduction

One of the options you have when you are running an installation of Windows NT is to reduce the number of unwanted files copied to the machine during the Text portion of the setup. The main benefit is the amount of time saved as well as reduction of network traffic. In the two examples that follow, we avoid copying 25 Mbytes of files during the Text-mode setup phase. When multiplied over large numbers of installations, this technique can lead to a significant time saving.

Peer Web Services

Peer Web Services is one Windows NT option that you cannot install during an unattended process. The option for installing this service simply doesn't exist in this mode. If Peer Web Services is required, you would have to install it after the initial setup, but more often than not, this service is unused. You can remove the file copy that takes place for this service during the unattended setup process.

To make sure that these files are not copied to the local system during the Text mode setup process, edit the `DOSNET.INF` file, which controls which optional folders are copied to the machine during Text-mode setup. Example 8.1 shows how to prevent the `\Inetsrv` folder from being copied by simply placing a semicolon (;) before the optional folder name.

EXAMPLE 8.1 The `DOSNET.INF` file edited to control optional folder copies

```
[OptionalSrcDirs]
;Inetsrv
Drvlib.nic
```

Third-Party Network Drivers

As you can see from Example 8.1, another optional folder that is copied by default to the local machine is the `\Drvlib.nic` folder. This folder contains drivers for all of the supported third-party network cards for Windows NT. This folder can be omitted from the copy in the same manner as the `\Inetsrv` folder. Simply place a semicolon before the folder name in the `DOSNET.INF` file.

Obviously, if the NIC that you are using in the machine requires a driver from the `\Drvlib.nic` folder, then the folder must be supplied. You can still remove all other files and folders from the `\Drvlib.nic` folder so that when it is copied, only the required drivers are placed on the machine; you will still realize a performance gain.

Optional Installation Features

When performing a Windows NT installation you can choose from many optional installation features and options. You can choose these accessories and components during a manual installation of Windows NT.

During the unattended installation, you may wish to take advantage of the same choices and select which options are installed. You do this by manipulating a setup file that corresponds to the options you wish to include or exclude.

The installation of the different accessories is controlled by a number of `.inf` files that correspond to the grouping of the accessories, as shown in Figure 8.1.

There are eight `.inf` files loosely corresponding to the option groups available for setup. These `.inf` files are listed in the `SYSSETUP.INF` file in the `[BaseWinOptionsInfs]` section.

- `Accessor.inf`—Contains settings to control the installation of the Accessories group. Items such as Calculator, Clock, and Paint are installed through this file.
- `Communic.inf`—Contains settings to control the installation of the Communications add-on items such as Chat and HyperTerminal.
- `Games.inf`—Contains the settings for the optional games such as Freecell (but not Pinball).
- `Mmopt.inf`—Contains settings for multimedia options and sound schemes.
- `Multimed.inf`—Contains the settings for multimedia programs.
- `Optional.inf`—Contains the settings for the Accessibility options.
- `Pinball.inf`—Contains settings for the Pinball game.
- `Wordpad.inf`—Contains the settings for the Wordpad program.

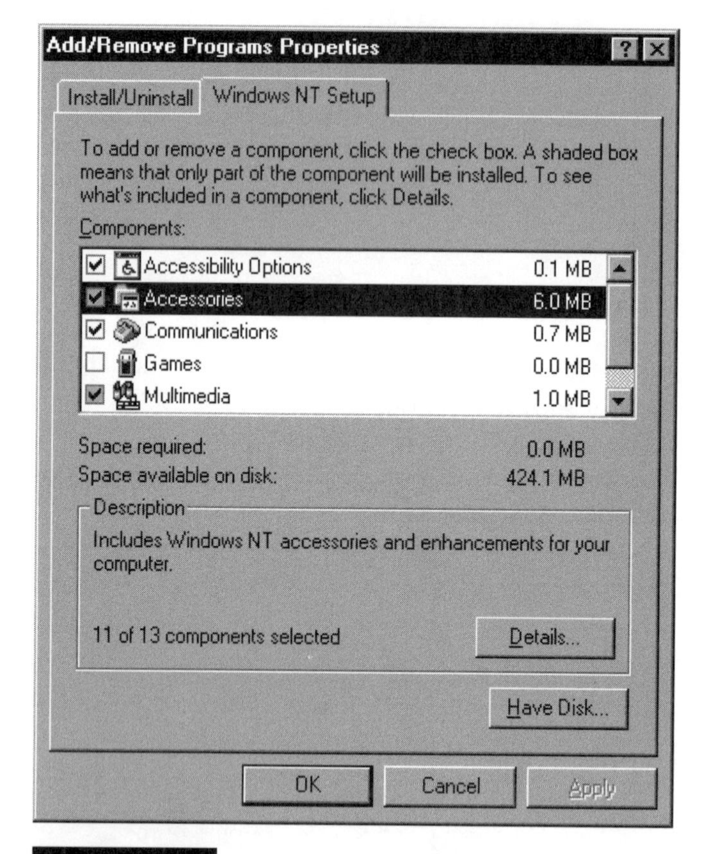

FIGURE 8.1 Options and Accessories for Windows NT setup

The structure of the files described above allows for multiple options to be arranged within sections of the file and for each section to contain a setting that determines the circumstances under which the option is installed. Example 8.2 is an extract from the `Communic.inf` file.

EXAMPLE 8.2 Extract of the `Communic.inf` file from Windows NT Workstation

```
[Chat]
OptionDesc     = %Chat_DESC%
Tip            = %Chat_TIP%
IconIndex      = 16 ;Net Client mini-icon for dialogs
Parent         = CommApps
InstallType    = 14 ;Typical, Portable, Custom
CopyFiles      = ChatCopyFilesSys, ChatCopyFilesHelp
AddReg         = ChatAddReg
UpdateInis     = ChatInis
```

```
Uninstall       = ChatUninstall
Upgrade         = ChatUpgrade
Detect          = %11%\winchat.exe

[Dialer]
OptionDesc      = %Dialer_DESC%
Tip             = %Dialer_TIP%
IconIndex       = 47 ;Phone mini-icon for dialogs
Parent          = CommApps
InstallType     = 14 ;Typical, Portable, Custom
CopyFiles       = DialerCopyFilesProg, DialerCopyFilesHelp
AddReg          = DialerAddReg
UpdateInis      = DialerInis
Uninstall       = DialerUninstall
Upgrade         = DialerUpgrade
Detect          = %24%\%Dialer_DIR%\dialer.exe

[Hypertrm]
OptionDesc      = %Hypertrm_DESC%
Tip             = %Hypertrm_TIP%
IconIndex       = 35 ;Phone mini-icon for dialogs
Parent          = CommApps
InstallType     = 14 ;Typical, Portable, Custom
CopyFiles       = HypertrmCopyFilesProg, HypertrmCopyFilesSys,
                  HypertrmCopyFilesHelp, HypertrmCopyFilesConfig
DelFiles        = HypertrmDelFilesProg
AddReg          = HypertrmAddReg
UpdateInis      = HypertrmInis
Uninstall       = HypertrmUninstall
Upgrade         = HypertrmUpgrade
Detect          = %24%\%Hypertrm_DIR%\hypertrm.exe
```

The extract from the file shown above contains three distinct sections representing the three available installation options in the Communications component of the optional components for Windows NT.

Example 8.2 is a small extract from the `Communic.inf` file. In reality, the three sections shown above are not located together. The file also contains registry entries that must be updated during setup and all other relevant information for this component. For the purposes of the ZAK customization, these other entries are unimportant.

InstallType

The `InstallType` setting determines when an option should be installed. The setting can have one of three possible values, `0`, `10`, or `14`.

- `0`—Specifies that the option should be installed if the setup type is Manual (as chosen in the GUI portion of the setup).

- 10—Specifies that the option should be installed if the setup type is either Typical or Custom.
- 14—Specifies that the option should be installed if the setup type is Typical, Custom, or Portable.

The unattended installation for Windows NT uses an installation type of Typical. Any item with an InstallType set to either 10 or 14 will be installed in an unattended operation. Any item with an InstallType set to 0 will be ignored.

Controlling the Options and Accessories Process

To control which options are installed during an unattended installation, you must first do some preparatory work.

1. In the \I386 folder of the ZAK distribution point, expand the relevant compressed .inf file that you wish to amend. For the Communic.inf file, type Expand communic.in_ communic.inf
2. Next, rename the .IN_ file so that it is not expanded during the setup process.
3. Finally, edit the relevant .inf file, and change the InstallType setting to match your wishes.

Preventing a Single Option from Installing

In the file shown in Example 8.2, each of the separate options that can be chosen by a check mark in the manual installation process is represented by section headers enclosed in square brackets "[ ]". The [Chat] section controls the installation of the Microsoft Chat program. By default the Install-Type setting for this option is 14 so that it is installed in Typical, Portable, and Custom setups.

If you wish this option to be installed when you run an unattended setup, then you can either leave the setting alone or change it to 10 which will also install in a Typical setup. If you do not want this option to install then set the InstallType value to 0. This setting prevents the installation because the unattended install runs in Typical mode and not Manual mode. Table 8.1 shows the eight different .inf files listed in the SYSSETUP.INF file and includes the optional installation components and their default InstallType setting.

TABLE 8.1 Activated Default Computer settings for the ZAK

File	Option	Default InstallType Setting
Accessor.inf	Calculator	10
	Character Map	10
	Clipboard Viewer	14
	Clock	14
	Desktop Wallpaper	0
	Document Templates	10
	Mouse Pointers	0
	Object Packager	14
	Paint	10
	Quick View	10
	Open GL Screen Savers	10
	Standard Screen Savers	10
Communic.inf	Chat	14
	Phone Dialer	14
	HyperTerminal	14
Games.inf	Freecell	0
	Mine Sweeper	0
	Solitaire	0
Pinball.inf	Pinball	0
Mmopt.inf	Media Options	10
	Musica Sound Scheme	0
	Jungle Sound Scheme	0
	Robotz Sound Scheme	0
	Utopia Sound Scheme	0
Multimed.inf	CD Player	14
	Media Player	14
	Sound Recorder	14
	Volume Control	14
Optional.inf	Accessibility Options	14
Wordpad.inf	Wordpad	10

Preventing a Full Options Category from Installing

To exclude all of the options in a particular category, such as Games, from being installed, simply place a semicolon before the `.inf` file name in the `SYSSETUP.INF` file. As a result, the complete category is ignored in the setup process. In Example 8.3, the `Games.inf` file is set to be ignored. As described in the preceding steps, the `SYSSETUP.IN_` file may have to be expanded in the `\I386` folder before you can amend the contents.

EXAMPLE 8.3 The `[BaseWinOptionsInfs]` section of the `SYSSETUP.INF` file

```
[BaseWinOptionsInfs]
accessor.inf
communic.inf
;games.inf
imagevue.inf
mmopt.inf
msmail.inf
multimed.inf
optional.inf
pinball.inf
wordpad.inf
```

Uniqueness Database Files

One of the problems in performing ZAK computer installations that you may have noticed by now is that for every computer you wish to install by this method, you have to supply certain unique information. Information such as computer name and license number need to be changed for each machine before the GUI portion of the setup starts. This means either creating a separate unattended install answer file for each computer (laborious and prone to error) or finding an automated way to achieve the desired result.

Uniqueness database files (UDBs) answer the need for an automated solution. A UDB can hold the unique information for many client computers and can substitute the values contained in the answer file. In this way, the answer file can provide most of the information, and can provide the UDB with any transient values.

A UDB file is built around an index of strings known as UniqueIDs. UniqueIDs are a reference to the computer that requires substitute values. When the `Winnt.exe` or `Winnt32.exe` command is used, an additional parameter must be supplied. The parameter is in the form `/UDF:ID[,`*`UDB_Filename`*`.UDB]`

The /UDF parameter supplies a unique ID for the computer that is going to be installed. This means that now you need to change only the command line for each individual setup instead of the answer file. The ID portion of the parameter can be any unique ID. It can be a number or a computer name. The UDB file name and path should be supplied; otherwise, during the setup, the technician is prompted to insert a disk containing the file. If the name and path are supplied, the file is copied to the local drive during Text-mode setup and this enables the setup to continue in unattended mode. However, any problems in matching the UniqueID supplied in the command line with one contained in the file will cause the setup to prompt for another file. If this prompt is answered with Cancel, the setup continues but uses the default values supplied in the unattended setup answer file.

The parameter for supplying a UDB is /UDF. The file extension for the UDB is .UDB. These are different and a common cause of error.

File Structure

The UDB is a plain text file that can be created with any text editor. The general format follows that of the unattended installation answer file (Unattend.txt in the case of the test environment). Section headers are enclosed in square brackets [ ], and each section header contains a value or values that may in turn point to further section headers.

[UNIQUEIDS]

The [UniqueIDs] section header is the first required entry. This section lists the UniqueIDs that will be referred to in the command-line call and associates UniqueIDs with the sections that will be replaced in the Unattend.txt file. The format is shown below.

```
[UniqueIDs]
ID1 = Section1, Section2
ID2 = Section1, Section3
ID3 = Section1, Section2, Section3, Section4
```

The UniqueIDs listed can be in almost any form. They can be user names, computer names, or references of some kind. The only rules are that you cannot use asterisk (*), space, comma, or equal sign (=).

[SECTIONS]

The remaining sections in this file are those referred to in the UniqueIDs section. You have a choice of format for these sections because there are two different ways of applying settings.

- **General sections**. These sections replace the corresponding section of the answer file for every UniqueID listed in the file. The section name is the same as that of the corresponding section in the answer file (`[Unattended]`, for example). If the section in the answer file contains five entries and you only list two entries in the section of the UDB, then the UDB will supply the two entries and the answer file will supply the other three.
- **ID-specific sections**. These sections also replace the corresponding section of the answer file, but only for a specific listed UniqueID. The section is named by a UniqueID and then by the section name from the answer file. A colon separates the two portions of the name. An example form of this section header type is `[ID1:Unattended]`. If a section exists for a named ID and answer file section combination, and also the general section as described above, the settings from the specific section are used.

EXCLUDED SECTIONS

Certain sections from the answer file cannot be included in the UDB file. These are:

```
[Display]
[KeyboardDrivers]
[MassStorageDrivers]
[Modem]
[OEM_Ads]
[OEMBootFiles]
[PointingDeviceDrivers]
```

Construction of a Uniqueness Database

Sections and keys in the UDB file can affect the parsing of the unattended install answer file in three ways.

- **Adding a Key**. A key that is not present in the answer file can still be added to the installation run. Place the relevant line in the UDB file under the correct section header, and then reference the section in the UniqueIDs section. When the installation is run for the UniqueID computer, the UDB file will be input, the section referenced, and the line read. The line will then be included in the installation even though it does not exist in the answer file. This technique has the same result as the addition of the line to the answer file although the answer file is never actually modified with this technique.

- **Replacing a Key**. If a key is included in a section in both the UDB file and the answer file, the entry in the UDB file takes precedence and is used for the UniqueIDs that reference the section. This has a net effect the same as replacing the line in the answer file, although the answer file is not changed with this technique.
- **Excluding a Key**. A key and its associated value can be excluded from the installation. Place the same key in the UDB, but leave the right-hand side of the equal sign empty. This has the net effect of removing the line from the answer file without amending that file.

You can create a UDB file from scratch in a plain text file by using any text editor. Follow the format discussed earlier in the File Structure section. Example 8.4 shows a UDB file followed by an example answer file to use as reference.

EXAMPLE 8.4 Sample UDB file

```
[UniqueIDs]
ZAKpc01 = Userdata, Network, TRParameters
ZAKpc02 = Userdata, Network, TRParameters
ZAKpc03 = Userdata, Network

[ZAKpc01:Userdata]
ComputerName = ZAKpc01
ProductID = 111-xxxxxx1

[ZAKpc01:TRParameters]
Netaddress = "40005000aaa1"

[ZAKpc02:Userdata]
ComputerName = ZAKpc02
ProductID = 111-xxxxxx2

[ZAKpc02:TRParameters]
Netaddress = "40005000aaa2"

[ZAKpc03:Userdata]
ComputerName = ZAKpc03
ProductID = 111-xxxxxx3

[Network]
JoinDomain = Pacific
```

In the UDB file shown in Example 8.4, three separate UniqueIDs are defined. Each of these UniqueIDs will be used in turn on the WINNT or WINNT32 command line when the installation is started. For the unattended installation, the `WINNT.EXE` command is used from a DOS boot disk. If the file in Example 8.4 named `Accounts.UDB` exists on the Network boot disk, the command line looks like this:

```
N:\i386\winnt.exe /U:a:\unattend.txt /S:n:\i386
   /UDF:ZAKpc01,a:\Accounts.UDB
```

In the preceding command, `N:` is the drive letter mapped to the network share point for the AppStation users. The `/U` switch supplies the unattended install answer file name and path, and the `/S` switch specifies the source name and path for NT system files. The `/UDF` parameter supplies the UniqueID for this computer and the path and file name of the `.UDB` file. For each subsequent computer, the only part of the command to be changed would be the UniqueID (ZAKpc01 in this case).

The relationship between the files shown in Examples 8.4 and 8.5 has three notable features.

- `[ID:Userdata]`—Defined separately for each UniqueID. A `[ZAKpc01:Userdata]` section contains settings solely for the use of the UniqueID specified. The `ComputerName` and `ProductID` keys contain values and so will replace the same keys in the answer file shown in Example 8.5. The other entries in the `[Userdata]` section of the answer file will still be applied, because they are not specified in the UDB. The same application method is applied to the other UniqueIDs. If the UDB is not loaded or specified for some reason, the computer name will be set to "Replaced" and the installation will hold, asking for a valid Product ID.
- `[ID:TRParameters]`—Defined separately for each UniqueID. The one key contained in this section, `Netaddress`, sets a different network address for both of the UniqueIDs that are defined to use this section. This key is not specified in the answer file, so if the UBD file was not processed, a network card would retain its burned in address. The two entries in the `[TRParameters]` section of the answer file are applied to all installations.
- `[Network]`—Defined once without a UniqueID prefix. All three UniqueIDs are set to use this section. Since it is a general section and there are no `[ID:Network]` sections to take precedence, the entries here will be set for all three UniqueIDs at installation. All three installations

will join the computers to the "Pacific" domain. Any problems with the UDB not loading or not being specified will cause installations to try and join the "TestDomain," as specified in the answer file. The outcome can be controlled. You can define the TestDomain so that the installations continue, or you can allow the installation to fail so that you know there is a problem. The keys in the [Network] section of the answer file that are not specified in the UDB file will be applied from the former.

EXAMPLE 8.5 Sample answer file

```
[Unattended]
OemPreinstall = no
ConfirmHardware = no
NtUpgrade = no
Win31Upgrade = no
TargetPath = WINNT
OverwriteOemFilesOnUpgrade = no

[UserData]
FullName = "administrator"
OrgName = "Mycompany"
ComputerName = replaced
ProductID = "XXX-XXXXXXX"

[GuiUnattended]
OemSkipWelcome = 1
OEMBlankAdminPassword = 1
TimeZone = "(GMT-05:00) Eastern Time (US & Canada)"

[Network]
InstallAdapters = AdaptersSection
InstallProtocols = ProtocolsSection
JoinDomain = TestDomain

[ProtocolsSection]
TC = TCParameters

[TCParameters]
DHCP = yes

[AdaptersSection]
IBMTRP = TRParameters,c:\ibmtrp

[TRParameters]
MaxTxFrameSize = 4096
DataRate = "M16"
```

System Tools

You use the tools described in this section during the ZAK installation and customization process. By default, the tools are called by command files. You can adjust the usage of these tools to suit your own requirements.

Attrib.exe

The `Attrib.exe` utility displays or sets attributes on files or folders. The + and - signs before the attribute letters signify that an attribute should either be set (+) or should be removed (-). If the command is used with only a file or folder name parameter, the current attributes are listed. The ZAK uses the `Attrib.exe` command extensively in the `Hide.cmd` command file to hide major parts of the local file system from the user.

SYNTAX

`Attrib.exe [ +a | -a | +h | -h | +r | -r | +s | -s |` *file/foldername* `| /s ]`

ATTRIBUTES • The attributes for this command can be `+/-a` (set/remove archive bit), `+/-h` (set/remove hidden attribute), `+/-r` (set/remove read-only attribute) and `+/-s` (set/remove system file attribute). Any number of attributes can be set or removed in one command call.

FILE/FOLDERNAME • The *file/foldername* parameter can be any valid file or folder for which you set, remove, or view attributes.

/S • The `/s` parameter indicates that the listed attributes should be set or removed on subfolders.

Cacls.exe

The `Cacls.exe` program displays or changes ACLs on files and folders held on an NTFS partition. This program is used extensively in the default ZAK behavior where it is run from the `Acls.cmd` file (in turn called from the `Zakb1wrk.cmd` file). Look at this command file for examples of how to use the `Cacls.exe` program.

SYNTAX

`Cacls.exe` *file/foldername* `[/C | /D` *user* `| /E | /G` *username:permission* `|` `/P` *username:permission* `| /R` *username* `| /T ]`

FILE/FOLDERNAME • The name of the file or folder to which the command applies. Wildcards can be used so that the command is applied to multiple files or even all files in the current folder and subfolders.

/C • The `/C` switch ensures that the command continues if an error is encountered. This is important if you are using the command within a batch file during an unattended installation.

/D USERNAME1 [USERNAME2...] • This switch denies access of the specified user to the file or folder structure. The username parameter can be a single user or a group, and multiple users can be listed in the one command call.

/E • The `/E` switch enables editing of an existing ACL as opposed to replacing the ACL.

/G USERNAME1:PERMISSION [USERNAME2:PERMISSION...] • This switch grants the specified permissions to the user. Multiple users can have permissions granted in one command call. The *username* parameter can be a user or group name. The *permission* parameter for each user can be `N` (No Access), `R` (Read), `C` (Change), `F` (Full Control).

/P USERNAME1:PERMISSION [USERNAME2:PERMISSION...] • This switch replaces permissions for the specified user on the file or folder structure. The *username* parameter can be a single user or a group, and multiple users can be listed in one command call. The *permission* parameter for each user can be `N` (No Access), `R` (Read), `C` (Change), `F` (Full Control).

/R USERNAME1 [USERNAME2...] • This switch completely revokes a user's permissions to a file or folder structure. The *username* parameter can be a single user or a group, and multiple users can be listed in one command call.

/T • The `/T` switch specifies that the command should be applied to the named files or folders in the current folder and in all subfolders.

Con2Prt.exe

`Con2Prt.exe` connects network printers for a particular user. It can also be used to disconnect all connected printers. The `Con2Prt.exe` program is used by the ZAK in the logon scripts provided for both TaskStation and AppStation users.

SYNTAX

`Con2Prt.exe [ /f | /cd \\`*printserver*`\`*printer1* `| /c \\`*printserver*`\`*printer2* `\\`*printserver*`\`*printer3*`...]`

Example: `Con2Prt.exe /f /cd \\IBSNT04\HP4_152 /c \\IBSNT04\HP4_Acc /c \\IBSNT04\Hpcolor`

/F • The `/f` switch removes all connected printers. If this switch is used, it must be the first switch and must be placed before any other switches.

/CD • The `/cd` switch connects the defined printer and sets it as the default printer for this user. If the `/cd` switch is used more than once, the next instance connects the printer but does not set it as the default printer.

/C • The `/c` switch connects network printers that will not be set as default printers. The `/c` switch can be repeated to cover multiple network printer connections.

FloppyLock

FloppyLock is a system service that controls access to the floppy drive. The system service is installed with the `INSTsrv` program and then can be used to control access to the floppy drive even after system restarts. When the service is installed and running on a Windows NT Server, only administrators can use the floppy drive. On an NT Workstation, only administrators and power users have access to the floppy drive. The default ZAK behavior runs the FloppyLock service installation from the `Zakb1wrk.cmd` command file.

INSTsrv.exe

`INSTsrv.exe` installs a system service in a quiet mode. The program is used in the ZAK to install the FloppyLock service described above.

SYNTAX

`INSTsrv` *servicename* `[`*exelocation* `| REMOVE | -a` *username* `| -p` *password*`]`

Example: `INSTsrv.exe Floppylocker %SystemRoot%\system32\floplock.exe -a \\thisDomain\administrator -p mypassword`

SERVICENAME • The `servicename` parameter is the name of the service as it will appear in the list of installed services within Control Panel.

EXELOCATION • The `exelocation` parameter is the full path and filename of the executable that sits behind the system service.

REMOVE • The `remove` parameter removes an installed system service. The following example removes the service called TestService from a Windows NT computer.

Example: `INSTsrv TestService REMOVE`

-A USERNAME • This switch provides a user name for the system service to run under.

-P PASSWORD • This switch provides the relevant password for the username switch described above.

Regedit.exe

`Regedit.exe` is a registry editing tool that enables you to make changes in the registry in quiet mode. This means that the registry changes can be scripted. `Regedit.exe` is used by the `Zakb1wrk.cmd` and the `AppCmds/TskCmds.cmd` command files to make registry changes for various keys and values.

SYNTAX

`Regedit.exe [ /s |` *filename*`.reg]`

/S • The `/s` switch runs the `regedit` command in quiet mode. The switch is required if you want to include the command in a script.

FILENAME.REG • The file name is the name of a text file containing a registry key or keys that must be changed with this command. Examples of the contents of these `.reg` files can be seen in the `C:\ZakAppDist\Netsys\I386\%OEM%\$$\Zak\Scripts` folder. The `.reg` files contained in this folder are all used during the ZAK client installation.

Do not double-click on one of these files to edit it. A `.reg` file type is associated with the registry editor by default, and double-clicking the file will merge the contents into your local registry.

Shutdown.exe

The `shutdown` command shuts down a Windows NT computer either locally or remotely. A text message can be displayed when the shutdown occurs; this message can be a maximum 127 characters long and must be enclosed in double quotes "". The shutdown command is used in the `Zakboot1.cmd` command file to shut down the computer with a 20-second delay and restart it after the Microsoft Office installation so that the machine is ready for logon by the user. The command line used for this procedure is shown in the example below.

Example: `SHUTDOWN /c /r /t:20`

SYNTAX

`Shutdown.exe [ \\`*Computername* `| /a | /c | /l | /r | /t:xxx | /y |` "*text message max 127 chars*"

\\COMPUTERNAME • The *Computername* parameter is supplied if the local machine is not the target of the shutdown command.

/A • The `/a` switch aborts a system shutdown that has been instigated but has not reached the end of the countdown period specified by the `/t:`*xxx* switch. After the countdown has finished and the shutdown is in progress, the `/a` switch cannot stop the shutdown.

/C • The `/c` switch forces any running applications to close during the shutdown. Using this switch means that running programs do not display any save data dialog boxes but are closed down immediately. This switch could lead to loss of data if used unwisely.

/L • The `/l` switch specifies that this is a local shutdown. This switch closes down the machine on which the command is run. The local computer is the default target for the shutdown unless a computer name is supplied so this switch is not necessary.

/R • This switch specifies that the computer should restart after the shutdown completes.

/T:xxx • This switch provides a countdown in seconds (*xxx*) before the shutdown starts. The default setting is 20 seconds.

/Y • This switch ensures that any questions arising from the shutdown command are answered as Yes.

SysDiff.exe

`SysDiff.exe` is a system difference tool used with the ZAK to install applications that cannot be set up in quiet mode. As you know, for an application to be installed along with the operating system in an unattended setup, the application must be able to be set up in quiet mode, that is, without requiring input from the user. When this is not possible, the SysDiff tool can be used to install the application.

The SysDiff tool works by taking a snapshot of a clean system before an application is installed, and then taking another after an application is installed. By comparing the two snapshots, the SysDiff tool can find the changes between the two snapshots and build a package containing these differences. The tool can then apply this package to a basic operating system installation, thus installing the application without requiring user input during the installation process. The onus of having to run in quiet mode is moved away from the application and onto the SysDiff tool. Because the SysDiff tool can work in quiet mode when it is applying a package to a system, it can be used to replace the application setup during an unattended system setup.

SysDiff has its limitations. It cannot apply an application that requires a system service to be created or amended. Device drivers cannot be added with SysDiff either.

INSTALLATION

The SysDiff tool is provided on the Windows NT 4.0 retail distribution media and also on the ZAK distribution media. You install the tool by simply copying the `SysDiff.exe` file and the `SysDiff.INF` file to any location on your machine. These files are already provided in the ZAK distribution points in the `C:\ZakAppDist\Netsys\I386\$OEM$\$$\Zak\Tools` folder.

SYNTAX

SysDiff has six possible command-line parameters and some optional switches. The command line syntax is `SysDiff.exe [/Snap | /Diff | /Apply | /Dump | /Inf | /Log:`*logfile name* `| /U | /C | /M ]`

/SNAP • The `/Snap` parameter runs SysDiff in snap mode, which takes a snapshot of the local system. The snapshot is output to the file name defined as *snap-shot-file* in the command syntax. The output file can have any valid file name.

Example: `SysDiff.exe /Snap` S*nap-shot-file*

/DIFF • The `/Diff` parameter runs SysDiff in difference mode, which compares the current system to the snapshot and creates a package of the differences, including files, registry settings, and contents of `.INI` files.

Example: `SysDiff.exe /Diff` *Snap-shot-file Package-file*

/APPLY • The `/Apply` parameter runs SysDiff in application mode, which applies the contents of a package file to the local machine. This parameter can be run after an unattended installation to apply applications at this point. The default ZAK machine setup or both TaskStation and AppStation computers use a form of this command to apply the Internet Explorer package.

Example: `SysDiff.exe /Apply` *Package-file*

/DUMP • The `/Dump` parameter runs SysDiff in dump mode, which outputs the contents of a package file into a readable text file. This parameter is used for troubleshooting. It can also be useful to acquaint you with the SysDiff tool; use it to look at package contents and understand how the internals of the process work.

Example: `SysDiff.exe /Dump` *Package-file Dump-file*

/INF • The `/Inf` parameter enables you to perform a slightly different type of installation than the `/Apply` parameter. Instead of copying the whole package file to the workstation as one file and then applying the contents, you can use the `/Inf` parameter to build a set of .Inf files for the package and create a folder structure below the `$OEM$` distribution point. This folder structure holds the files in their expanded form rather than in one package file. The files are then copied as part of the Windows NT setup procedure.

Example: `SysDiff.exe /Inf /m IE401.dif F:\I386`

/LOG • The `/Log` parameter defines the name of an optional log file that can be used with any of the other parameters.

Example: `SysDiff.exe /Diff /Log:C:\Winnt\Logs\Difference.log` *Package-file Dump-file*

/U • The `/U` switch forces all text output files to be created in UNICODE and can be used with any of the parameters shown above.

/C • The `/C` switch adds a comment to a package creation with the `/DIFF` parameter. When the package is then applied with the `/Apply` parameter, the comment is displayed for the user. This comment can be a short explanation of what the package is or why it is being applied. If the package is going to be applied with the `/Inf` mode parameter, then the comment should not be used because no separate package installation is carried out.

Example: `SysDiff.exe /Diff /Log:C:\Winnt\Logs\Difference.log /C:"Application Title"` *Snap-shot-file-file Package-file*

Note that the comment is enclosed in double quotes " ".

/M • Including a command made up from the `/M` switch with the `/Apply` parameter in a ZAK command file (usually the `Zakb1wrk.cmd` file) allows you to preinstall a package during the Windows NT setup process.

The `/M` switch redirects the changes that were captured during the `/Diff` mode run. For example, if Administrator is logged on when the `/Diff` mode is run, changes to the Start menu are captured from `\%SystemRoot%\Profiles\Administrator\Start Menu\Programs` folder structure. When the `/Apply` parameter is specified, these changes would normally be applied to exactly the same folder structure. When the `/M` switch is specified, these changes are redirected to the Default User profile on the new machine; thus all newly created users will have these changes placed in their profiles. The default ZAK behavior uses this switch to apply the Internet Explorer difference file from the `Zakb1wrk.cmd` command file.

NINE

Step-Through Customization

In This Chapter

- Introduction
- Project 1: Windows NT Installation
- Project 2: System Policies
- Summary

This chapter looks at two full customization projects for the ZAK. Using the test installation environment that was created in the first part of this book as a base, the chapter takes you through all of the steps involved in the customization process.

Starting from the user definition and moving through the design phase, the chapter looks at what needs to be accomplished, then moves to the actual customization work. At the end of the chapter, you should feel confident that you can take the default ZAK installation and mold the design and implementation routines into a significant tool to be used on your own site.

Introduction

The customization of the default ZAK behavior is necessary unless you are very lucky and the default setup of the task-based workers meets your needs exactly. However, the reality is that we all have different business applications to install and use, and the level of control imposed on users will vary according to company policy, user skill level, and any previous experience of user-related problems.

The projects that follow will take you through the many ways to modify the ZAK in a meaningful way so that you can get the most out of the structure and methodologies offered by the base kit.

Project 1: Windows NT Installation

This first project concentrates on the customization of the Windows NT installation process. The ZAK can help you control management costs in many ways. You can reduce the amount of time it takes to perform an installation. You can produce many installations that are exactly the same, thus providing a unified workstation environment to the user. You can install applications during the Windows NT setup process and further reduce the time it takes to roll out a machine. In this project, we develop a sample workstation definition. Then, we step through the amendments to the default ZAK installation process. The step-through exercises for this project take you through a whole cycle of customizing a Windows NT installation. This cycle includes making changes to optional portions of the OS setup to tailor the end result to fit your requirements. Also included are instructions that customize the ZAK mode portion of the NT installation. During an unattended installation, applications are installed from this customized portion. Here, too, the most benefit can be gained when it comes to tailoring the workstation installation.

Prerequisites

The equipment prerequisites for this project are based on those from Chapter 2, in which the test environment was built. You should have completed the full test environment build described in Chapter 2 including the NT TaskStation and AppStation setups and all of the other ancillary tasks.

SERVER

The lab environment server requires the following equipment and setup characteristics:

- One primary domain controller (*no* backup domain controllers) with Windows NT Server 4.0 installed
- Service Pack 3 (or greater) installed
- 32 Mbytes RAM (or higher)
- CD-ROM drive
- NetBIOS name **IBSNT04**
- Domain name **NTDOM01**
- ZAK installation software
- At least 1 Gbyte free disk space

WORKSTATION

The test environment requires the following workstation setup.

- One workstation machine
- Windows NT 4.0 Workstation distribution media
- NetBIOS named **TestPC1** is used
- Windows NT 4.0 Resource Kit
- Office 97 distribution media
- Office 97 Resource Kit
- Floppy disk drive in each machine
- Minimum of 300 Mbytes free disk space on clean hard drive; no OS installed
- Unattend-aware network interface card in each machine
- MS-DOS boot disk for each different network interface card type

Customization Goals

The following sections contain all of the workstation definitions that are used for this lab installation type. The changes from the base ZAK workstation build are significant; they include replacing portions of the distribution point (useful when new service packs come along), controlling the optional component installations to reduce clutter in the menu system, and using Sys-Diff to install an application. The changes made to the ZAK distribution point for this project will be made in the `C:\ZakAppDist` folder structure, which we created in Chapter 2 when setting up the NT AppStation.

SERVICE PACK REPLACEMENT

- Service Pack 4 will be applied in place of Service Pack 3.

OPTIONAL COMPONENTS

- The Games components and Pinball will not be installed.
- The Communications components will not be installed.
- Multimedia programs and options will not be installed.
- The Accessories components group will be reduced as follows:
  - Calculator included.
  - Clock included.
  - Quick View included.
  - All other Accessories components will not be installed.

- Accessibility options will be installed.
- Wordpad will be installed.
- The Microsoft Exchange Client icon setup will be excluded from the installation.

EXCLUDING THE COPY OF UNWANTED OPTIONAL SOFTWARE

- Exclude Peer Web Services from the installation.
- Exclude the copy of third-party network drivers from the installation.
- Exclude Internet Explorer 2 from the installation.

ADJUSTING FILE SYSTEM SECURITY

- Add/Remove controls from the `Acls.cmd` command file.
- Add/Remove controls from the `Hide.cmd` command file.

SYSDIFF INSTALLATION: INTERNET EXPLORER

- Replace Internet Explorer 3 with an Internet Explorer 4 package in the distribution point.

Service Pack Replacement

From time to time, parts of the distribution point for the ZAK client setup may need to be replaced, for example, to update the Service Pack to the latest release. The replacement of the Service Pack distribution is quite simple.

The first step is to remove the existing Service Pack files from the server. These are located in the AppStation distribution point under the `C:\ZakAppDist\netsys\I386\$OEM$\$$\SP` folder. Next, you copy the files from the Service Pack 4 CD to the distribution point.

1. Start NT Explorer on the Domain controller.
2. Navigate to the **C:\ZakAppDist\netsys\I386\$OEM$\$$\SP** folder.
3. Select the whole contents of the folder and choose **File** > **Delete**.
4. Confirm all of the deletions as necessary.
5. Place the Service Pack 4 CD in the drive on the server.
6. Copy the contents of the folder **X:\I386** to the **C:\ZakAppDist\netsys\I386\$OEM$\$$\SP** folder.

The service pack files from SP4 will only be applied to new machine installations. Existing machines must be updated in another manner. One way you can do this is to use the SysDiff program to build a Service Pack package or you can run a service pack update remotely in quiet mode on the workstation.

The service pack is installed during the ZAK workstation installation process from the `AppCmds.cmd` command file and is run in quiet mode so that no responses are required.

Optional Components

The optional components of Windows NT 4.0 are a mixture of unproductive programs such as games, multimedia add-ons, and accessories, some of which may be useful. For this next exercise, I have listed the components that I find most useful in my own environment and have listed those components that could be considered to be distracting while adding little or no value to the system. All of these components can be controlled by access control systems such as profiles and policies, but a question you should ask yourself is "Why install a component that you don't want used?" The exclusion of some optional components can also speed up installation.

Although the installation of the optional components can be controlled, the creation of shortcuts in the Accessories group still takes place. Although this looks untidy, the contents of the Start Menu folders should be controlled by user profiles or system policies, so it makes little difference.

To control which components are installed, you must edit the appropriate `.inf` files, which control the installation behavior.

1. Open a **DOS prompt** on the Server.
2. Navigate to the **C:\ZapAppDist\Netsys\I386** folder. This is the source folder that we use for these exercises.
3. Type **Expand.exe SYSSETUP.IN_ SYSSETUP.INF** and press **Enter**. This command expands the compressed file into a usable state.
4. Rename the **SYSSETUP.IN_** file to **SYSSETUP.OLD**.
5. Edit the **SYSSETUP.INF** file with any text editor, and find the **[BaseWinOptionsInfs]** section.
6. Place a semicolon before the **Games.inf**, **Pinball.inf**, **Communic.inf**, **Mmopt.inf**, **Multimed.inf**, and **Msmail.inf** entries. The semicolon excludes these entire options categories from the installation.
7. Save the **SYSSETUP.INF** file.

The resulting `SYSSETUP.INF` file contains a `[BaseWinOptionsInfs]` section that looks like the one listed in Example 9.1. Rename the compressed file so the expanded file is automatically used during an installation.

EXAMPLE 9.1 The [BaseWinOptionsInfs] section after editing

```
[BaseWinOptionsInfs]
accessor.inf
;communic.inf
;games.inf
imagevue.inf
;mmopt.inf
;msmail.inf
;multimed.inf
optional.inf
;pinball.inf
wordpad.inf
```

In the second stage in the customization of the Optional Components installation, we select the options from within the Accessories category that will be installed and we tag those that will not.

1. Open a **DOS prompt** on the Server.
2. Navigate to the **C:\ZapAppDist\Netsys\I386** folder. This is the source folder that we use for these exercises.
3. Type **Expand.exe ACCESSOR.IN_ ACCESSOR.INF <Enter>**. This command expands the compressed file into a usable state.
4. Rename the **ACCESSOR.IN_** file to **ACCESSOR.OLD**. If the compressed file doesn't exists at installation time, the expanded file is used.
5. Edit the **ACCESSOR.INF** file with any text editor.
6. Navigate to the **[Calc]** section. Set the **InstallType** option to **10**.
7. Navigate to the **[Clock]** section. Set the **InstallType** option to **10**.
8. Navigate to the **[Quick View]** section. Set the **InstallType** option to **10**.
9. Go to each of the following sections in turn and change the **InstallType** setting to **0**. This setting excludes them from the Typical mode setup performed during an Unattended installation.

   - [CharMap]
   - [ClipBook]
   - [Deskpaper]
   - [MousePoint]
   - [ObjectPkg]
   - [Paint]
   - [ScreenSave]
   - [SSOpenGL]
   - [SSStandard]
   - [Templates]

10. Save the file.

As a result of the preceding editing, only the components of Accessories that have had the InstallType set to 10 will be installed, as we see later in the project when the client installation is performed.

Excluding the Copy of Unwanted Optional Software

Peer Web Services is one of the optional items that we can exclude from the Windows NT setup, thereby saving the time it takes to copy the source files to the local workstation. If your installation does not require this service, it is a good idea to exclude it. Even if the service is required, it cannot be installed through an unattended installation but must be installed after the installation.

Another item that can be excluded is the copying of the third-party network card driver folders, if you know that the driver for your network cards can be found in another place. This exclusion can also save time.

1. Start Windows Explorer on the Server.
2. Navigate to the **C:\ZapAppDist\Netsys\I386** folder.
3. Double-click the **DOSNET.INF** file to edit it in Notepad. This file does not require expanding.
4. Navigate to the **[OptionalSrcDirs]** section.
5. Place a semicolon before the **Inetsrv** entry and the **Drvlib.nic** entry.
6. Save the file. You may have to change the read-only attribute to save the file and then make the file read-only again.

Example 9.2 shows the section after proper editing.

EXAMPLE 9.2 The `[OptionalSrcDirs]` section after editing

```
[OptionalSrcDirs]
;inetsrv
;drvlib.nic
```

Removing the entries under the `[OptionalSrcDirs]` section prevents the source files from being copied to the workstation. This could save a large amount of time over many installations. Internet Explorer is the final exclusion that we will make in this part of the project. During the initial installation, Internet Explorer 2.0 is installed. The ZAK then replaces this with Internet Explorer 3.02. Later in this project, we will build a package to install Internet Explorer 4.01. The upshot here is that we do not need Internet Explorer 2.0 installed. Again, removing this item can save time over many installations. The following instructions are based on the `SYSSETUP.INF` file having been expanded in the previous section.

1. Edit the **SYSSETUP.INF** file in the `C:\ZapAppDist\Netsys\I386` folder with any text editor and find the **[Infs.Always]** section.
2. Place a semicolon before the **Iexplore.inf** entry.
3. Save the file.

Example 9.3 shows the section after proper editing.

EXAMPLE 9.3 The `[Infs.Always]` section after editing

```
[Infs.Always]
;Iexplore.inf, DefaultInstall
```

Adjusting File System Security

Both the `Acls.cmd` file and the `Hide.cmd` file apply file system security to the local workstation. They are run from the `Zakb1wrk.cmd` command file during the ZAK mode portion of the installation. You can adjust both of these files to meet your particular needs for local file system security.

ACLS.CMD

File system security is an important consideration when it comes to rolling out network-connected machines. The role of the machine needs to be considered along with the contents of the local hard disk(s). Historically, these have been the two main considerations for deciding how much security needs to be applied to the local workstation. If the workstation contained only applications and no data, then security was generally left at the default setting (minimal). This practice led to machines being interfered with and resulting downtime both of which cost the organization real money.

When looking at a ZAK deployment, consider the result of intrusion into your system. The `Acls.cmd` file applies strengthened security standards to the local machine. You should consider using this command file in your final deployment to secure system files and any other possible danger areas from unwanted intrusion by users.

The `Acls.cmd` file only contains entries regarding files and folders that the default ZAK knows about. If you install further applications, then you must manually add the relevant files and folders to this file and set the relevant level of protection.

You can avoid applying any of the settings in this command file by commenting the entry out in the `Zakb1wrk.cmd` file. The final two entries in a standard `Zakb1wrk.cmd` file call the `Acls.cmd` and the `Hide.cmd` files. An `@REM` comment placed before the `Acls.cmd` command file call prevents the file from running.

HIDE.CMD

The `Hide.cmd` file uses the `ATTRIB +H` command to apply the `Hidden` attribute to the entire file system on the local drive. This command can cause a problem with some applications if certain files are hidden. If you choose to use this functionality, you may have to experiment a little when deciding which files to hide.

The functionality here is possibly better implemented by a system policy that hides the drive itself. Again, some applications may not like this, but my experiences in this area show that the system policy is received better by more applications than simply hiding individual files and folders.

To remove the functionality completely, comment out the command file (with an `@REM`) in the `Zakb1wrk.cmd` command file.

SysDiff Installation—Internet Explorer

`SysDiff.exe` is the system difference tool provided by Microsoft. The tool's main purpose is to take a snapshot of a base system before an application is installed. You can then compare this snapshot with the updated system after the application is installed and output the differences to a package file. This file can then be applied to other base systems (systems without the application installed), and the result is an application installation.

The question arises then, "Why not run the application installation?" The main use of SysDiff is for unattended installation or installations where quiet mode is required. Some applications do not support a quiet mode installation, so the conversion from an application installation process to a SysDiff application is necessary. The SysDiff application can then be run in quiet mode as required.

This exercise illustrates the procedures for installing the Internet Explorer 4.01 application on a Windows NT workstation with SysDiff. This application has been chosen simply as an exercise. The same rules and procedures apply to the use of SysDiff on any application, not just Internet Explorer. You can easily amend the instructions that follow and apply them to any application that you wish.

PREPARING THE BASE INSTALLATION

Complete the following preparatory steps in order. At the end of this section, you will have a clean base installation from which to take a snapshot. Normally, you should perform this AppStation installation in the same way as the planned installations for future uses of the ZAK. The reason for this is that SysDiff works best when the snapshot is taken from a system that resembles the installation(s) that the snapshot will be applied to.

1. Ensure that you have followed the instructions in the second portion of the *Excluding the Copy of Unwanted Optional Software* section to exclude the Internet Explorer 2 installation on the workstation. There is little point in going through with this installation when Internet Explorer 4 is going to be installed.
2. Edit the **Zakb1wrk.cmd** file found in the **C:\ZakAppDist\Netsys\I386\$OEM$\$$\Zak\Scripts** folder on the server, and comment out (use **@REM** before the command) the command call for both **Acls.cmd** and **Hide.cmd**. These command files can interfere with the application installation we do for this exercise. You can remove the comments later and include the commands in future installations if required.
3. Edit the **Zakb1wrk.cmd** file described in the previous step and comment out the line **%SystemRoot%\zak\tools\sysdiff /apply /m %SystemRoot%\zak\scripts\msie302.dif**. This command uses SysDiff to apply a package containing Internet Explorer 3.02. This is the line that will be replaced later in the customization process so that Internet Explorer 4.01 is applied instead. For this exercise, there is no point in installing the earlier version of the product.
4. Perform a full AppStation client installation as described in *Part One* of this book. Ensure that only the AppStation installation is performed. No other configuration work should be done on the machine. We install the AppStation client because the changes we made in the previous sections were all made in the AppStation distribution folder structure. This machine is going to be used as the base installation from which we will take a snapshot. The main reason for this choice is that the Internet Explorer package file installation will be included in the AppStation setup process. It is critical that the snapshot be taken when the machine is in the same stage of preparedness as future installations will be when the SysDiff file is applied during the ZAK setup process.
5. When the installation is complete, log on to the workstation locally as Administrator. Do not log on to the workstation as any of the defined ZAK users; doing so may make changes to the machine that are not desired at the moment.
6. Copy the files **SysDiff.exe** and **SysDiff.inf** from the Windows NT Server CD in the folder **\Support\Deptools\I386** to the root of the local workstation **C: drive**. Do this via floppy disk rather than by connecting network drives. The fewer system changes, the better from this point onward. The SysDiff tool is also provided on the ZAK distribution media.

The resulting AppStation client machine should have been through the AppStation setup but should have missed some of the final ZAK mode stages. Internet Explorer 3.02 has not been installed. The file system has not had the security applied and is still visible because the `Hide.cmd` file was not run. If you chose to implement all of the changes described in the earlier sections of this chapter, then only the named optional Accessories applications are available (Calculator, Clock, and Wordpad) along with those applications, such as Notepad, that are always installed. The Accessories folder should have far fewer subfolders because of the full options groups, such as Games, that were excluded. Figure 9.1 shows a sample Accessories folder after this installation has been completed.

SYSTEM SNAPSHOT

Now that you have prepared a base system, you need to take a snapshot. To do this, you should be logged on locally as Administrator. No applications should be running. Ensure that no extra network drives have been connected or any system changes made in any way since you logged on. This check is important.

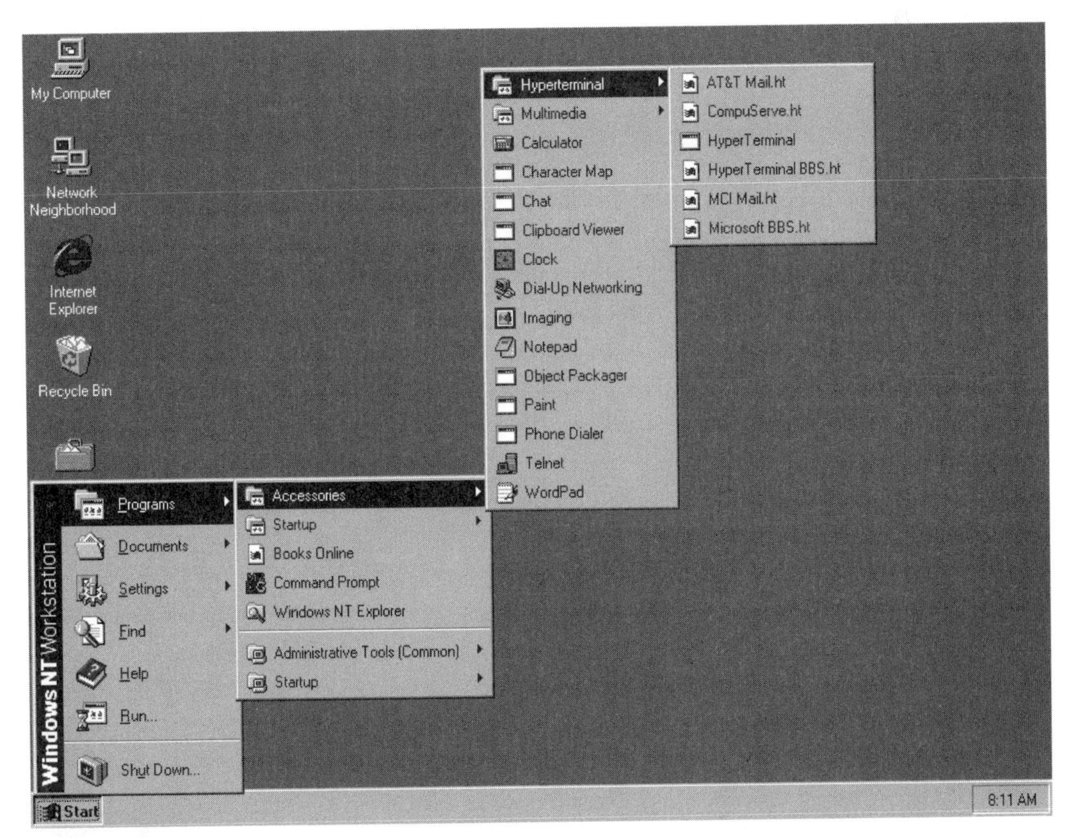

FIGURE 9.1 Accessories folder has fewer entries because of the reduced nature of the installation

1. Start a **Dos Prompt** session.
2. Change directory to the root of the **C: Drive**.
3. Enter the command **SysDiff /Snap C:\AppStat.snp** and press Enter. The SysDiff application starts, and three progress boxes are displayed. One box shows the progress of the File and Folder snapshot, one shows the progress of the Registry snapshot, and the third shows the `.INI` file snapshot. Figure 9.2 shows the snapshot in progress.
4. At the end of the snapshot process, an indicator tells you that the snapshot was successful and names the output file (in this case, **C:\AppStat.snp**).

INSTALL THE APPLICATION

As mentioned earlier, the application could be almost any that you wish to install via SysDiff. All applications are developed in different ways, so you will need to thoroughly test all applications on which you wish to use SysDiff.

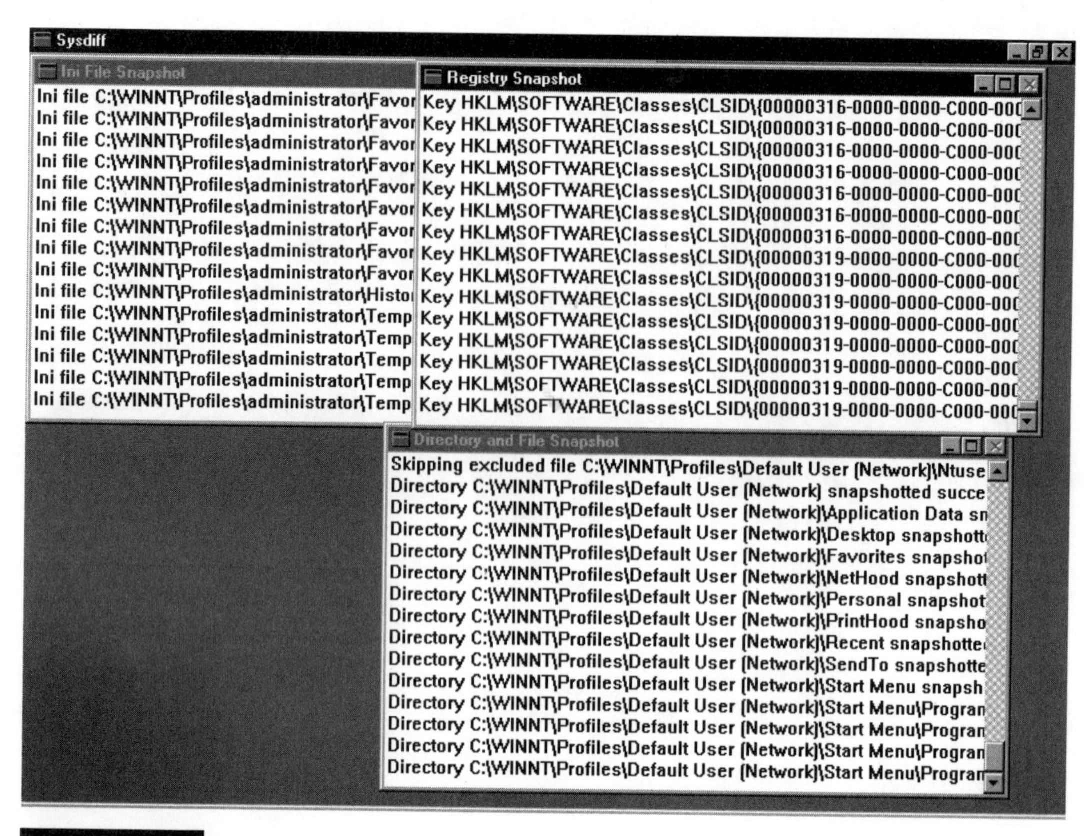

FIGURE 9.2 Snapshot in progress using SysDiff

Some applications may not install properly with SysDiff. Swapping between the `/Apply` method of application and the `/INF` method may cure some of the difficulties you may encounter.

Internet Explorer 4.01 is the application being installed here. For this exercise, I have the source software on CD. If you need to install from the network and are forced to map a drive, then ensure that the drive mapping is removed before running the `/Diff` process. If the drive mapping is not removed, the `/Diff` process will note that a network drive that was not there before is mapped and will include the mapping in the installation package.

This is the time when most problems occur with SysDiff. Now that you have a snapshot of the system, any single change in the system may be recorded as a difference and so included in the installation package. You must make sure that changes are limited to those required by the application.

1. Place the source media in the CD drive, or map a network drive to the source.
2. Start the application setup, in this particular case, by running the **Ie4setup.exe** program. The details of the installation are irrelevant because you could just as easily use some other productivity tool such as an Accounts package. However, during this installation I have not only installed the software but also configured it so that all further installations will be preconfigured.
3. Complete the installation and reboot the machine. Some change is almost inevitable on the first reboot after an application is installed, so it is better to reboot before you run the `/Diff`.

CAPTURE THE DIFFERENCES

It is important to capture the system differences as soon as possible after the application is installed. Many unwanted changes can occur by accident, and these can influence the make-up of the final package file.

1. Start a **Dos Prompt** session.
2. Change directory to the root of the **C: Drive**.
3. Enter the command **SysDiff /Diff /C "Internet Explorer 4.01 package Installation" C:\AppStat.snp C:\IE401.dif** and press Enter. The SysDiff application starts and the differences between those stored in the **AppStat.snp** snapshot file and the current system settings are recorded in the **IE401.dif** package file. The `/C` switch adds a comment to the package file, which is displayed when it is applied by `/Apply` mode.
4. At the end of the difference process, an indicator tells you that the process was successful and names the output file (in this case, **C:\IE401.dif**).

5. Copy the **C:\IE401.dif** file to the network distribution point for the AppStation computer. This will be the **C:\ZakAppDist\Netsys\I386\$OEM$\$$\Zak\Scripts** folder on the server. The folder should contain the **MSIE302.dif** file (the ZAK-supplied Internet Explorer 3.02 package). There is no reason why network drives cannot be mapped at this point.

RUNNING THE WORKSTATION INSTALLATION: OPTION 1

Now that you have created the package file for Internet Explorer 4.01, you need to include it in the ZAK-mode installation process. Internet Explorer is installed on the workstation in the final part of the installation. The installation command is included in the `Zakb1wrk.cmd` command file found in the `C:\ZakAppDist\Netsys\I386\$OEM$\$$\Zak\Scripts` folder.

1. On the Server, edit the **`Zakb1wrk.cmd`** command file and go to the Internet Explorer installation command line that was previously commented out. It should read `@REM %SystemRoot%\zak\tools\sysdiff /apply /m %SystemRoot%\zak\scripts\msie302.dif`.
2. Replace the file name **MSIE302.dif** with the new filename **IE401.dif**. Since the new file was placed in the same folder as the old, the remainder of the command can be left intact.
3. Remove the comment **`@REM`** from the front of the command. This command exists twice in the file. The first occurrence is in the descriptive portion of the file, and the second is in the active command portion. Ensure that you uncomment the entry in the active command portion of the file.
4. You may wish to uncomment the entries that run the `Acls.cmd` and the `Hide.cmd` files at this point.
5. Save the file and exit. The active command portion of the file should now look like that shown in Example 9.4.
6. Run the AppStation installation to look at the results. You can run the installation on the same base machine that you used for the snapshot and Internet Explorer setup. Your default AppStation installation should format the workstation hard disk so that it is clean before the setup takes place.

EXAMPLE 9.4 The amended `Zakb1wrk.cmd` command file

```
@rem uncomment the following line if you want sms
@rem cmd /c \\opktest3\sms_shr\runsms.bat
@net use O: \\IBSNT04\NETAPPS /user:NTDOM01\administrator w1rkhab0
cmd /c %SystemRoot%\zak\scripts\off97.cmd
cmd /c %SystemRoot%\zak\scripts\cleanup.cmd
@rem uncomment the following line if you want sms
```

```
@rem cmd /c copy %SystemRoot%\zak\scripts\smsrun32.lnk
%SystemRoot%\"profiles\All Users\Start Menu\PROGRAMS\STARTUP"
%SystemRoot%\zak\tools\sysdiff /apply /m %SystemRoot%\zak\scripts\IE401.dif
cmd /c rmdir /s /q %SystemRoot%\sp
REGEDIT.EXE /S %SystemRoot%\zak\scripts\noautlog.REG
%SystemRoot%\zak\tools\instsrv FloppyLocker %SystemRoot%\system32\floplock.exe
@net user administrator password
@REM cmd /c %SystemRoot%\zak\scripts\acls.cmd
@REM cmd /c %SystemRoot%\zak\scripts\hide.cmd
```

The Internet Explorer 4.01 installation now takes place during the ZAK-mode portion of the Windows NT workstation unattended setup. Remember that the ZAK-mode portion runs after the full NT installation has finished, using the autologon feature to gain access to the machine.

Make sure you have copied the difference package files to the server distribution point before beginning a new installation. Otherwise, you may lose your package file and have to start over, because the first step in the network boot disk formats the drive.

RUNNING THE WORKSTATION INSTALLATION: ALTERNATIVE APPLICATION

The second way to install software that you have packaged with `SysDiff.exe` is to install it as part of the Windows NT primary installation. The `/Apply` mode installation discussed above copies the single package file to the local workstation during the Text-mode portion of the setup, and the command file to perform the installation is called during the ZAK mode portion of the setup.

A second method of installing a software package is to use the `/Inf` mode parameter of SysDiff. In this mode, the files are extracted from the package and placed as a folder structure under the `$OEM$` folder structure of the ZAK distribution point. The necessary folder structure and files are placed here along with a `.INF` file that describes the registry entries/deletions and any `.INI` file changes. For compatibility, all of the files placed in this structure are named in their DOS 8.3 format. A file named `$$Rename.txt` holds the DOS format to a long filename format translation table. A command is added to the `CMDLINES.TXT` file to run the application installation.

This method of installation can be useful, but it is more prone to errors than is the `/Apply` mode. If an application will not install in `/Inf` mode, then `/Apply` mode may well work. The steps to perform a `/Inf` mode application are outlined below.

1. Install a base installation, perform a system snapshot, install the package, and build a difference file, as shown earlier in this section.
2. Run the command `SysDiff.exe /inf /m` *package_filename OEM_folder_root*. The OEM_folder_root parameter is the path to the `I386` folder on the distribution point that already contains the `$OEM$` folder.
3. Ensure that the command to run the application installation has been automatically placed in the **CMDLINES.TXT** file. A sample command would be `rundll32 setupapi,InstallHinfSection Default-Install 128 .\ie401.INF` where a suffix of the `ie401.INF` parameter indicates the name of the difference file that was used to build the application folder structure.
4. The workstation installation can be run, and the application should install as part of the Windows NT setup.

When you first attempt this method you may come across problems that require user intervention. For example, if any of the files that you are installing in the application are older than already installed files (such as those from a service pack), you may be prompted to keep the newer file. You must work through this type of problem, noting the file name and your decision (keep or overwrite). Then, either you can replace the file in the `\system32` folder of the distribution point with the file from the `$OEM$` folder structure, or you can remove the file from the `$OEM$` structure so the copy attempt doesn't take place.

It is worth noting here that in Microsoft's default kit, the `/Apply` mode method of installing Internet Explorer is used, so this is probably not a good application to use as an experiment with the `/Inf` mode.

MULTIPLE APPLICATION INSTALLATIONS

To install more applications in the same way, follow the steps outlined below.

1. Perform the base machine installation.
2. Run **SysDiff** in **/Snap** mode to take a snapshot of the system.
3. Install **Application1,** taking all of the precautions against unwanted changes outlined in the previous sections.
4. Run **SysDiff** in **/Diff** mode, and move the output package file to the server distribution point.
5. On another base installation, install the application, using **SysDiff /Apply**. Test this installation thoroughly for any problems.
6. When you are satisfied with the first package, apply the package to a base installation.

7. Run **SysDiff** in **/Snap** mode and take another snapshot of the system. This snapshot is post installation and testing of Application1.
8. Install **Application2,** taking the same precautions against unwanted changes.
9. Run **SysDiff** in **/Diff** mode to record the differences in a package file.
10. Apply this application package to a "base installation + Application1 machine," and thoroughly test the system.
11. Move the package files to the server distribution point.
12. Repeat the "snapshot, installation, difference" routine for further applications as needed. You should move your base system on with each application so that the next application is placed on top of the previous one.
13. Place the **SysDiff /Apply** commands in the **Zakb1wrk.cmd** command file in the order that the files were created, one command for each package file.

It is best to install only one application in each SysDiff package. Unwanted results may occur if you attempt to install more than one application between the snapshot and difference phase of the routine.

I cannot overstress the need for a sanitized system. Packages should be built from clean installations, and a clean test environment should be used.

When you get used to the power of the SysDiff tool you will realize just how versatile it really is. Instead of installing an application with the tool, you could simply copy files. For example, if all of your users are required to use an online fax product and they must all use the same cover sheet, you could copy the template file to the server by using SysDiff. You could take a snapshot of a system and then place the templates in the correct folder. The difference file would only contain the template files. Then, you could use SysDiff in a login script to place the files on existing machines, and in the ZAK command files to place the files on new installations.

Project 2: System Policies

This second project looks at the customization process for the policies supplied with the ZAK. As discussed in previous chapters, system policies provide the strictest method of applying control to the desktop. You can still gain benefits however, by simply using user profiles to present a uniform look and feel and to eliminate some of the distractions that might otherwise cost production time. The final choice needs to be an informed one. Consider the level of user competency, corporate regulations, user relations (will your users think that you are trying to be "Big Brother"), and your TCO-related goals when deciding what amount of control should be put in place.

Prerequisites

The equipment prerequisites for this project are based on those from the previous project. As with the previous project, the full test environment build described in Chapter 2, including the NT TaskStation and AppStation setups and all of the other ancillary tasks, should be completed before continuing.

SERVER

The lab environment server requires the following equipment and setup characteristics.

- One primary domain controller (*no* backup domain controllers) with Windows NT Server 4.0 installed
- Service Pack 3 (or greater) installed
- 32 Mbytes RAM (or higher)
- CD-ROM drive
- NetBIOS name **IBSNT04**
- Domain name **NTDOM01**
- ZAK installation software
- At least 1 Gbyte free disk space

WORKSTATION

The test environment requires the following workstation setup.

- One workstation machine
- Windows NT 4.0 Workstation distribution media
- NetBIOS named **TestPC1** is used
- Windows NT 4.0 Resource Kit
- Office 97 distribution media
- Office 97 Resource Kit
- Floppy disk drive in each machine
- Minimum of 300 Mbytes free disk space on clean hard drive; *no* OS installed
- Unattend-aware network interface card in each machine
- MS-DOS boot disk for each different network interface card type

Customization Goals

The following list contains all of the workstation definitions that are used for this lab installation type. The changes from the base ZAK environment behavior include the following: using system policies to change the desktop look presented to different user types and using user profiles to provide a less stringent level of control for one user group in particular. The changes made to the ZAK distribution point for this lab will be made in the `C:\ZakAppDist` folder structure created in Chapter 2 during the NT App-Station setup. If you have made changes to this structure since it was created (possibly by following the exercises in Project 1), then you should restore the structure from backup or remove the structure and re-create it to start from a clean base installation.

USER DEFINITION

- Define the different user groups according to the level of control that is needed.

TEMPLATE AMENDMENT

- Make a change to one of the supplied templates.

POLICY CREATION

- Create global groups that match the user definitions created in the first part of the project.
- Add test users to the new global groups.
- Begin a new policy file.
- Set up policies for the global groups.

BUILD POLICIES FOR EACH GLOBAL GROUP

- Create the global groups mentioned above.
- Add global group policy icons and Administrator policy icon.
- Define the Default User policy.
- Define the Default Computer policy.
- Define the group policies.
- Define the Administrator policy.

User Definition

One of your tasks for using ZAK is to define your user groups. The criteria for user definitions vary, but some of the basics include job responsibilities, required applications, user proficiency level, and a measurement of the required level of control that you wish to impose.

For this exercise, we define four groups.

- **Accounts**. This group needs to run a specific accounting package from a mainframe. No other system access is required.
- **Sales**. The Sales staff require a limited number of applications for their job responsibilities. Microsoft Office is used along with mainframe access to a sales system.
- **Marketing**. Marketing staff require the access that Sales staff have plus functionality provided by Windows NT such as Calculator, Paint, and other Accessories.
- **Managers**. The Managers group needs access to any of the applications that are used by members of the first three groups. In addition, the managers would like to avoid the restrictions of imposed control by IS staff.

Template Amendment

The `ZAKwinnt.adm` template file contains a setting that allows you to control which drives (local and network) are visible to the user. By hiding drives, you prevent users from browsing drives and possibly deleting or moving files.. This kind of control is best left to NTFS permissions if possible, but take an example of an application that writes temporary files to the network location that holds the application. Users might need full access to the location for the application to work correctly. In this case, you could hide the drive so that users couldn't browse the folders and possibly cause problems.

By default, the only offerings for hiding drives in this template are for all the drives, the `C:` drive, the `U:` drive, the `O:` drive or combinations of these. You can find the section that controls this setting in the `ZAKwinnt.adm` file by searching for the reverse alphabet string `"zyxwvut"`.

In our exercise, we add two more options to the drive exclusion list. The first additional option allows a user to see only local drives up to and including `E:`, and the second option allows users to see every alternate drive (evens only). This second option allows users to see `B:`, `D:`, `F:`, `H:`, etc., if they exist.

The relevant section from the `ZAKwinnt.adm` file is shown in Example 9.5.

EXAMPLE 9.5 An extract from the `ZAKwinnt.adm` file

```
KEYNAME Software\Microsoft\Windows\
     CurrentVersion\Policies\Explorer
    PART !!HideDrivesOption  DROPDOWNLIST
    VALUENAME "NoDrives"
    ITEMLIST
     Name !!HideDrives_all   VALUE NUMERIC 67108863
     Name !!HideDrives_C     VALUE NUMERIC 67108859 ; (67108863 - 4)
     Name !!HideDrives_U     VALUE NUMERIC 66060287
     Name !!HideDrives_CU    VALUE NUMERIC 66060283
     Name !!HideDrives_COU   VALUE NUMERIC 66043899
    END ITEMLIST
```

Corresponding entries in the `[strings]` section of the file define the used strings, designated by the `!!` prefix.

To calculate the numeric value for this key, you must represent each letter of the alphabet with a binary number, as shown below.

```
z y x w v u t s r q p o n m l k j i h g f e d c b a
1 1 1 1 1 1 1 1 1 1 1 1 1 1 1 1 1 1 1 1 1 1 1 1 1 1
```

A number "1" representing the drive letter means that the drive is hidden from the user. A "0" makes the drive visible. To calculate the number required, place a 0 to represent visible drives and a 1 to hide all others. Then, change the resulting 26-bit binary number to a decimal value. For example, to show drives `V:` and `U:` only, place a 0 to represent these; the binary result is 11110011111111111111111111 (63963135d).

The notes contained within the `ZAKwinnt.adm` file are slightly misleading in this section. They say that setting the third lowest bit to 0 will hide the `C:` drive. In fact, this setting will hide all drives *except* the `C:` drive. To hide just the `C:` drive, change all bits to 0 and then set the third-lowest bit to 1.

The value set to all 1's in binary represents 67108863 decimal. This hides all drives.

1. Make a safe copy of the `ZAKwinnt.adm` file.
2. Using Calculator in Scientific mode, find the decimal equivalent of 11111111111111111111100000. This should be 67108832d.
3. Next, find the decimal equivalent of 01010101010101010101010101. This should be 22369621d.

4. Place an entry in the `ZAKwinnt.adm` file just above the `END ITEMLIST`. This entry should be

   – `Name !!HideDrives_Below_FVALUE NUMERIC 67108832`

5. Place a further entry below the previous one. This entry should read

   – `Name !!HideDrives_Evens  VALUE NUMERIC 22369621`

6. Find the `"HideDrives"` entries in the `[strings]` section. Add an entry

   – `HideDrives_Below_F="Show Only Local Drives up to and including E:"`

7. Add a second entry

   –`HideDrives_Evens="Show only even Drives beginning at B:"`

8. Save the file.

The steps outlined above add two options to the **ZAK Policies** > **Windows NT** > **Drives** > **Restrictions** category within user-related policies. You will now be able to set these policies in the following exercises.

Policy Creation

For this exercise, create a new policy file. The policy file will contain group policies for each of the four groups identified above, plus a Default User policy, a Default Computer policy, and an individual user policy for the Administrator user. The Administrator policy will be used to free the account from any constraints placed on all users by virtue of the Default User policy.

CREATE THE NEW POLICY FILE

1. Log on to the server and start the Policy Editor.
2. Select **Options > Policy Template**.
3. Add the following templates from the ZAK distribution source.
   - `Common.adm.`
   - `Off97nt4.adm.`
   - `Winnt.adm.`
   - `ZAKwinnt.adm.`
4. Select **OK**.
5. Select **File > New Policy**.
6. Select **File > Save As**, and enter the file name **NTconfig.pol**. This file should be located in the **Netlogon** share of the server for the policy to apply properly.

The policy file has been created and saved, based on the four loaded templates. The `Off97nt4` template has been included here because one or more of the defined user models will require access to applications and the ZAK provides this template by default. This template could just as easily be replaced or accompanied by another application template, a custom-built template, or excluded altogether. It is included here for the exercise.

Building Group Policies

The default content of a system policy is a Default Computer policy and a Default User policy. All the settings exposed within each of these policies are set to be ignored by default. The net result of using this policy at the moment would be to leave all settings as they are. The policy would have no effect.

CREATING USERS/GLOBAL GROUPS

1. Use User Manager for Domains to create four global groups named **Accounts**, **Sales**, **Marketing,** and **Managers**.
2. Create five test domain users named **AccUser1**, **SalUser1**, **MarUser1**, **MarUser2,** and **ManUser1**.
   - AccUser1 should be a member of the Accounts global group.
   - SalUser1 should be a member of the Sales global group.
   - MarUser1 and MarUser2 should be members of the Marketing global group.
   - ManUser1 should be a member of all four global groups.

We will use the users and groups defined above to test the customized policy models that will be created later in this project.

ADDING POLICIES TO THE FILE

1. With the policy file open, select **Edit** > **Add Group**.
2. Browse the global groups, and double-click the **Accounts**, **Sales**, **Marketing**, and **Managers** global groups.
3. Select **OK** and **OK** again to add all four groups to the policy.
4. Select **Edit** > **Add User**.
5. Browse the domain users, and double-click the **Administrator** user.
6. Select **OK** and **OK** again.
7. Select **Edit** > **Add Computer**.
8. Browse the domain computers and double-click the **IBSNT04** computer.
9. Save the policy.

Figure 9.3 illustrates the results of the preceding process.

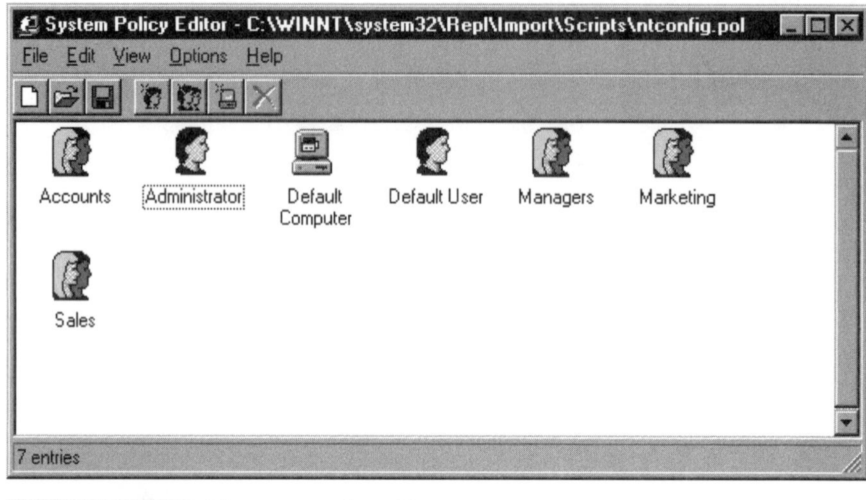

FIGURE 9.3 The new policy file

The preceding steps add four group icons and one individual user icon to the policy file. At this point, the policies behind each of the icons will all be set to ignore every exposed setting.

The reason for browsing for users, groups, or computers is that there is no spell checker here. If you enter a name incorrectly, it will be accepted but the policy will not be applied in the way that you may plan.

ARRANGE GROUP POLICY

We arrange the group policies in order so that we can be certain of the application order for conflicting settings.

1. With the policy file open, select **Options** > **Group Priority**.
2. The order of Priority from highest (top) to lowest (bottom) should be set to:
   — Managers.
   — Marketing.
   — Sales.
   — Accounts.
3. Select **OK.**
4. Save the policy.

DEFAULT USER POLICY

Use the Default User policy as a base that contains settings you wish to apply to all users. The only users who will not have settings read from this policy are those that have an individual policy enabled. This does not mean that the settings in the Default User policy will definitely be used. For example, if a user logs on and does not have an individual policy set, the Default User policy contents will be applied. The settings applied here could then be overwritten by group policy settings so that the Default User settings are never seen by the user.

Some of the goals that we should achieve with this policy are:

- To deny all users access to the **Screen Saver**, **Appearance,** and **Settings** tabs in **Control Panel** > **Display**. Users can cause problems by changing settings here. These problems require IS intervention to fix and so increase costs. The **Screen Saver** is included so that a corporate default can be put in place and a default time that cannot be amended by the user is set.
- To put in place shell restrictions to remove unwanted access to items on the **Start Menu** and in **My Computer** and **Network Neighborhood**.
- To disable **Registry editing** tools and **Task Manager**.
- To locate **Office 97 Template** files in the same network location for all office users.
- To automatically activate **Word 97 Macro Virus** protection.
- To set Internet settings to contain the address of the local **Proxy Server**.

The settings described above will form a base from which further policy settings can be built. The only users who will avoid having these policy settings used are those who have an individual policy and so do not parse the Default User policy. At the moment the only user in this category is Administrator.

1. With the policy file open, double-click the **Default User** icon.
2. Expand the **Control Panel** > **Display** category, and place a check mark in the **Restrict display** box.
3. Place a check mark against:
   — Hide Screen Saver tab.
   — Hide Appearance tab.
   — Hide Settings tab.

4. Expand the **Shell > Restrictions** category. Place a check mark against:
   - — Remove Run command from Start Menu.
   - — Remove folders from Settings on Start Menu.
   - — Remove Taskbar from Settings on Start Menu.
   - — Remove Find command from Start Menu.
   - — Hide Network Neighborhood.
   - — No Entire Network in Network Neighborhood.
   - — No workgroup contents in Network Neighborhood.
   - — Don't save settings at exit.
5. Expand the **System > Restrictions** category. Place a check mark against:
   - — Disable Registry editing tools.
6. Expand the **Office 97 > Common** category. Place a check mark against:
   - — User Templates. Enter a network path for common templates to be stored in. This should be accessible and configured as read-only for all Office users.
7. Expand the **Word 97 > Tools_Options > General** category. Place a check mark against:
   - — Macro Virus Protection.
8. Expand the **Windows** category. Place a check mark against:
   - — Internet Settings. Place the IP address in the Proxy Server box, and select Proxy Enable.
9. Expand the **Windows NT Shell > Restrictions** category. Place a check mark against:
   - — Disable context menus for the Taskbar.
   - — Remove the *Map Network Drive* and *Disconnect Network Drive* options.
10. Expand the **Windows NT System** category. Place a check mark against:
    - — Run logon scripts synchronously. Note the warning about the Computer section setting taking precedence. Computer policies are applied after User policies and so Computer policies take precedence.
    - — Disable Task Manager.
11. Select **OK.**
12. Save the policy.

If you log on to the domain using MarUser2 as the test subject, you can see the restrictions that have been put in place. Do not use any of the other defined users for this test. Look at the restrictions placed on the Start Menu functionality. Look at the available Display options in Control Panel. Try and start a registry editing tool. These are the base settings that will be applied to all users. You can use group policies or individual policies to move on from these base settings and make adaptations that fit groups or users.

DEFAULT COMPUTER POLICY

The nature of the ZAK is to impose control over users so the Computer policies are not used extensively. You may decide to change this and use the system policy to place tighter controls over the computer as well as the user. The goals achieved with this policy are:

- To provide a hidden share to all workstation drives so that remote administrative connections can be made.
- To display a Logon Banner with a "Legal Notice" for all authenticating users.

The settings defined in this policy are used if there is no individual computer policy. This is an "either or" situation. Only one or the other is applied.

1. With the policy file open, double-click the **Default Computer** icon.
2. Expand the **Windows NT Network** > **Sharing** category. Place a check mark against:
   - Create hidden drive shares (workstation).
3. Expand the **Windows NT System > Logon** category. Place a check mark against:
   - Logon Banner. The caption will appear at the top of the displayed dialog box and the *Text* will appear within the dialog box. Change the contents as required.
4. Save the policy.

The logon banner will appear between the <CTRL ALT DEL> secure attention sequence and the appearance of the dialog box for credentials. The user must select OK before the logon can continue. Note that this may not be the case if the default GINA module is not used for authentication.

ACCOUNTS GROUP POLICY

The Accounts group will have the most restrictive setup. Access to only one program is needed for this type of user. The program that the Accounts department users need to access is based on a mainframe. The goals achieved with this policy are:

- To change the startup shell for the Accounts users.
- To limit the view of the network drives for the Accounts users.

Connectivity to the mainframe is made with the Telnet program. This could just as easily be a terminal emulation program of some sort.

1. With the policy file open, double-click the **Accounts** icon.
2. Expand the **Windows NT Shell** > **Custom User Interface** category. Place a check mark against:
   - Custom Shell. Enter the string `Telnet.exe` in the dialog box. This presupposes that TCP/IP will be an installed component of the workstation and that the Telnet program can be found in the path.
3. Expand the **ZAK Policies > Windows NT > Drives > Restrictions** category. Place a check mark against:
   - Show only selected drives. Use the drop-down list to select "Don't show any drives."
4. Save the policy file.

Figure 9.4 shows how the screen looks to Accounts users.

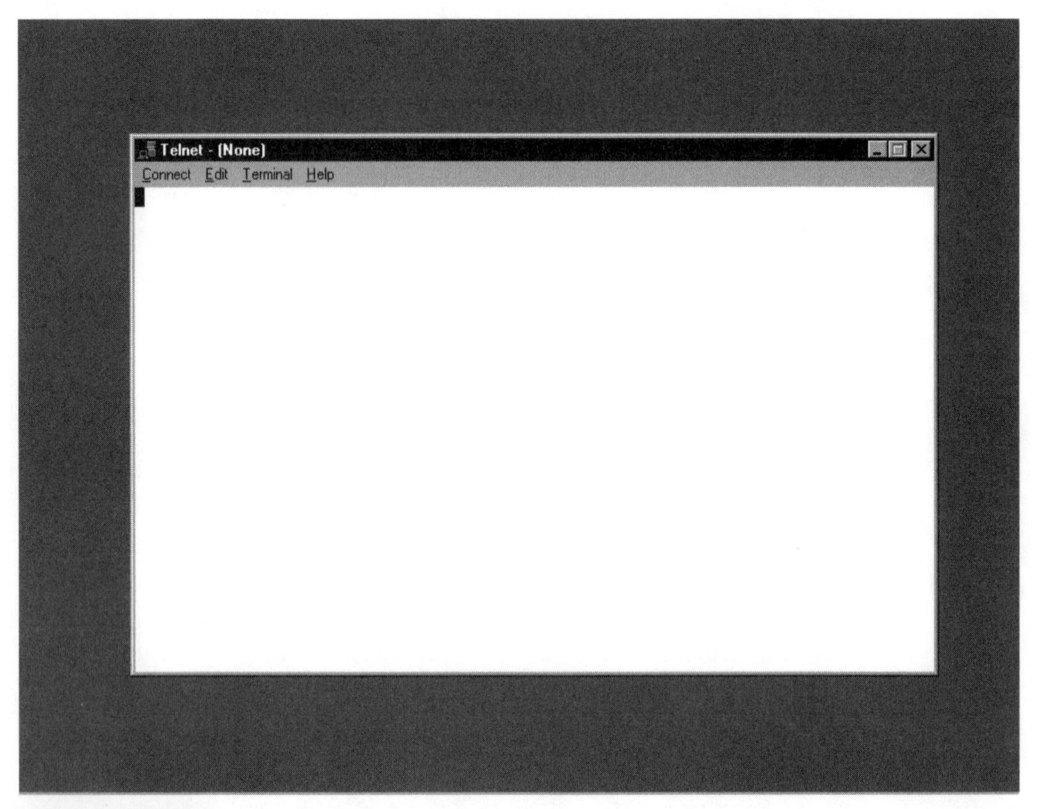

FIGURE 9.4 The screen for the Accounts users

The changes to group policies being made in this section have an impact only on users who belong to the specified global group.

SALES GROUP POLICY

The Sales group have a fairly restricted desktop and computer access policy in the same way as the Accounts group. Access to mainframe applications is required, but so is access to other applications. This means that the shell cannot be changed in the same way as in the previous section. Access to desktop programs, such as Notepad and Calculator, stored locally on the machine is not necessary for the job type, but the programs are not protected from use either. The goals achieved with this policy are:

- To point the Sales group to a custom Programs folder containing shortcuts to all necessary applications.
- To hide items on the desktop.
- To grant the Sales group access to see all local drives.

Connectivity to the mainframe is made with the Telnet program. This could just as easily be a terminal emulation program of some sort.

1. With the policy file open, double-click the **Sales** icon.
2. Expand the **Shell** > **Restrictions** category. Place a check mark against:
   - Hide all items on the desktop.
3. Expand the **Windows NT Shell > Custom Folders** category. Place a check mark against:
   - Hide Start Menu subfolders. This hides the normal Start Menu subfolder views so that custom menus can be used.
   - Custom Programs folder. The default entry in the dialog box is **%USERPROFILE%\Start Menu\Programs**. You should create a central location that contains shortcuts to all necessary applications such as MS Office 97 and Telnet and place the path in this box. The user should have a drive mapped in the logon script to this share.
4. Expand the **Windows NT Shell > Restrictions** category. Place a check mark against:
   - Remove common program groups from Start menu.
5. Expand the **ZAK Policies > Windows NT > Drives > Restrictions** category. Place a check mark against:
   - Show only selected drives. Use the drop-down list to select *Show Only Local Drives up to and including E:*
6. Save the policy file.

Central control of application access is gained by means of the Custom Programs folder created through the previous instructions. You can amend the contents of the folder as necessary in one place and have this reflected for all of the Sales group.

The *Remove common program groups* setting removes unwanted content from the Start Menu and subfolder. The *Hide all items on desktop* setting removes the items that may otherwise cause distraction from the desktop. These settings are not necessary for the Accounts users because these people have only the Telnet program as a shell and so cannot see the menus or desktop.

If the settings in this policy are not superseded, the Sales users will not be able to see any network drives through My Computer or Explorer. Applications such as Word 97 or Excel 97 will not display network drives in dialog boxes. These drives are available, however, and if a user does have a network drive mapped and an application needs to access the drive, this access should not be a problem.

Figure 9.5 illustrates how Sales users view their desktop.

FIGURE 9.5 The desktop for the Sales users

The available Start Menu options only allow access to the programs available from the Custom Programs location.

MARKETING GROUP POLICY

The Marketing group requires more access to the local machine than those defined previously. They need accessories such as Notepad, Wordpad, and Calculator. The goal achieved with this policy is:

- To point the Marketing group to a Custom Programs folder containing shortcuts to all necessary applications.

1. With the policy file open, double-click the **Marketing** icon.
2. Expand the **Windows NT Shell > Custom Folders** category. Place a check mark against:
   - Hide Start menu subfolders.
   - Custom Programs folder. You should create a central location and copy the Programs folder, subfolders, and contents from a local machine (from the Default Users profile location) to the network location. Adjust the contents of the central copy to suit your needs. Place the path in this box. The user should have a drive mapped in the logon script to this share.
3. Expand the **Windows NT Shell > Restrictions** category. Place a check mark against:
   - Remove common program groups from Start menu.
4. Save the policy file.

As with the settings for the Sales group, a central location holds the menu contents and shortcuts for the users. The central menu structure for this group simply has more items available for use. The contents can be adjusted to fit the needs of many different user groups. Figure 9.6 illustrates how Marketing users view their desktop.

MANAGERS GROUP POLICY

The users in the Managers group will have only the restrictions placed on them from the Default User policy. As the Managers users will also be members of all of the other groups (for NTFS permissions to be assigned per group), we must negate some of the settings that will be inherited from these groups. The goals achieved with this policy are:

- To place settings in the policy to negate unwanted settings from previously applied group policies.
- To provide the Managers group with a centrally configured Programs folder.

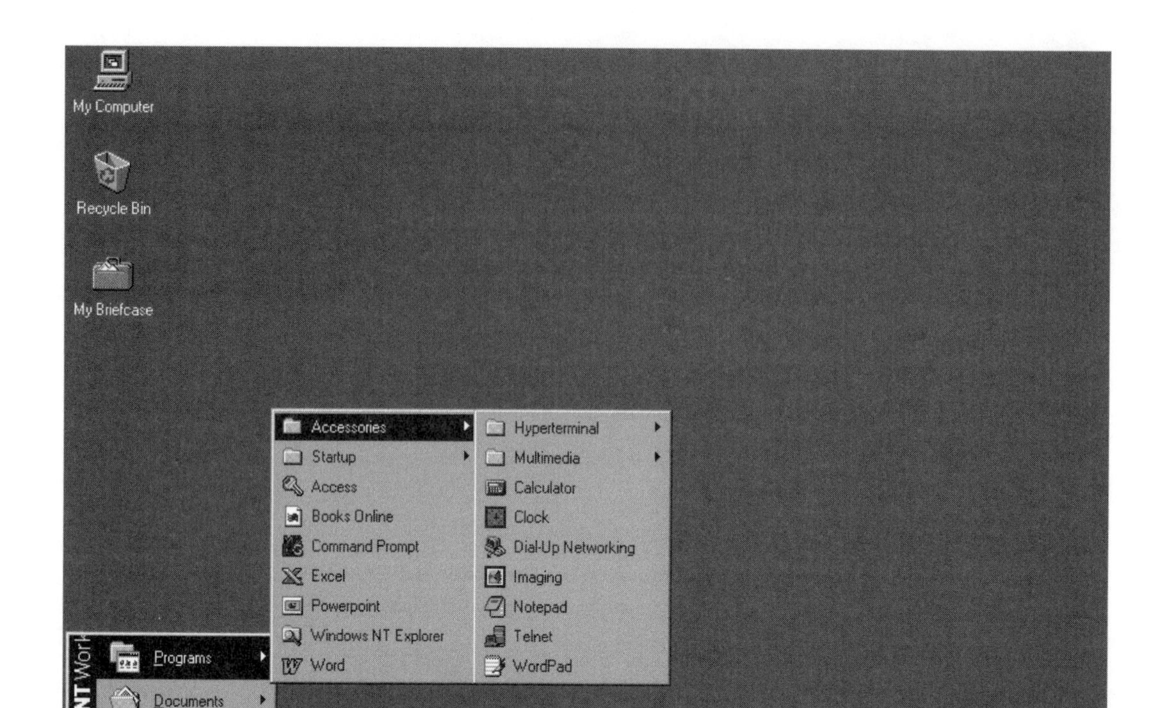

FIGURE 9.6 Marketing users' desktop

1. With the policy file open, double-click the **Managers** icon.
2. Expand the **Windows NT Shell > Custom User Interface** category. Change the box content from grayed-out (ignored) to empty with white background (disabled) for:
   - Custom Shell. This change negates the setting applied from the Accounts group policy.
3. Expand the **Shell > Restrictions** category. Change the box content from grayed-out (ignored) to empty with white background (disabled) for:
   - Hide all items on the desktop. This will negate the setting brought forward from the Sales policy.
4. Expand the **Windows NT Shell > Custom Folders** category. Place a check mark against:
   - Hide Start Menu subfolders. This selection hides the normal Start Menu subfolder views so that custom menus can be used.

- Custom Programs folder. You should create a central location and copy the Programs folder, subfolders, and contents from a local machine (from the Default Users profile location) to the network location. Adjust the contents of the central copy to suit your needs. Place the path in this box. The user should have a drive mapped in the logon script to this share.

5. Expand the **Windows NT Shell > Restrictions** category. Place a check mark against:
   - Remove common program groups from Start menu. This setting should still be used because a Custom Programs folder is being used.
6. Expand the **ZAK Policies > Windows NT > Drives > Restrictions** category. Change the box content from grayed-out (ignored) to empty with white background (disabled) for:
   - Show only selected drives. This setting negates the setting passed through from the Marketing group policy.
7. Save the policy file.

The Managers users are presented with the same desktop and available programs folders as the Marketing group. The difference in the policies is necessary because the members of the Managers group are also members of the other three groups, whereas members of Marketing are not.

ADMINISTRATOR USER POLICY

The Administrator user policy ensures that the controls applied by the Default User policy are not applied to this user. No changes to the default policy need be made. All settings in the policy are grayed out (ignored), but this setting is okay. The very fact that the individual user policy exists means that when the user logs on to the domain, the Default User policy is not loaded.

Summary

You can use the two projects in this chapter as the basis for your own customization project. Remember that the ZAK will not fit your requirements exactly, so you must plan the customization process carefully to ensure that you achieve the desired results.

Most of the information in our two projects can be replaced with your own variations on the theme. More time spent performing the exercises will pay dividends when it is time to roll out the product and use the design methodologies of the ZAK to lower the costs associated with running your own Windows NT installation.

PART FOUR

Appendices

In This Part

APPENDIX A

Network Interface Cards

NICs Supported by Windows NT NCadmin Tool

Description	Driver
3Com EtherLink	ELNK
3Com EtherLink 16	ELNK16
3Com EtherLink II or IITP (8 or 16-bit)	ELNKII
3Com EtherLink III	ELNK3
3Com EtherLink Plus	ELNKPL
3Com EtherLink/MC	ELNKMC
3Com TokenLink	TOKLNK
Advanced Micro Devices AM2100/AM1500T	AM2100
Amplicard AC 210/AT	NE2000
Amplicard AC 210/XT	NE1000
ARCNET Compatible	SMCARC
Artisoft AE-1	NE1000
Artisoft AE-2 (MCA) or AE-3 (MCA)	NE2000
Artisoft AE-2 or AE-3	NE2000
Cabletron E2000 Series DNI	CBL20XX
Cabletron E2100 Series DNI	CBL21XX
DEC (DE100) EtherWorks LC	DEPCA
DEC (DE101) EtherWorks LC/TP	DEPCA

Description	Driver
DEC (DE102) EtherWorks LC/TP_BNC	DEPCA
DEC (DE200) EtherWorks Turbo	DEPCA
DEC (DE201) EtherWorks Turbo/TP	DEPCA
DEC (DE202) EtherWorks Turbo/TP_BNC	DEPCA
DEC (DE210) EtherWorks MC	DEPCA
DEC (DE211) EtherWorks MC/TP	DEPCA
DEC (DE212) EtherWorks MC/TP_BNC	DEPCA
DEC DEPCA	DEPCA
DEC EE101 (Built-In)	DEPCA
DEC Ethernet (All Types)	DEPCA
DECpc 433 WS (Built-In)	DEPCA
Exos 105	AM2100
HP PC LAN Adapter/16 TL Plus (HP27252)	HPLANP
HP PC LAN Adapter/16 TP (HP27247A)	HPLANB
HP PC LAN Adapter/16 TP Plus (HP27247B)	HPLANP
HP PC LAN Adapter/8 TL (HP27250)	HPLANB
HP PC LAN Adapter/8 TP (HP27245)	HPLANB
IBM PCMCIA-NIC	PCMNIC
IBM Token Ring	IBMTOK
IBM Token Ring (All Types)	IBMTOK
IBM Token Ring (MCA)	IBMTOK
IBM Token Ring 4/16Mbs	IBMTOK
IBM Token Ring 4/16Mbs (MCA)	IBMTOK
IBM Token Ring II	IBMTOK
IBM Token Ring II/Short	IBMTOK
Intel EtherExpress 16 (MCA)	EE16
Intel EtherExpress 16 or 16TP	EE16
Intel TokenExpress 16/4	OLI164
Intel TokenExpress EISA 16/4	OLI164
Intel TokenExpress MCA 16/4	OLI164
IPX/SPX Support Driver	IPXMONO
National Semiconductor AT/LANTIC Ethernode 16-AT3	NE2000
National Semiconductor Ethernode *16AT	NE2000
NCR Token Ring 16/4 Mbs ISA	NCRTR
NCR Token Ring 16/4 Mbs MCA	NCRTR
NCR Token Ring 4 Mbs ISA	NCRTR
NE1000 Compatible	NE1000
NE2000 Compatible	NE2000
Novell/Anthem NE/2	NE2000

Description	Driver
Novell/Anthem NE1000	NE1000
Novell/Anthem NE1500T	AM1500
Novell/Anthem NE2000	NE2000
Novell/Anthem NE2100	AM2100
Olicom 16/4 Token Ring Adapter	OLI164
Proteon ISA Token Ring (1340)	PRO4
Proteon ISA Token Ring (1342)	PRO4
Proteon ISA Token Ring (1346)	PRO4AT
Proteon ISA Token Ring (1347)	PRO4AT
Proteon MCA Token Ring (1840)	PRO4
Proteon Token Ring (P1390)	P1390
Proteon Token Ring (P1392)	P1392
Pure Data PDI508+ (ArcNet)	SMCARC
Pure Data PDI516+ (ArcNet)	SMCARC
Pure Data PDI9025-32 (Token Ring)	OLI164
Pure Data PDuC9025 (Token Ring)	OLI164
Racal NI6510	NI65
RadiSys EXM-10	SMCMAC
SMC ARCNET PC100,PC200	SMCARC
SMC ARCNET PC110,PC210,PC250	SMCARC
SMC ARCNET PC120,PC220,PC260	SMCARC
SMC ARCNET PC130/E	SMCARC
SMC ARCNET PC270/E	SMCARC
SMC ARCNET PC600W,PC650W	SMCARC
SMC ARCNET PS110,PS210	SMCARC
SMC ARCNETPC	SMCARC
SMC EtherCard (All Types except 8013/A)	SMCMAC
SMC EtherCard PLUS (WD/8003E)	SMCMAC
SMC EtherCard PLUS 10T (WD/8003W)	SMCMAC
SMC EtherCard PLUS 10T/A (MCA) (WD 8003W/A)	SMCMAC
SMC EtherCard PLUS 16 With Boot ROM Socket (WD/8013EBT)	SMCMAC
SMC EtherCard PLUS Elite (WD/8003EP)	SMCMAC
SMC EtherCard PLUS Elite 16 (WD/8013EP)	SMCMAC
SMC EtherCard PLUS Elite 16 Combo (WD/8013EW or 8013EWC)	SMCMAC
SMC EtherCard PLUS Elite 16T (WD/8013W)	SMCMAC
SMC EtherCard PLUS TP (WD/8003WT)	SMCMAC
SMC EtherCard PLUS With Boot ROM Socket (WD/8003EB)	SMCMAC
SMC EtherCard PLUS With Boot ROM Socket (WD/8003EBT)	SMCMAC
SMC EtherCard PLUS/A (MCA) (WD 8003E/A or 8003ET/A)	SMCMAC

Description	Driver
SMC EtherCard PLUS/A (MCA,BNC/AUX) (WD 8013EP/A)	SMCMAC
SMC EtherCard PLUS/A (MCA,TP/AUX) (WD 8013EW/A)	SMCMAC
SMC StarCard PLUS (WD/8003S)	SMCMAC
SMC StarCard PLUS With On Board Hub (WD/8003SH)	SMCMAC
SMC StarCard PLUS/A (MCA) (WD 8003ST/A)	SMCMAC
Tulip NCC-16	NCC16
Xircom Pocket Ethernet I	XIRC1
Xircom Pocket Ethernet II	XIRC
Zenith Data Systems NE2000 Compatible	NE2000
Zenith Data Systems Z-Note	ZNOTE

Drivers Supplied in the \I386 Directory

Drivers in the **boldface** rows are Unattend Aware.

Options Name	Literal String	.INF File
ELNKMC	3Com 3C523 EtherLink/MC Adapter	oemnadem.inf
ELNKII	**3Com EtherLink II Adapter (also II/16 and II/16 TP)**	**oemnade2.inf**
ELNK3EISA	3Com EtherLink III EISA Adapter	oemnadee.inf
ELNK3ISA509	**3Com EtherLink III ISA/PCMCIA Adapter**	**oemnade3.inf**
ELNK3MCA	3Com EtherLink III MCA Adapter	oemnaden.inf
ELNK16	**3Com EtherLink16/EtherLink16 TP Adapter**	**oemnade1.inf**
AM1500T	**Advanced Micro Devices AM2100/AM1500T Adapter**	**oemnadam.inf**
AMDPCI	AMD PCNET Family Ethernet Adapter	oemnadap.inf
MAPLE	COMPAQ 32-Bit DualSpeed Token Ring Controller	oemnadnf.inf
NETFLX	COMPAQ NetFlex/NetFlex-2 ENET-TR Controller	oemnadnf.inf
BONSAI	COMPAQ NetFlex-2 DualPort ENET Controller	oemnadnf.inf
RODAN	COMPAQ NetFlex-2 DualPort TR Controller	oemnadnf.inf
DURANGO	COMPAQ NetFlex-2 TR Controller	oemnadnf.inf
LT200	**COPS/DayStar Digital LocalTalk Adapter**	**oemnadlt.inf**
LT200MC	COPS/DayStar Digital LocalTalk Adapter (MCA)	oemnadlm.inf
DE425	DEC DE425 EtherWORKS Turbo EISA Adapter	oemnaddt.inf
DE434	DEC DE434 EtherWORKS Turbo PCI TP Adapter	oemnaddt.inf
DE435	DEC DE435 EtherWORKS Turbo PCI Adapter	oemnaddt.inf
DE450	DEC DE450 EtherWORKS Turbo PCI Adapter	oemnaddt.inf
DE500	DEC DE500 Fast Ethernet PCI Adapter	oemnaddt.inf
DEC100	**DEC EtherWORKS LC Adapter**	**oemnadd1.inf**
DECETHER WORKSTURBO	**DEC EtherWORKS Turbo Adapter**	**oemnadd2.inf**
DEC422	DEC EtherWORKS Turbo EISA Adapter	oemnadd4.inf

Options Name	Literal String	.INF File
DEC101	**DEC EtherWORKS Turbo/LC Adapter**	**oemnadd1.inf**
DEC300	DEC FDDIcontroller/EISA	oemnadd3.inf
DEFPA	**DEC FDDIcontroller/PCI**	**oemnaddf.inf**
MULTIA	DEC multia's Ethernet Controller	oemnaddt.inf
DC21040	DEC PCI Ethernet DECchip 21040	oemnaddt.inf
DC21041	DEC PCI Ethernet DECchip 21041	oemnaddt.inf
DC21140	DEC PCI Fast Ethernet DECchip 21140	oemnaddt.inf
DC21142	DEC PCI Fast Ethernet DECchip 21142	oemnaddt.inf
DECSTAT	**DEC Turbo Channel Ethernet Adapter**	**oemnadde.inf**
DATAFIREST	Digi DataFire - ISA1S/T Adapter	oemnaddi.inf
DATAFIREU	Digi DataFire - ISA1U Adapter	oemnaddi.inf
DATAFIRE4ST	Digi DataFire - ISA4S/T Adapter	oemnaddi.inf
PCIMACISA	Digi PCIMAC - ISA Adapter	oemnaddi.inf
PCIMACMC	Digi PCIMAC - MC Adapter	oemnaddi.inf
PCIMAC4	Digi PCIMAC/4 Adapter	oemnaddi.inf
NE2000IBMCOMPAT	**IBM Ethernet PCMCIA and Compatible Adapter**	**oemnadni.inf**
IBMTOK	**IBM Token Ring (ISA/PCMCIA) Adapter**	**oemnadtk.inf**
IBMTOKMC	**IBM Token Ring 4/16 Adapter /A**	**oemnadtm.inf**
IBMTOKA	**IBM Token Ring Adapter /A**	**oemnadtm.inf**
IBMTOK2ISA	**IBM Token Ring Network 16/4 ISA Adapter II**	**oemnadt2.inf**
EE16	**Intel Ether Express 16 LAN Adapter**	**oemnadin.inf**
EE16MC	Intel Ether Express MCA Adapter	oemnadim.inf
IEEPRO	**Intel EtherExpress PRO Ethernet Adapter**	**oemnadep.inf**
MSMDGMPSM16	**Madge Smart 16 Ringnode**	**oemnadma.inf**
MSMDGMPATP	**Madge Smart 16/4 AT Plus Ringnode**	**oemnadma.inf**
MSMDGMPISA	**Madge Smart 16/4 AT Ringnode**	**oemnadma.inf**
MSMDGMPEISA	**Madge Smart 16/4 EISA Ringnode**	**oemnadma.inf**
MSMDGMPISACP	**Madge Smart 16/4 ISA Client Plus Ringnode**	**oemnadma.inf**
MSMDGMPPNP	**Madge Smart 16/4 ISA Client PnP Ringnode**	**oemnadma.inf**
MSMDGMPISAC	**Madge Smart 16/4 ISA Client Ringnode**	**oemnadma.inf**
MSMDGMPMCA	**Madge Smart 16/4 MC Ringnode**	**oemnadma.inf**
MSMDGMPMC32	**Madge Smart 16/4 MC32 Ringnode**	**oemnadma.inf**
MSMDGMPPC	**Madge Smart 16/4 PC Ringnode**	**oemnadma.inf**
MSMDGMPPCI	**Madge Smart 16/4 PCI Ringnode**	**oemnadma.inf**
MSMDGMPPCIBM	**Madge Smart 16/4 PCI Ringnode (BM)**	**oemnadma.inf**
MSMDGMPPCMCIA	**Madge Smart 16/4 PCMCIA Ringnode**	**oemnadma.inf**
MICRODYNEPCMCIA	**Microdyne NE4000 PCMCIA Adapter**	**oemnadni.inf**
LOOP	**MS Loopback Adapter**	**oemnadlb.inf**
NE2000MCA	**NE/2 and Compatible MC Adapter**	**oemnadnm.inf**
NPEISA	Network Peripherals FDDI EISA	oemnadnp.inf

Options Name	Literal String	.INF File
NPMCA	Network Peripherals FDDI MCA	oemnadfd.inf
NE1000	**Novell NE1000 Adapter**	**oemnadn1.inf**
NE2000	**Novell NE2000 Compatible Adapter**	**oemnadn2.inf**
NE2000SOCKETEA	**Novell NE2000 Socket EA Adapter**	**oemnadn2.inf**
NE3200	Novell NE3200 EISA Adapter	oemnadne.inf
NE4000PCMCIA	**Novell NE4000 PCMCIA Adapter**	**oemnadni.inf**
AM1500T1	**Novell/Anthem NE1500T Adapter**	**oemnadam.inf**
AM1500T2	**Novell/Anthem NE2100 Adapter**	**oemnadam.inf**
P189X	**ProNET-4/16 p189X NIC**	**oemnadpm.inf**
P1390	**Proteon p139X Adapter**	**oemnadp3.inf**
P1990	**Proteon p199X Adapter**	**oemnadp9.inf**
WD8003EA	SMC (WD) 8003E /A	oemnadwm.inf
WD8003WA	SMC (WD) 8003W /A	oemnadwm.inf
WD8013EPA	SMC (WD) 8013EP /A	oemnadwm.inf
WD8013WPA	SMC (WD) 8013WP /A	oemnadwm.inf
SMCISA	**SMC (WD) EtherCard**	**oemnadwd.inf**
UBPC	**Ungermann-Bass Ethernet NIUpc Adapter**	**oemnadub.inf**
UBPCEOTP	**Ungermann-Bass Ethernet NIUpc/EOTP Adapter**	**oemnadub.inf**
UBPS	Ungermann-Bass Ethernet NIUps Adapter	oemnadum.inf

Drivers Supplied in the \DRVLIB\NETCARD\X86 and \I386\DRVLIB.NIC Directories

Drivers in the **boldface** rows are Unattend Aware.

Options Name	Literal String
3C508	3Com 3C508 ISA 16-bit Ethernet Adapter
ELINK527	3Com 3C527 EtherLink/MC 32 Adapter
3C592	**3Com EtherLink III EISA Bus-Master Adapter (3C592)**
3C590	**3Com EtherLink III PCI Bus-Master Adapter (3C590)**
3C597	**3Com Fast EtherLink EISA 10/100BASE-T Adapter (3C597)**
3C595	**3Com Fast EtherLink PCI 10/100BASE-T Adapter (3C595)**
3C905	**3Com Fast EtherLink XL Adapter (3C905)**
FLNK	3Com FDDILink EISA LAN Adapter
TLNK3EISA	3Com TokenLink III ISA Adapter in EISA mode (3C619B)
ACCNT	**Accton EN166x MPX2 PnP Ethernet Adapter**
ACCTONEN2216	**Accton EN2216 Ethernet PCMCIA Adapter**
ALANE0	**Adaptec ATM LAN Emulation Adapter**
AT1700	Allied Telesyn AT1700 Ethernet Adapter

Options Name	Literal String
AT1700	Allied Telesyn AT1720 Ethernet Adapter
A2560PCI	Allied Telesyn AT-2560 Series PCI/100 Ethernet Adapter
ANDTOK	Andrew ISA IIA Token Ring Adapter
E21XX	Cabletron E21XX Ethernet Adapter
E22XX	Cabletron E22XX Ethernet Adapter
F30XX	Cabletron F30XX FDDI Adapter
F70XX	Cabletron F70XX FDDI Adapter
T20XX	Cabletron T20XX Token Ring Adapter
EMPCI	Cogent eMASTER+ PCI Adapter
CPQNDIS	Compaq Ethernet LAN Card
NetFlex3	Compaq NetFlex-3 Controller
$enet	Compex ENET16 P/PNP Ethernet Adapter
IRMAtrac	DCA IRMAtrac Token Ring Adapter
DigiSyncFR	Digi SyncPort Frame Relay Adapter
DigiSyncX25	Digi SyncPort X.25 Adapter
DLINKDE220	**D-Link DE-220 ISA Ethernet Adapter**
DLINKDE650	**D-Link DE-650 Ethernet PCMCIA Adapter**
Diehl_DIVA	Eicon DIVA ISDN ISA Adapter
Diehl_DIVAPCM	Eicon DIVA PCMCIA ISDN Adapter
Diehl_DIVAPRO	Eicon DIVA PRO ISDN Adapter with Advanced DSP
Diehl_S2M	Eicon Primary Rate ISDN Adapter
Diehl_QUADRO	Eicon QUADRO ISDN Adapter
Diehl_SCOM	Eicon SCOM ISDN Adapter
Diehl_WAN	Eicon Virtual WAN-Miniport ISDN Interface
ECCARDS	Eicon WAN Adapters
HPTXPCI	HP 10/100TX PCI Ethernet Adapter
HP27245	HP 27245A PC LAN Adapter/8 TP
HPMCA	HP 27246A MC LAN Adapter/16 TP
HP27247A	HP 27247A PC LAN Adapter/16 TP
HP27247B	HP 27247B PC LAN Adapter/16 TP Plus
HP27250	HP 27250 PC LAN Adapter/8 TL
HP27252A	HP 27252A PC LAN Adapter/16 TL Plus
J2573A	HP DeskDirect (J2573A) 10/100 ISA LAN Adapter
J2577A	HP DeskDirect (J2577A) 10/100 EISA LAN Adapter
J2585A	HP DeskDirect (J2585A) 10/100 PCI LAN Adapter
J2585B	HP DeskDirect (J2585B) 10/100 PCI LAN Adapter
J2970A	HP DeskDirect (J2970A) 10BaseT/2 PCI LAN Adapter
J2973A	HP DeskDirect (J2973A) 10BaseT PCI LAN Adapter
IBMFEPCI	IBM 100/10 PCI Ethernet Adapter
IBMTOK4	**IBM Auto 16/4 Token Ring ISA Adapter**

Options Name	Literal String
STREAMER	IBM Auto LANStreamer PCI Adapter
IBMISAETHER	**IBM ISA Ethernet Adapter**
IBMENIIN	IBM LAN Adapter/A for Ethernet
QUADENET	IBM PeerMaster Server Adapter
STREAMER	IBM Streamer Family Adapters
ETH16I	ICL EtherTeam16i Adapter
ETH32	ICL EtherTeam32 Adapter
E100BPCI	**Intel 82557-based 10/100 Ethernet PCI Adapter**
E10PCI	Intel EtherExpress PRO/10 PCI LAN Adapter
EPRONT	Intel EtherExpress PRO/10+ ISA Adapter
E10PPCI	**Intel EtherExpress PRO/10+ PCI Adapter**
E100BEXP	**Intel EtherExpress PRO/100B PCI Adapter**
FL32	Intel Flash32 EISA LAN Adapter
TKXP16	Intel TokenExpress 16/4 Adapter
TKXP32	Intel TokenExpress Server Adapter
LINKSYSE16	**LinkSys Ether16 LAN Card**
LINKSYSEC2T	**LinkSys EthernetCard PCMCIA**
LEC	**Madge ATM LAN Emulation Client**
BLUTOK	**Madge Blue+ Token Ring Adapter**
CC10BT	Megahertz CC10BT/2 Ethernet PCMCIA Adapter
XJEM3288	**Megahertz XJEM3288 Ethernet+Modem PCMCIA Adapter**
NE100PCI	Microdyne NE10/100 PCI Adapter
MGSL	MicroGate SyncLink Internet Adapter
NSCNE4100	**National Semiconductor InfoMover NE4100**
NCRTOK	NCR StarLAN 16/4 Token Ring Adapter
NPAT2	Network Peripherals FDDI - AT2
NPAT3	Network Peripherals FDDI - AT3
NCPF	Network Peripherals NuCard PCI FDDI
NiwRAS	Niwot Networks NiwRAS Adapter
GOCARD	Olicom Ethernet GoCard
OCE2XM	Olicom Ethernet ISA/IV Adapter
O100PCI	Olicom Ethernet PCI 10/100 Adapter
OCE4XMP10	**Olicom Ethernet PCI/II 10 Adapter**
OCE4XMP100	**Olicom Ethernet PCI/II 10/100 Adapter**
GOCARDMF	Olicom GoCard ET/Modem 288
PCMCIA	**Olicom GoCard TR 16/4**
COMBO	**Olicom GoCard TR/Modem 144**
OCTK16	**Olicom Token Ring 16/4 Adapter**
OCTK32	Olicom Token Ring Server Adapter

Options Name	Literal String
OTCJODNT	Ositech Jack of Diamonds Trumpcard
ES3210	Racal Interlan ES3210 EISA Ethernet Adapter
NI6510	Racal InterLan XLerator/EB/NI6510 Adapters
RTL8029	Realtek RTL8029 PCI Adapter
RnsFDDI	RNS 2200 PCI FDDI LAN Controller
SMC8216	SMC 8216 EtherCard Elite16 Ultra
SMC8416	SMC 8416 EtherEZ
SMC8432	SMC 8432 EtherPower PCI Ethernet Adapter
SMC9232	SMC 9232 Fast Ethernet Adapter
SMC9332	SMC 9332 EtherPower10/100 PCI Fast Ethernet Adapter
SMC8232	SMC EISA EtherCard Elite32 Ultra Adapter
ACLSER	Star Gate ACL/Avanstar Family Adapter
SKTOKNT	SysKonnect SK-NET 4/16+ Token Ring Adapter
SKFENT	SysKonnect SK-NET EISA FDDI Adapter
SKFPNT	SysKonnect SK-NET FDDI PCI Adapter
SKETHNT	SysKonnect SK-NET G16 Ethernet Adapters
SKETHNT	SysKonnect SK-NET G32+ Ethernet Adapters
SKFINT	SysKonnect SK-NET ISA FDDI Adapter
SKFMNT	SysKonnect SK-NET MCA FDDI Adapter
SKTOKNT_PCI	SysKonnect SK-NET Token Ring PCI Adapter
SKTOKNT	SysKonnect SK-NET TR4/16+ Token Ring Adapter
TC$4045e	Thomas-Conrad TC4045 Token Ring Adapter
TC$4046e	Thomas-Conrad TC4046 Token Ring Adapter
AL56	U.S. Robotics Allegra 56 Frame Relay
ALT1	U.S. Robotics Allegra T1 Frame Relay
USRBRI	U.S. Robotics Sportster ISDN Adapter
WAVELAN_ISA	WaveLAN ISA Bus Adapter
WAVELAN_MCA	WaveLAN MCA Bus Adapter
CENDIS3	Xircom CreditCard Ethernet
CE2XPS	Xircom CreditCard Ethernet IIps
CEM28XPS	Xircom CreditCard Ethernet+Modem 28.8
CM2NDIS3	Xircom CreditCard Ethernet+Modem II
CTNDNT	Xircom CreditCard Token Ring
XCSPE2	Xircom Pocket Ethernet II
XCSPE3	Xircom Pocket Ethernet III

APPENDIX B

Sample Unattend.txt Files

Sample 1

```
; Microsoft Windows NT Workstation Version 4.0 and
; Windows NT Server Version 4.0
;
; Sample Unattended Setup Answer File for IBM PCI
; Token Ring Adapter
;
; This file contains information about how to
; automate the installation
; or upgrade of Windows NT Workstation and Windows
; NT Server so the
; Setup program runs without requiring user input.
;

[Unattended]
OemPreinstall = no
OemSkipEULA = Yes
ConfirmHardware = no
NtUpgrade = no
Win31Upgrade = no
TargetPath = WINNT
OverwriteOemFilesOnUpgrade = no
```

```
[UserData]
FullName = "administrator"
OrgName = "IBM"
ComputerName = MACHINE1
ProductID = "XXX-XXXXXXX"

[GuiUnattended]
OemSkipWelcome = 1
OEMBlankAdminPassword = 1
TimeZone = "(GMT-05:00) Eastern Time (US & Canada)"

[Display]
ConfigureAtLogon = 0
BitsPerPel = 16
XResolution = 640
YResolution = 480
VRefresh = 70
AutoConfirm = 1

[Network]
InstallAdapters = AdaptersSection
InstallProtocols = ProtocolsSection
JoinDomain = ntdomain

[ProtocolsSection]
TC = TCParameters

[TCParameters]
DHCP = yes

[AdaptersSection]
IBMTRP = TRParameters,c:\ibmtrp

[TRParameters]
Netaddress = "40005000ABCD"
MaxTxFrameSize = 4096
DataRate = "M16"
```

Sample 2

```
[unattended]
OemPreinstall = no
OemSkipEULA = Yes
NoWaitAfterTextMode = 0
NoWaitAfterGuiMode = 1
FileSystem = ConvertNTFS
targetpath = Winnt

[UserData]
FullName = "NetPC User"
OrgName = " "
ComputerName = "************** CHANGE THIS LINE ************"
ProductID = "111-1111111"

[GuiUnattended]
OemSkipWelcome = 1
OemBlankAdminPassword = 1
TimeZone = "(GMT-08:00) Pacific Time (US & Canada); Tijuana"

[OEM_Ads]
Banner = "Windows NT 4.0 ZAK CLIENT SETUP"

[Network]
DetectAdapters = DetectParams
InstallProtocols = ProtocolsSection
; ********** CHANGE THE FOLLOWING LINES**********************
; Change the "NetPC Domain" to the domain ZAK clients will be joining.
; On the CreateComputerAccount change the NetPCAdmin to an administrative
; account that lets the computer create a computer account in the domain
; you will be joining; in the NetPCAdminPassword give the account password
; ********** CHANGE THE FOLLOWING LINES**********************
JoinDomain = "NetPC Domain"
CreateComputerAccount = NetPCAdmin,NetPCAdminPassword

[DetectParams]
DetectAdapters = ""
DetectCount = 1

[ProtocolsSection]
TC = TCPIPParams

[TCPIPParams]
DHCP = yes

[Display]
BitsPerPel = 8
XResolution = 800
YResolution = 600
VRefresh = 60
AutoConfirm = 1
```

Sample 3

```
; Microsoft Windows NT Workstation Version 4.0 and
; Windows NT Server Version 4.0
; (c) 1994 - 1996 Microsoft Corporation. All rights reserved.
;
; Sample Unattended Setup Answer File
;
; This file contains information about how to automate the installation
; or upgrade of Windows NT Workstation and Windows NT Server so the
; Setup program runs without requiring user input.
;

[Unattended]
OemPreinstall = no
OemSkipEULA = Yes
ConfirmHardware = no
NtUpgrade = no
Win31Upgrade = no
TargetPath = WINNT
OverwriteOemFilesOnUpgrade = no

[UserData]
FullName = "Your User Name"
OrgName = "Your Organization Name"
ComputerName = COMPUTER_NAME

[GuiUnattended]
TimeZone = "(GMT-08:00) Pacific Time (US & Canada); Tijuana"

[Display]
ConfigureAtLogon = 0
BitsPerPel = 16
XResolution = 640
YResolution = 480
VRefresh = 70
AutoConfirm = 1

[Network]
Attend = yes
DetectAdapters = ""
InstallProtocols = ProtocolsSection
JoinDomain = Domain_To_Join

[ProtocolsSection]
TC = TCParameters

[TCParameters]
DHCP = yes
```

APPENDIX C

Answer File OEM Key Options

Answer File Key/Value Pairs for OEM

This section contains listings of the key/value pairs for certain entries in the Unattend.txt file. Use these listings to find the relevant entry for your installation.

[Unattended]

KEYBOARDLAYOUT

The following is a list of all the valid keyboard layout names for the retail version of Windows NT 4.0.

```
"Albanian"
"Belarusian"
"Belgian Dutch"
"Belgian French"
"Brazilian (ABNT)"
"Bulgarian"
"Bulgarian Latin"
"Canadian English (Multilingual)"
"Canadian French"
"Canadian French (Multilingual)"
"Croatian"
"Czech"
```

```
"Czech (QWERTY)"
"Danish"
"Dutch"
"Estonian"
"Finnish"
"French"
"German"
"German (IBM)"
"Greek"
"Greek Latin"
"Greek (220)"
"Greek (220) Latin"
"Greek (319)"
"Greek (319) Latin"
"Hungarian"
"Hungarian 101-key"
"Icelandic"
"Irish"
"Italian"
"Italian (142)"
"Latin American"
"Latvian"
"Latvian (QWERTY)"
"Lithuanian"
"Norwegian"
"Polish (Programmers)"
"Polish (214)"
"Portuguese"
"Romanian"
"Russian"
"Russian (Typewriter)"
"Serbian Cyrillic"
"Serbian Latin"
"Slovak"
"Slovak (QWERTY)"
"Slovenian"
"Spanish"
"Spanish variation"
"Swedish"
"Swiss French"
"Swiss German"
"Turkish F"
"Turkish Q"
"Ukrainian"
"United Kingdom"
"US"
"US-Dvorak"
"US-Dvorak for left hand"
"US-Dvorak for right hand"
"US-International"
```

[COMPUTERTYPE]

The following is a list of all the valid computer device names for the retail version of Windows NT 4.0.

```
"AST Manhattan SMP","RETAIL"
"Compaq SystemPro Multiprocessor or 100% Compatible","RETAIL"
"Corollary C-bus Architecture","RETAIL"
"Corollary C-bus Micro Channel Architecture","RETAIL"
"IBM PS/2 or other Micro Channel-based PC","RETAIL"
"MPS Uniprocessor PC","RETAIL"
"MPS Multiprocessor PC","RETAIL"
"MPS Multiprocessor Micro Channel PC","RETAIL"
"NCR System 3000 Model 3360/3450/3550","RETAIL"
"Olivetti LSX5030/40","RETAIL"
"Standard PC","RETAIL"
"Standard PC with C-Step i486","RETAIL"
"Wyse Series 7000i Model 740MP/760MP","RETAIL"
```

[PointingDeviceDrivers]

The following is a list of all the valid pointing device (mouse) names for the retail version of Windows NT 4.0.

```
"Logitech Mouse Port Mouse" = "RETAIL"
"Logitech Serial Mouse" = "RETAIL"
"Microsoft BallPoint Serial Mouse" = "RETAIL"
"Microsoft "(Green Buttons) or Logitech Bus Mouse" = "RETAIL"
"Microsoft InPort Bus Mouse" = "RETAIL"
"Microsoft Mouse Port Mouse (includes BallPoint)" = "RETAIL"
"Microsoft Serial Mouse" = "RETAIL"
"No Mouse or Other Pointing Device", = "RETAIL"
```

[MassStorageDrivers]

The following is a list of all the valid mass storage devices for the retail version of Windows NT 4.0.

```
"Adaptec AHA-151X/AHA-152X/AIC-6X60 SCSI Adapter" = "RETAIL"
"Adaptec AHA-154X/AHA-164X SCSI Host Adapter" = "RETAIL"
"Adaptec AHA-174X EISA SCSI Host Adapter" = "RETAIL"
"Adaptec AHA-274X/AHA-284X/AIC-777X SCSI Adapter" = "RETAIL"
"Adaptec AHA-294X/AHA-394X/AIC-78XX SCSI Controller" = "RETAIL"
"Adaptec 2920/2905 / Future Domain 16XX/PCI/SCSI2Go" = "RETAIL"
"AMD PCI SCSI Controller/Ethernet Adapter" = "RETAIL"
"AMIscsi SCSI Host Adapter" = "RETAIL"
"BusLogic FlashPoint" = "RETAIL"
"BusLogic SCSI Host Adapter" = "RETAIL"
"Compaq 32-Bit Fast-Wide SCSI-2/E" = "RETAIL"
"Compaq Drive Array" = "RETAIL"
"Dell Drive Array" = "RETAIL"
```

```
"DPT SCSI Host Adapter" = "RETAIL"
"Future Domain TMC-7000EX EISA SCSI Host Adapter" = "RETAIL"
"Future Domain 8XX SCSI Host Adapter" = "RETAIL"
"IBM MCA SCSI Host Adapter" = "RETAIL"
"IDE CD-ROM (ATAPI 1.2)/PCI IDE Controller" = "RETAIL"
"Mitsumi CD-ROM Controller" = "RETAIL"
"MKEPanasonic CD-ROM Controller" = "RETAIL"
"Mylex DAC960/Digital SWXCR-Ex Raid Controller" = "RETAIL"
"NCR 53C9X SCSI Host Adapter" = "RETAIL"
"NCR 53C710 SCSI Host Adapter" = "RETAIL"
"NCR C700 SCSI Host Adapter" = "RETAIL"
"Olivetti ESC-1/ESC-2 SCSI Host Adapter" = "RETAIL"
"QLogic PCI SCSI Host Adapter" = "RETAIL"
"Symbios Logic C810 PCI SCSI Host Adapter" = "RETAIL"
"Sony Proprietary CD-ROM Controller" = "RETAIL"
"UltraStor 14F/14FB/34F/34FA/34FB SCSI Host Adapter" = "RETAIL"
"UltraStor 24F/24FA SCSI Host Adapter" = "RETAIL"
```

[GuiUnattended]

[TIMEZONE]

```
"(GMT) Greenwich Mean Time; Dublin, Edinburgh, London"
"(GMT+01:00) Lisbon, Warsaw"
"(GMT+01:00) Paris, Madrid"
"(GMT+01:00) Berlin, Stockholm, Rome, Bern, Brussels, Vienna"
"(GMT+01:00) Prague"
"(GMT+02:00) Eastern Europe"
"(GMT+02:00) Athens, Helsinki, Istanbul"
"(GMT-03:00) Rio de Janeiro"
"(GMT-04:00) Atlantic Time (Canada)"
"(GMT-05:00) Eastern Time (US & Canada)"
"(GMT-06:00) Central Time (US & Canada)"
"(GMT-07:00) Mountain Time (US & Canada)"
"(GMT-08:00) Pacific Time (US & Canada); Tijuana"
"(GMT-09:00) Alaska"
"(GMT-10:00) Hawaii"
"(GMT-11:00) Midway Island, Samoa"
"(GMT+12:00) Wellington"
"(GMT+10:00) Brisbane, Melbourne, Sydney"
"(GMT+09:30) Adelaide"
"(GMT+09:00) Tokyo, Osaka, Sapporo, Seoul, Yakutsk"
"(GMT+08:00) Hong Kong, Perth, Singapore, Taipei"
"(GMT+07:00) Bangkok, Jakarta, Hanoi"
"(GMT+05:30) Bombay, Calcutta, Madras, New Delhi, Colombo"
"(GMT+04:00) Abu Dhabi, Muscat, Tbilisi, Kazan, Volgograd"
"(GMT+03:30) Tehran"
"(GMT+03:00) Baghdad, Kuwait, Nairobi, Riyadh"
"(GMT+02:00) Israel"
"(GMT-03:30) Newfoundland"
"(GMT-01:00) Azores, Cape Verde Is."
"(GMT-02:00) Mid-Atlantic"
```

```
"(GMT) Monrovia, Casablanca"
"(GMT-03:00) Buenos Aires, Georgetown"
"(GMT-04:00) Caracas, La Paz"
"(GMT-05:00) Indiana (East)"
"(GMT-05:00) Bogota, Lima"
"(GMT-06:00) Saskatchewan"
"(GMT-06:00) Mexico City, Tegucigalpa"
"(GMT-07:00) Arizona"
"(GMT-12:00) Enewetak, Kwajalein"
"(GMT+12:00) Fiji, Kamchatka, Marshall Is."
"(GMT+11:00) Magadan, Soloman Is., New Caledonia"
"(GMT+10:00) Hobart"
"(GMT+10:00) Guam, Port Moresby, Vladivostok"
"(GMT+09:30) Darwin"
"(GMT+08:00) Beijing, Chongqing, Urumqi"
"(GMT+06:00) Alma Ata, Dhaka"
"(GMT+05:00) Islamabad, Karachi, Sverdlovsk, Tashkent"
"(GMT+04:30) Kabul"
"(GMT+02:00) Cairo"
"(GMT+02:00) Harare, Pretoria"
"(GMT+03:00) Moscow, St. Petersburg"
```

Example

```
[Unattended]
OEMPreinstall = Yes
ComputerType = "Standard PC","RETAIL"
KeyBoardLayout = "US-International"
[PointingDeviceDrivers]
"Microsoft Serial Mouse" = "RETAIL"
[MassStorageDrivers]
"Adaptec AHA-294X/AHA-394X/AIC-78XX SCSI Controller" = "RETAIL"
[KeyBoardDrivers]
"XT, AT, or Enhanced Keyboard (83-104 keys)" = "RETAIL"
```

APPENDIX D

Manual Installation Synopsis

Character Mode

- Boot your machine from either the first of the three Windows NT startup diskettes or from the Windows NT 4.0 bootable CD (if your computer's BIOS supports El Torito Bootable CD-ROM - no emulation mode - format). This installation will start automatically on an Intel x86-based computer. Follow the on-screen prompts.
- Sufficient drivers are loaded to start a base, multiprocessor version of Windows NT.
- You are presented with a welcome screen. To continue with the installation, press Enter. During this screen and those that follow, you can get context help by pressing the F1 key and you can exit setup by pressing the F3 key. You can use the R option in this screen to repair a damaged installation of Windows NT.
- Mass storage devices are detected next. All IDE and ESDI devices are automatically detected. Hard disks are not detected at this point. You are given the opportunity to install any devices that are not listed.

- If your primary hard disk is not an IDE or ESDI device (usually when your HDD is SCSI) and it is not recognized by BIOS, then you may have to specify the device here and select an appropriate driver. Your installation will fail if there is no available, active device on which to install.
- If your CD-ROM device is not automatically detected and listed here, then you must choose S to specify the device and either select from the provided list or provide a driver. The installation will fail if the source files are not available.
- You must accept the End User License Agreement to continue the installation.
- Old versions of Windows are detected, and you are asked whether to upgrade or install a fresh version.
- The setup process detects the make-up of your computer and presents an appropriate list. You can change this list if it is not correct.
- The next step is to choose your disk partitioning requirements. You can decide on the format of the partition(s) at this time. FAT or NTFS partitions are supported under Windows NT 4.0 on an Intel x86-based computer.
- If in the previous step you chose a FAT partition on which to install Windows NT, you are given the opportunity of converting to NTFS.
- The next step is to select the folder into which Windows NT will be installed. The default offering of `\WINNT` is usually sufficient.
- The hard disks are checked for corruption before the installation of the operating system files.
- Setup now begins to copy system files that are needed for your setup; it prompts you to press Enter to restart the computer when it has finished. This is the end of the character-mode setup phase.

Graphical Mode

- The system reboots into a mini-single-processor version of Windows NT or multiprocessor version if your computer contains more than one processor.
- This phase of the installation process initializes and copies more files from the CD-ROM.
- The Windows NT Setup Wizard is invoked.
- The first phase of the Setup Wizard gathers information about your computer.

- You are asked to choose the installation method. The choices are Typical, Portable, Compact, and Custom.
- You are asked for your name and organization name.
- Next, you enter the CD key that is usually found on the back of the CD case for the distribution media.
- You are asked for a computer name and the password to be used for the default Administrator account on the computer.
- You are now asked whether you wish to create an Emergency Repair Disk (ERD); then, you are given the choice of adjusting the components that will be installed.
- The Gathering Information process is complete, and the next stage is to install Networking.
- You are given the choice of participating in a network.
- If you chose to connect to the network, you next define your network adapter(s). You do this with an automatic search or by providing drivers.
- When your adapter(s) is defined, you must select the protocols you wish to use.
- At this stage, extra files are copied, the protocols are bound to the adapter, and the network portion of NT is started.
- You choose to connect this machine to a Workgroup or a Domain. You supply credentials that are capable of creating a Domain account for the computer if this is your choice.
- The last portion of the graphical-mode phase is now started. This finishing phase asks for time-zone information and displays adapter setup information.
- Files are now copied to complete the installation.
- The configuration is saved.
- Temporary files are removed and the installation is finished.

APPENDIX E

ZAK Command Script Listings

Acls.cmd

```
@rem This script will put more stringent security
@rem on a Windows NT 4.0 appstation client
@rem

@rem
@rem SYSTEM DRIVE AND ALL FILES/DIRECTORIES ON
@rem SYSTEM DRIVE
@rem
=====================================================
@rem
@rem NOTE THAT THIS FILE ONLY COVERS DIRECTORIES AND
@rem FILES WE KNOW
@rem ABOUT ON THE ZERO ADMINISTRATION CLIENT.  IF
@rem THERE ARE ADDITIONAL
@rem APPLICATIONS INSTALLED ON THE ZERO
@rem ADMINISTRATION CLIENT THEN YOU
@rem NEED TO ADD LINES FOR THE DIRECTORIES CREATED.

@rem
@rem SYSTEM DRIVE
@rem ===========
@rem
```

```
pushd %SystemDrive%\
cacls.exe . /G administrators:f system:f everyone:r
<%SystemRoot%\zak\scripts\yesfile
cacls.exe * /C /G administrators:f system:f everyone:r
<%SystemRoot%\zak\scripts\yesfile

@rem
@rem BOOT FILES
@rem ==========
@rem only system and administrator need access to the boot files
@rem

cacls.exe boot.ini /G administrators:f system:f
<%SystemRoot%\zak\scripts\yesfile
cacls.exe ntbootdd.sys /G administrators:f system:f
<%SystemRoot%\zak\scripts\yesfile
cacls.exe ntdetect.com /G administrators:f system:f
<%SystemRoot%\zak\scripts\yesfile
cacls.exe ntldr /G administrators:f system:f
<%SystemRoot%\zak\scripts\yesfile

@rem
@rem PROGRAM FILES
@rem =============
@rem
@rem First recurse through and just give read access to everyone to everything
@rem in the Program Files

cacls.exe "Program Files" /c /t /g administrators:f system:f everyone:r
<%SystemRoot%\zak\scripts\yesfile

@rem Remove ability to view or use anything under windows NT accessory
@rem directory

cacls.exe "Program Files\Windows NT" /c /t /g administrators:f system:f
<%SystemRoot%\zak\scripts\yesfile

@rem open up the office and templates subdirectories of msoffice
@rem for new file additions
@rem
@rem for the template directory there on the nec98 platform it is called Template
@rem and on other platforms it is called Templates

cacls.exe "Program Files\Microsoft Office\Office" /e /g everyone:c
<%SystemRoot%\zak\scripts\yesfile
cacls.exe "Program Files\Microsoft Office\Templates" /e /g everyone:c
<%SystemRoot%\zak\scripts\yesfile
cacls.exe "Program Files\Microsoft Office\Template" /e /g everyone:c
<%SystemRoot%\zak\scripts\yesfile
```

```
@rem
@rem TEMP DIRECTORY
@rem ==============
@rem change permission on temp directory to allow additions...
@rem

cacls.exe Temp /c /t /g everyone:c administrators:f system:f
<%SystemRoot%\zak\scripts\yesfile

@rem we have opened up the temp directory. this means however that somebody
@rem delete the directory as well.   we can prevent this by copying a file here
@rem and denying delete access to the file.  without being able to delete the
@rem file the temp directory cannot be deleted.

copy %SystemRoot%\zak\scripts\yesfile Temp\secure.dir
cacls.exe Temp\secure.dir /g administrators:f system:f
<%SystemRoot%\zak\scripts\yesfile
attrib +h Temp\secure.dir

@rem
@rem SMS DIRECTORIES
@rem ===============
@rem
@rem Uncomment these lines if installing SMS client
@rem

@rem cacls.exe ms /c /t /g everyone:c administrators:f system:f
<%SystemRoot%\zak\scripts\yesfile
@rem cacls.exe ms\sms\bin /c /t /g everyone:r administrators:f system:f
<%SystemRoot%\zak\scripts\yesfile

@rem
@rem SYSTEM DIRECTORY
@rem ================

cd %SystemRoot%
cacls.exe * /c /g administrators:f system:f everyone:r
<%SystemRoot%\zak\scripts\yesfile
cacls.exe . /g administrators:f system:f everyone:c
<%SystemRoot%\zak\scripts\yesfile

cacls.exe config      /t /c /g administrators:f system:f everyone:r
<%SystemRoot%\zak\scripts\yesfile
cacls.exe cursors     /t /c /g administrators:f system:f everyone:r
<%SystemRoot%\zak\scripts\yesfile
cacls.exe help      /t /c /g administrators:f system:f everyone:r
<%SystemRoot%\zak\scripts\yesfile
cacls.exe forms       /t /c /g administrators:f system:f everyone:r
<%SystemRoot%\zak\scripts\yesfile
cacls.exe inf       /t /c /g administrators:f system:f everyone:r
<%SystemRoot%\zak\scripts\yesfile
cacls.exe java      /t /c /g administrators:f system:f everyone:r
<%SystemRoot%\zak\scripts\yesfile
```

```
cacls.exe media       /t /c /g administrators:f system:f everyone:r
<%SystemRoot%\zak\scripts\yesfile
cacls.exe ShellNew    /t /c /g administrators:f system:f everyone:r
<%SystemRoot%\zak\scripts\yesfile
cacls.exe system      /t /c /g administrators:f system:f everyone:r
<%SystemRoot%\zak\scripts\yesfile
cacls.exe system32    /t /c /g administrators:f system:f everyone:r
<%SystemRoot%\zak\scripts\yesfile
cacls.exe SendTo      /t /c /g administrators:f system:f everyone:c
<%SystemRoot%\zak\scripts\yesfile


@rem everything under profiles is maintained whatever it was before this is
@rem not changed
cacls.exe profiles /g administrators:f system:f everyone:c
<%SystemRoot%\zak\scripts\yesfile

@rem we deny any access to .inf files, .exe files and .hlp files under system
cacls.exe *.inf /t /g administrators:f system:f <%SystemRoot%\zak\scripts\yesfile
cacls.exe *.exe /t /g administrators:f system:f <%SystemRoot%\zak\scripts\yesfile
cacls.exe *.hlp /t /g administrators:f system:f <%SystemRoot%\zak\scripts\yesfile
cacls.exe *.txt /t /g administrators:f system:f <%SystemRoot%\zak\scripts\yesfile
cacls.exe *.com /t /g administrators:f system:f <%SystemRoot%\zak\scripts\yesfile
cacls.exe *.cpl /t /g administrators:f system:f <%SystemRoot%\zak\scripts\yesfile

@rem
@rem LOCK ZAK RELATED STUFF
@rem ======================
@rem lock everything related to zak.  we want to keep zak around in case
@rem we need to reapply some zak stuff during upgrades, etc

cacls.exe %SystemRoot%\zak /t /c /g system:f administrators:f
<%SystemRoot%\zak\scripts\yesfile
cacls.exe %SystemRoot%\zakboot1.cmd /g system:f administrators:f
<%SystemRoot%\zak\scripts\yesfile
cacls.exe %SystemDrive%\%temp%\*.log /t /c /g system:f administrators:f <
%SystemRoot%\zak\scripts\yesfile


@rem
@rem EXCEPTIONS
@rem ==========
@rem



@rem
@rem EXCEPTIONS IN SYSTEM DIRECTORY
@rem ===============================
@rem open up the exceptions
@rem
```

```
cd %SystemRoot%
cacls.exe system32 /e /g everyone:c <%SystemRoot%\zak\scripts\yesfile
cacls.exe help /e /g everyone:c <%SystemRoot%\zak\scripts\yesfile
cacls.exe forms /e /g everyone:c <%SystemRoot%\zak\scripts\yesfile
cacls.exe cookies /t /c /g administrators:f system:f everyone:c
<%SystemRoot%\zak\scripts\yesfile
cacls.exe history /t /c /g administrators:f system:f everyone:c
<%SystemRoot%\zak\scripts\yesfile
cacls.exe occache /t /c /g administrators:f system:f everyone:c
<%SystemRoot%\zak\scripts\yesfile
cacls.exe repair /t /c /g administrators:f system:f
<%SystemRoot%\zak\scripts\yesfile
cacls.exe system32\viewers /t /c /e /g everyone:r
<%SystemRoot%\zak\scripts\yesfile

@rem
@rem do printers
@rem

cacls.exe system32\spool\printers /t /c /e /g everyone:c
<%SystemRoot%\zak\scripts\yesfile
cacls.exe system32\spool\drivers /t /c /e /g everyone:c
<%SystemRoot%\zak\scripts\yesfile

@rem
@rem allow write in the "Temporary Internet Files"
@rem

cacls.exe "Temporary Internet Files" /t /c /e /g administrators:f system:f
everyone:c <%SystemRoot%\zak\scripts\yesfile

@rem
@rem OPEN UP SPECIFIC FILE EXCEPTIONS
@rem

cd %SystemDrive%\
cacls.exe explorer.exe /t /e /g everyone:r
cacls.exe iexplore.exe /t /e /g everyone:r
cacls.exe userinit.exe /t /e /g everyone:r
cacls.exe nddeagnt.exe /t /e /g everyone:r
cacls.exe systray.exe /t /e /g everyone:r
cacls.exe runapp.exe /t /e /g everyone:r
cacls.exe net.exe /t /e /g everyone:r
cacls.exe net1.exe /t /e /g everyone:r
cacls.exe mapisvc.inf /t /e /g everyone:r
cacls.exe mapisp32.exe /t /e /g everyone:r
cacls.exe newprof.exe /t /e /g everyone:r
cacls.exe con2prt.exe /t /e /g everyone:r
cacls.exe fixprf.exe /t /e /g everyone:r
cacls.exe winhlp32.exe /t /e /g everyone:r
cacls.exe mspaint.exe /t /e /g everyone:r
cacls.exe mplay32.exe /t /e /g everyone:r
cacls.exe sndrec32.exe /t /e /g everyone:r
cacls.exe wordpad.exe /t /e /g everyone:r
```

```
cacls.exe packager.exe /t /e /g everyone:r
cacls.exe windows.hlp  /t /e /g everyone:r
cacls.exe taskmgr.exe  /t /e /g everyone:r
cacls.exe wangimg.exe  /t /e /g everyone:r

@rem
@rem Begin SMS Client Exceptions
@rem Uncomment these lines if installing SMS client
@rem

@rem cacls.exe appstart.exe  /t /e /g everyone:r
@rem cacls.exe inv32cli.exe  /t /e /g everyone:r
@rem cacls.exe smsrun32.exe  /t /e /g everyone:r
@rem cacls.exe wchat32.exe  /t /e /g everyone:r
@rem cacls.exe wslave32.exe  /t /e /g everyone:r
@rem cacls.exe wuser32.exe  /t /e /g everyone:r
@rem cacls.exe sms.ini  /t /e /g everyone:c

@rem
@rem End SMS Client Exceptions
@rem

@rem localized versions need access to internat.exe
cacls.exe internat.exe      /t /e /g everyone:r

@rem for FE versions to make IME files readable.
cacls.exe MSIME97M.exe  /t /e /g everyone:r

@rem so that logon scripts can be executed
cacls.exe cmd.exe /t /e /g everyone:r


@rem
@rem for 16 bit DOS/Win apps
@rem

cacls.exe %SystemRoot%\system32\ntvdm.exe   /e /g everyone:r
<%SystemRoot%\zak\scripts\yesfile
cacls.exe %SystemRoot%\system32\wowexec.exe /e /g everyone:r
<%SystemRoot%\zak\scripts\yesfile
cacls.exe %SystemRoot%\system32\command.com /e /g everyone:r
<%SystemRoot%\zak\scripts\yesfile

@rem Files Office tries to write to.

cacls.exe %SystemRoot%\forms\frmcache.dat /e /g everyone:c
cacls.exe %SystemRoot%\forms\msforms.twd /e /g everyone:c
cacls.exe outlook.prf /t /e /g everyone:r
cacls.exe artgalry.cag /t /e /g everyone:c
```

```
cacls.exe %SystemRoot%\*.acl /c /e /g everyone:c
<%SystemRoot%\zak\scripts\yesfile
cacls.exe outlook.prt /t /e /g everyone:c
cacls.exe xl8galry.xls /t /e /g everyone:c
cacls.exe gr8galry.gra /t /e /g everyone:c
cacls.exe custom.dic /t /e /g everyone:c
cacls.exe mlcfg32.cpl /t /e /g everyone:r
```

App/Tskcmds.cmd

```
@rem ******************
@rem Registry Changes/Additions
@rem ******************

cmd /c %SystemRoot%\REGEDIT.EXE /S %SystemRoot%\zak\scripts\newtemp.REG
cmd /c %SystemRoot%\REGEDIT.EXE /S %SystemRoot%\zak\scripts\runonce.REG
cmd /c %SystemRoot%\REGEDIT.EXE /S %SystemRoot%\zak\scripts\autolog.REG
cmd /c %SystemRoot%\REGEDIT.EXE /S %SystemRoot%\zak\scripts\nosavcon.REG

@rem ******************
@rem Apply Service pack
@rem ******************

cmd /c %SystemRoot%\sp\update /u /n /z


@rem ******************
@rem update system help files
@rem ******************
cmd /c copy %SystemRoot%\system32\windows.hlp %SystemRoot%\system32\windadm.hlp
cmd /c copy %SystemRoot%\zak\scripts\zak.hlp %SystemRoot%\system32\windows.hlp
```

Autologon.reg

```
REGEDIT4

[HKEY_LOCAL_MACHINE\SOFTWARE\Microsoft\Windows NT\CurrentVersion\Winlogon]
"AutoAdminLogon"="1"
;"DefaultDomainName"="Domain-Name"
;"DefaultUserName"="User-Name-Of-Administrative-Account-On-Domain-Name"
;"DefaultPassword"="Password-Of-Administrative-Account"
"DefaultUserName"="administrator"
"DefaultPassword"="Password"
"DefaultDomainName"="NTDOM01"
```

Cleanup.cmd

```
del /q "%SystemRoot%\profiles\All Users\Start Menu\PROGRAMS\STARTUP\*.*"
```

Cmdlines.txt

```
[commands]

;******************
;Run batch file that does all the cmdlines stuff
;******************
"cmd /c %SystemRoot%\zak\scripts\appcmds.cmd"
```

Hide.cmd

```
REM
REM This is used to hide the files on the system
REM

attrib +h /s %SystemDrive%\*.*
For /R %SystemDrive%\  %%i in (.) do attrib +h "%%i"

attrib -h /s %SystemRoot%\profiles\*.*
For /R %SystemRoot%\profiles %%i in (.) do attrib -h "%%i"

REM
REM Some directories and files don't get the right permissions because
REM they have already been marked as system.  We cover them specially here
REM

attrib +h +s %SystemRoot%\fonts
attrib +h +s %SystemRoot%\tasks
attrib +h +s %SystemRoot%\wintrust.hlp
attrib +h +s %SystemDrive%\boot.ini

REM unhide the zak\scripts directory files, otherwise we won't be able to
REM continue

attrib -h %SystemRoot%\zak\scripts\*.*

REM
REM unhide the exchange.prf file in the c:\temp directory.  this is in case it
REM got left behind
REM

attrib -h %SystemDrive%\temp\exchange.prf
```

Newtemp.reg

```
REGEDIT4

[HKEY_LOCAL_MACHINE\SYSTEM\CurrentControlSet\Control\Session Manager\
Environment]
"temp"="%SystemDrive%\\temp"
"tmp"="%SystemDrive%\\temp"
```

Noautolog.reg

```
REGEDIT4

[HKEY_LOCAL_MACHINE\SOFTWARE\Microsoft\Windows NT\CurrentVersion\Winlogon]
"DefaultUserName"=""
"AutoAdminLogon"="0"
"DefaultPassword"=""
```

NoSavcon.reg

```
REGEDIT4

[HKEY_CURRENT_USER\SOFTWARE\Microsoft\Windows NT\CurrentVersion\Network\
Persistent Connections]
"SaveConnections"="no"
```

Off97.cmd

```
O:\Off97\msoffice\setup.exe /b3 /qnt /gc+ %SystemDrive%\temp\offlog.txt
```

RunOnce.reg

```
REGEDIT4

[HKEY_LOCAL_MACHINE\SOFTWARE\Microsoft\Windows\CurrentVersion\RunOnce]
"boot1cmd"="cmd /c %SystemRoot%\\zakboot1.cmd"
```

Zakb1wrk.cmd

```
@REM   APPEND THE FOLLOWING ENTRIES
@REM   ============================
@REM
@REM
@REM - Do SMS Client setup.
@REM   Replace the server name and share name of the SMS server/share in
@REM   your environment.
@REM   cmd /c \\opktest3\sms_shr\runsms.bat
@REM
@REM - Connect up the network distribution point for network applications
@REM   net use <drive:> \\server\share /user:<user> <password>
@REM
@REM - Run office client setup:
@REM   cmd /c %SystemRoot%\zak\scripts\off97.cmd
@REM
@REM - Disconnect the drive
@REM   net use <drive:> /d
@REM
@REM - Remove stuff that Office put into the All Users Startup directory
@REM   cmd /c %SystemRoot%\zak\scripts\cleanup.cmd
@REM
@REM - Copy SMS client link into the startup group
@REM   cmd /c copy %SystemRoot%\zak\scripts\smsrun32.lnk
@REM   %SystemRoot%\"profiles\All Users\Start Menu\PROGRAMS\STARTUP"
@REM
@REM - Install IE3
@REM   %SystemRoot%\zak\tools\sysdiff /apply /m
@REM   %SystemRoot%\zak\scripts\msie302.dif
@REM
@REM - Remove the sp from the target
@REM   cmd /c rmdir /s /q %SystemRoot%\sp
@REM
@REM - Modify the registry to not autologon next time
@REM   REGEDIT.EXE /S %SystemRoot%\zak\scripts\noautolog.REG
@REM
@REM - Install floppy locker service
@REM   %SystemRoot%\zak\tools\instsrv FloppyLocker
@REM   %SystemRoot%\system32\floplock.exe
@REM
@REM - Change the local administrator password to what has been chosen
@REM   by the system administrator
@REM   net user administrator <password-entered-by-administrator>
@REM
@REM - Do system acls
@REM   cmd /c %SystemRoot%\zak\scripts\acls.cmd
@REM
@REM - Hide the files
@REM   cmd /c %SystemRoot%\zak\scripts\hide.cmd
@REM
```

```
@rem uncomment the following line if you want sms
@rem cmd /c \\opktest3\sms_shr\runsms.bat
net use O: \\IBSNT04\NETAPPS /user:NTDOM01\administrator password
cmd /c %SystemRoot%\zak\scripts\off97.cmd
cmd /c %SystemRoot%\zak\scripts\cleanup.cmd
@rem uncomment the following line if you want sms
@rem cmd /c copy %SystemRoot%\zak\scripts\smsrun32.lnk
%SystemRoot%\"profiles\All Users\Start Menu\PROGRAMS\STARTUP"
%SystemRoot%\zak\tools\sysdiff /apply /m %SystemRoot%\zak\scripts\msie302.dif
cmd /c rmdir /s /q %SystemRoot%\sp
REGEDIT.EXE /S %SystemRoot%\zak\scripts\noautolog.REG
%SystemRoot%\zak\tools\instsrv FloppyLocker %SystemRoot%\system32\floplock.exe
net user administrator password
cmd /c %SystemRoot%\zak\scripts\acls.cmd
cmd /c %SystemRoot%\zak\scripts\hide.cmd
```

Zakboot1.cmd

```
@REM   ZAKBOOT1.CMD
@REM
@REM   This file is executed on the first logon that happens after GUI
@REM   Setup completes.  It completes setting up of the ZAK Client including
@REM   installing InternetExplorer, Microsoft Office (Appstation Only) and
@REM   applying security to the files on the ZAK client and hiding the files
@REM   too.
@REM

@rem run the worker batch file to do all the ZAK work
cmd /c %SystemRoot%\zak\scripts\zakb1wrk.cmd

@rem
@rem delete the autolog.reg and worker batch file since they have the
@rem domain administrator password
@rem

cmd /c attrib -h %SystemRoot%\zak\scripts\zakb1wrk.cmd
cmd /c attrib -h %SystemRoot%\zak\scripts\autolog.reg
cmd /c del /f /q %SystemRoot%\zak\scripts\zakb1wrk.cmd
cmd /c del /f /q %SystemRoot%\zak\scripts\autolog.reg

@rem do the shutdown
shutdown.exe /C /R /T:20
```

GLOSSARY

Access Control Entry (ACE)
An ACE is an entry in an ACL. The ACL is made up of zero or more ACEs (a null ACL contains no entries). An ACE describes the access rights of a user or group to an object. It is made up of a trustee (user account or group), a set of access rights for the trustee, and a flag that indicates whether the rights are granted, denied, or audited.

Access Control List (ACL)
An object within the NT system is protected by an ACL. The ACL contains a list of ACEs that is checked when a user attempts to access an object. An ACL is used to protect files and folders on an NTFS partition as well as objects such as printers.

Access Control List—Discretionary
The discretionary ACL is controlled by the owner of the object and is used to grant or deny permissions to the object.

Access Control List—System
The system ACL is used to specify audit tracking information for an object and is controlled by the administrator. An ACE in a system ACL may specify that an audit record be generated in the Event Log when an access attempt on the object fails.

Answer File
Used in an unattended installation to provide input usually provided by the user.

Automatic Mode—Policy Application
The default mode of policy application whereby the policy file name is `NTconfig.pol` and the location is the Netlogon share of the authenticating server.

Generic Section Header
A user-defined section header name.

Graphical Identification and Authentication (GINA) DLL GINA is a replaceable portion of the Winlogon component of NT (the component that provides interactive logon support). GINA specifically provides identification and authentication support.

IIS Internet Information Server. Supplied with the retail version of Windows NT Server used for Web service provision.

Key A registry folder that contains subkeys or values. Also, an entry in a section of the unattended installation answer file.

Local User Profile A local user profile is stored on a single workstation, and the settings contained in that profile are only applied when the user logs on to that particular station.

Mandatory User Profile A mandatory user profile is a roaming profile that is set to be read only, so that the user cannot save changes to it. This can be used for a group of users who require the same desktop look and feel. Also, a mandatory user profile is a security measure preventing users from logging on without loading the restrictions in the profile.

Manual Mode—Policy Application The alternative policy application mode allowing an administrator to define the file name and location for the policy file.

Multi-homed More than one network adapter installed in a machine.

Quiet Mode An installation mode for the operating system or for an application in which the usual user input is not required.

Roaming User Profile A roaming user profile is a profile available to a user regardless of which workstation is logged on to. The profile is located in a central location accessible from all workstations.

Section Header Used in the unattended installation answer file to group together like settings under a heading. Syntax is a string name enclosed in square brackets "[ ]".

Security Account Manager (SAM) The Security Account Manager is responsible for controlling the user account database that stores all of the usernames, passwords, and access rights assigned within the system.

SID—Computer

A SID is a system identifier. Every computer in the domain except primary and backup domain controllers (PDC, BDC) is statistically guaranteed to have a unique SID within the domain. A SID is a 96-bit identifier that can be used to uniquely identify each individual computer. Domain controllers (PDC and BDC) are treated as one and share a common SID (one reason why a BDC installation requires the presence of a domain controller to copy the SID from).

SID—User/Group

User and group SIDs are generated from the computer SID with an extra number set concatenated to identify the unique user and groups of a machine or domain. Because of the quasi-unique property of the SID (the numbers are assigned sequentially), the SID is guaranteed to be statistically unique.

System Policy

A system policy is used to help control the look and feel of a user desktop. Settings controlled in this manner can be access to system tools, network availability, Start menu contents and location, and the ability to run programs.

Trusted System

The security features of a trusted system are built into the base product and do not exist as a separate entity. This makes it virtually impossible for anybody to interfere with the base set of rules for security.

User Profile

A user profile is a collection of settings that define users' preferences and desktop look on a workstation. The type of settings included here are color settings, Start menu contents, and desktop icons and shortcuts.

Value

An entry assigned to a key in the registry. Also, an entry assigned to a key in the unattended installation answer file. Separated from the key by an equals sign "=".

INDEX

C

D

E

F

G

H

I

K

L

M

N

O

P

R

S

T

U